Sex, Breath, and Force

Sex, Breath, and Force

Sexual Difference in a Post-Feminist Era

Edited by
Ellen Mortensen

LEXINGTON BOOKS

A division of
ROWMAN & LITTLEFIELD PUBLISHERS, INC.
Lanham • Boulder • New York • Toronto • Oxford

LEXINGTON BOOKS

A division of Rowman & Littlefield Publishers, Inc.
A wholly owned subsidiary of The Rowman & Littlefield Publishing Group, Inc.
4501 Forbes Boulevard, Suite 200
Lanham, MD 20706

PO Box 317
Oxford
OX2 9RU, UK

British Library Cataloguing in Publication Information Available

Library of Congress Cataloging-in-Publication Data

Sex, breath, and force : sexual difference in a post-feminist era / edited by Ellen
Mortensen.
    p. cm.
  ISBN-13: 978-0-7391-1032-4 (cloth : alk. paper)
  ISBN-10: 0-7391-1032-2 (cloth : alk. paper)
  ISBN-13: 978-0-7391-1467-4 (pbk. : alk. paper)
  ISBN-10: 0-7391-1467-0 (pbk. : alk. paper)
  1. Sex differences. 2. Feminist theory. I. Mortensen, Ellen. II. Title.
HQ1075.S467 2006
305.4201--dc22   2005035075

Printed in the United States of America

⊖™ The paper used in this publication meets the minimum requirements of American
National Standard for Information Sciences—Permanence of Paper for Printed Library
Materials, ANSI/NISO Z39.48–1992.

Contents

Acknowledgments

The publication of this book has been made possible in part due to a research grant awarded by the Norwegian Research Council (NFR) to pursue the research project *Sexual Difference—Beyond Constructionism*. All of the contributions have been written in the context of this four-year project and have never been previously published.

I would like to thank Kjell Soleim at the Centre for Women's and Gender Research (SKOK) at the University of Bergen for leading the research project in its earliest phases. Birger Angvik, Gry Brandser, Vibeke Erichsen, Reidar K. Lie and Paal Bjørby were likewise active paticipants in the group in the early stages and I would like to thank them for their respective input. In addition, I am indebted to the other members of the KVIK research group who have not contributed to the book: Cathrine Holst, Randi Gressgård and Kari Jegerstedt. Jegerstedt has also worked as an editorial assistant to the book. And last, but not least, I would like to thank Rune Smistad for his gentle professionalism in the formatting and preparation of the manuscript, and Kirsten Bang at SKOK for helping out with the administrative tasks connected to the project.

Bergen, January 2006

Ellen Mortensen

Introduction

A marked shift has occurred in the field of feminist theory in the course of the last few years. Theoretical schools and discourses—such as psychoanalysis—that previously enjoyed a hegemonic position now seem to be in decline, while other theoretical movements and modes of inquiry are moving to center stage. Feminist theory is today characterized by contestation and heterogeneity, and could be construed as a turbulent maelstrom of *polemos*. While the question of "sexual difference" has gained renewed resonance in Europe, where the question figures centrally in ontological, theoretical and political inquiries, it seems to have lost some of its former aura of attraction in the U.S., at least in certain circles.

At this time when groups and alliances seem irreconcilable and are pitted against each other in an atmosphere of animosity—where queer theorists combat the heterosexism in traditional feminist scholarship, where African-American feminists and other ethnic groups combat racism in feminism, where post-structuralists fight the strict rationalism of feminist epistemology, where non-Western post-colonial feminists fight against Eurocentrism in feminist theory—we feel the need to slow down the pace, lower the volume, and return to the less spectacular act of questioning. We are puzzled by the recent development and ask: Is the notion of "sexual difference" obsolete or is it still productive? Are we in need of a more fundamental, ontological questioning of gender, beyond the confines of parity? Has the conceptual edifice of psychoanalysis crumbled or does it still provide productive possibilities for reflection, rethinking and critique? Does sexual difference have any validity in feminist politics today? How do current forms of sexual practices open up toward new modes of questioning gender and sexuality? And more importantly, how does technology enframe our thinking on gender and sexuality if we concede that technology determines what is and what grants becoming in our age? Under this new regime, what are the conditions of possibility for thinking the question of sexual difference?

Attempts have been made to establish a dialogue between Northern

1

European and Anglo-American scholars and theorists precisely on the question
of sexual difference. It is important to show that intellectual work is not con-
fined to the Anglo-American or the Parisian scenes with their rising and falling
stars, but that important intellectual and theoretical work is also being done
elsewhere, as for instance in the peaceful corner of Northern Europe where
many of the contributors to the current volume reside. This book assembles
essays from scholars from five different countries who range from well-reput-
ed professors to younger, doctoral—and post-doctoral fellows. The essays vary
in topic and scope, all the while retaining a focus on sexual difference as the
overarching problematic.

The majority of the essays were originally presented either in seminars,
colloquia or conferences held as part of a four-year research project entitled,
Sexual Difference—Beyond Constructionism, hosted and organized by the
Centre for Women's and Gender Research (SKOK) at the University of Bergen,
Norway. The project was funded by the Norwegian Research Council, which
made it possible for scholars from the other Nordic countries as well as from
the United States to participate in the project at different times during the four-
year period.

From the U.S., three scholars were invited to participate: Elizabeth
Grosz, Kelly Oliver and Jodi Dean. All three contributors deal with, or have in
the past dealt with psychoanalysis in some fashion or another; today they hold
different positions concerning its continued validity as a theoretical framework.
For her part, Elizabeth Grosz has of late taken an explicit stance against psychoanalysis as a valid parameter for questioning gender and sexuality. This
move counts as a radical change, given the fact that she has spent the better part
of her career working with Lacanian psychoanalysis. Nowadays she is above
all inspired by the theories of Henri Bergson and Gilles Deleuze as she calls for
more experimental modes of thinking, ones that would reach beyond received
paradigms of thought, toward a becoming of sexual difference that is not yet
articulated.

In the essay included in this volume, "The Force of Sexual Difference,"
Grosz argues for a rethinking of the question of sexual difference beyond the
parameters of psychoanalysis and phenomenology. Her focus is not on sexual
difference as it relates to the body or to gender identity. Rather, she advocates
a radical questioning of sexual difference as matter, force and difference—in
time. To aid her in this endeavor, Grosz invokes Luce Irigaray and her understanding of a future ontology of sexual difference, as well as Gilles Deleuze and
his thinking on the force of difference in becoming. By making the two thinkers
speak together, but in difference, Grosz calls for an understanding of sexual
difference that pays heed to the complexities of time. She tries to circumvent
spacialized notions of temporalities in terms of "the past," "the present" and
"the future." Rather, Grosz argues, we need to think sexual difference in its
complex temporality, where the three notions of time—the past, the present and

the future—coexist in the same event, as both actual and virtual time in dynamic and productive difference.

Kelly Oliver, for her part, has taken an opposite stance in regard to psychoanalysis, finding renewed insights in it despite its apparent demise. In dealing with female depression and sublimation in Western culture, she advocates for the usefulness of psychoanalysis through the works of Freud and Kristeva, as ways of elucidating the racial and gendered aspects of depression. For Oliver, oppression is an undeniable factor in depression since the melancholia of depression results from a double loss: first, a loss of a sense of oneself as an agent and, second, a loss of the sense of oneself as lovable or loved. It is important to study the specific workings of depression for individuals or groups of people who are devalued and oppressed in patriarchal culture, since the conditions of possibility for sublimation of their affects and drives in meaningful language are meager and fraught with obstacles.

Contesting received notions of publicity, Jodi Dean introduces in her essay "Secrets and Drives" an inquiry into technoculture in late capitalism. Critical theory, which is based on the belief in the value and efficacy of enlightenment thought, she argues, is mistaken in its analysis of contemporary technoculture. Dean convincingly makes the claim that the notion of the public rests on the logic of the secret, which in fact divides the public into those who know and those who believe the knowers. Instead of providing a challenge to capitalism, critical theory and the belief in the enlightenment of the public, inevitably feeds into the machinery of late capitalism and thus solidifies its hegemonic position. What characterizes technoculture in global capitalism today, Dean claims, is the faltering of meaning and communication, due to the information overload. In order to analyze the current state of affairs in technoculture, Dean turns to Lacanian psychoanalysis, which she claims has greater explanatory powers in these matters than critical theory. According to Lacanian theorists like Žižek and Copjec, the collapse in communication is caused by the weakening of the symbolic system, which has occurred as a consequence of the global spread of information. Technoculture, which assures the never-ending circulation of contesting truths and insights, bits and fragments of mobile and fluid truths and identities, does not function as a structure of desire in a symbolic system, but rather as a closed, repetitive circuit of drive, with a promise of instant satisfaction. In this circuit of drive, the Imaginary and the Real become merged in such a way that the Symbolic is undermined and weakened. Consequently, technoculture fails to symbolize the world for us, and the production of knowledge only produces an increased need for more knowledge, understood as information.

At the same time technoculture captures us in a swirl of endless circulating sound bites, which ultimately end up signifying nothing. Contrary to the critical theorist's belief in the progressive potential of critique—in leading to truth and in the enlightenment of the public—Dean calls for sobriety in our revolutionary hopes of what critique of symbolic systems may engender. She insists that the workings of technoculture operate not in the service of freedom and knowledge for the public, but rather in the interest of capitalist economy and its voracious hunger for profit. We are in dire need, she argues, of developing new modes of inquiry for dealing with the challenges of technoculture in the future.

The Norwegian philosophers Kristin Sampson and Vigdis Songe-Møller both meditate on the questions concerning femininity in its relation to maternity and materiality in Plato and Aristotle respectively. In her essay "A Difference of Origin," Sampson performs an inquiry into Plato's *Timaeus* and the complex accounts of parenthood and origin in this text. By attributing special attention to the Platonic notion of the *chôra*, and by invoking diverging interpretations of this term in the reception of Plato, Sampson critiques Plato's notion of a one-parent (paternal) structure of origin that has come to dominate Western metaphysics.

Similarly, Vigdis Songe-Møller questions Aristotle's ideological projection of the feminine as imperfect or deviant nature. In a careful reading of the four causes of that which is, *ousia*, in Aristotle's works, Songe-Møller is able to unveil the way in which Aristotle tries to separate the feminine from the masculine, precisely by identifying the feminine with passivity, matter and death. But in so doing, he ends up investing the feminine with a fundamental ambiguity. On the one hand, as the material principle in reproduction, woman stands for death, but on the other hand, as necessary for reproduction, she stands for life. This ambiguity—as both life and death—is never resolved in Aristotle and has survived in the philosophical tradition that followed in the wake of his thinking.

In the Nordic countries, the work of Luce Irigaray has found sustained resonance among feminist theorists and philosophers. Hence, both Johanna Oksala from Finland and Ellen Mortensen from Norway rely in part on Irigaray in their respective investigations of the ontology of sexual difference. Oksala resides in the neighborhood of Heidegger's thinking on the ontological difference between Being and beings when she calls for a need to pursue ontological questions. Oksala's analysis couples Heidegger's thinking on the question concerning technology, and the way in which beings come to be objectified as "standing-reserve," with Foucault's notion of technologies of the self. By so doing, she unveils the fundamental historicity, not only of ontology, but also of the way in which we as living beings are implicated and determined by ontology. Last, but not least, Oksala invokes Irigaray and her thinking on breath in her attempt at redefining what is, an Eastern-inspired, utopian vision of a future ontology, one in which our entire being—corporeal as well as spiritual—is implicated, precisely through a cultivation of breath.

Mortensen likewise turns to Irigaray, notably in her attempt to question Nietzsche's notion of will to power as an alternative avenue to think sexual difference. Mortensen asks if it is possible to envision will to power in the feminine, and marshals—on the one hand—the insights gained by Irigaray in her reading of Nietzsche, and—on the other hand—Heidegger's seminal work on his fellow philosopher, in particular his insistence that all of Nietzsche's thinking can be subsumed under the rubric "will to power as art." Ultimately, the inquiry into Nietzsche's notion of will to power opens up a new path of thinking sexual difference, Mortensen claims, beyond the confines of subjective perspectivism: a free, aesthetic releasement of being, a "letting-be-in the-open"— in the feminine.

The Finnish philosopher Sara Heinämaa explores yet another avenue for thinking sexual difference, one that she arrives at through Simone de Beauvoir and her critique of phenomenology. By retracing some of the key concepts of phenomenology—be it the phenomenology of perceived objects according to Husserl and Merleau-Ponty or the "psychoanalysis of things" according to Sartre—Heinämaa uncovers the way in which Beauvoir redefines these concepts, and in particular, the concepts that deal with feminine embodiment, love and desire. Heinämaa performs a very careful reading of Beauvoir's *The Second Sex* and some of her novels in order to prove that Beauvoir in no way accepts the male phenomenologists' versions of these themes. Contrary to the masculine mode of experiencing embodiment, love and desire, which is characterized by a polarity between attraction and repulsion, activity and passivity, Beauvoir posits that the feminine mode of experiencing the very same phenomena is characterized by a fundamental ambiguity. Furthermore, according to Heinämaa, Beauvoir describes feminine desire as fundamentally other to the "means and ends"- mechanism that is dominant in masculine desire. Feminine desire is, Beauvoir claims, different by virtue of its vacillation, ambiguity and open-ended fluctuation in a never-ending movement of ebb and flow.

Like Heinämaa, the Swedish theorist Lisa Käll gathers important insights from Merleau-Ponty's notion of otherness when pondering the question of sexual difference. In her article "Traces of Otherness," Käll, argues that Merleau-Ponty's notion of reversible flesh provides an understanding of otherness that is situated beyond the confines of parity. Merleau-Ponty discovers in the difference between touching and being touched in the flesh of the self a fundamental ontology of ambiguity through which sexual difference can be rethought and no longer reduced to the male/female opposition which permeates our thinking and being in the world.

The political implications of the question of sexual difference are highlighted in the contributions of Tiina Rosenberg from Sweden who deals explicitly with the question of heteronormativity, or more precisely, how heteronormativity pertains to the reception of the Swedish film by Lukas Moodysson, *Show Me Love.* Rosenberg critiques the reception of the film and the almost unanimous silencing of the blatant lesbian theme in the film. By using, among others, Iris Marion Young's social theories of difference coupled with the concept of heteronormativity from queer theory, Rosenberg unveils the mechanisms whereby lesbianism is incorporated into the dominant culture. The effect of this incorporation is a tacit privileging and solidification of the heterosexual norm that prevails in Swedish culture.

In her essay, "Differences That Matter? Or: What Is Feminist Critique" the Norwegian philosopher Cathrine Egeland explores the political dimensions of sexual difference, and focuses in this context on the disagreements among feminist theorists concerning the notion of critique. Egeland identifies the different arguments and traces the fault lines that have emerged in the debate. By identifying the diverse positionings—that of Benhabib, Moi, Butler, Braidotti and Irigaray—Egeland makes a critical assessment of their respective arguments. She concludes that Irigaray's notion of critique as intervention—an intervention from within discourses—is perhaps the most fruitful feminist strategy for thinking sexual difference in the future.

This collection of essays brings together a plethora of philosophers and theories, which at least in part converge in a common concern for the question of sexual difference. At times the theorists contradict each other and may even be said to threaten each other's positions. It is our conviction, however, that open contestation of ideas and of theories is one of the assets and strengths of feminist theory today. We hope that *Sex, Breath, and Force* will prove to be a valuable contribution to feminist theory in its intention to embrace the spirit of productive *polemos* as well as endorse the pursuit of free and thorough meditation.

Ellen Mortensen

The Force of Sexual Difference

Elizabeth Grosz

> A revolution in thought and ethics is needed if the work of sexual difference is to take place. We need to reinterpret everything concerning the relations between the subject and discourse, the subject and the world, the subject and the cosmic, the microcosmic and the macrocosmic... In order to make it possible to think through, and live, this difference, we must reconsider the whole problematic of space and time. (Irigaray, *An Ethics of Sexual Difference*, 6-7)

We have entered a new millennium, and it is time to rethink some of the key questions that have occupied feminist, queer and postmodern theories of subjectivity, identity and 'gender'. Indeed, I believe that it is time to move beyond the very language of identity and gender, to look at other issues left untouched, questions unasked, assumptions unelaborated, that feminist and queer politics need to address in order to revitalize themselves and to propel themselves into new conceptions of desire, power, pleasure, and into the development of new practices. Among these underdeveloped and unasked questions are those deemed the most offensive and disputed within the last decades: not the body, which of course is now the most valorized and magical of conceptual terms, but messy biology, matter, materiality, which have had to be organized and contained (as body) and dematerialized (through language); not ideology, which again has been privileged as the object of intellectual analysis, but force, energy, affect, which are nowhere discussed but relegated to abjection and the outside position of the Real; and not gender, which is again the contained, represented, socialized ideal, but sexual difference, that untidy and ambiguous invocation of the pre-structuring of being by irreducible difference. Matter, force and difference remain elided in contemporary political discourses and theoretical analyses, they remain too destabilizing, too difficult to direct into concerted political pathways, to provide the basis of a new politics. Yet matter, force and difference, or matter as force and difference, remain the prerogatives of science and are either treated fearfully and with distrust, or ignored all together.

In this paper, I want to look at that which both preconditions and destabilizes gender and bodies, that which problematizes all identity, that which discourse and representation cannot contain and politics cannot direct: sexual difference as force; and force as itself divided, differentiated, sexualized. In this process I want to bring together two strange and at times potentially antagonistic bed-fellows: Luce Irigaray and Gilles Deleuze, who, while they may share little in common, are nevertheless directly linked through the preeminence they grant to difference as force, to the force of difference. While clearly I do not have the space and time to develop a nuanced and detailed reading of the works of each on the question of difference, I do want to present an impressionistic overview of the ways in which an understanding of difference, difference not tied to opposition, difference not determined by identity, difference not subsumed by comparison, can disturb and displace the politics of identity on which most feminist, queer and minority politics is based, and can provide new research questions and new political experiments by which these political programs may revitalize themselves.

Instead of exploring the phenomenology, the experiential, the subjective ingredients of sexual difference, what it is like to live as a woman or a man, a lesbian or a heterosexual, as black or as white—which the feminist investment in psychoanalysis and phenomenology has privileged for the last three decades or more—it may be time to explore instead what such approaches leave out, what we might understand as the physics of sexual difference, its materiality, its force, its ontological weight and above all, its time. Lying beyond and framing these primarily epistemological approaches is the pressing but forgotten question of ontology. Far from providing an alternative to the positivistic approaches of contemporary analytic philosophy, structuralism and post-structuralism have shared uncritically in its reduction of ontology to epistemology, and in its reduction of materiality to representation. Through, for example, the Lacanian conception of the Real, all that is beyond representation, beyond symbolization, is equated with the ineffable; and through Derrideanism, the outside, that which is beyond the text, that which incapable of being construed as writing or trace—force, unconfigured matter, nature—is inevitably returned back to the text and to writing, reterritorialized, blunted as surprise, excess, or immanence.

It is for this reason I believe that Deleuze's work, which is not particularly feminist, may be of tremendous use for feminist politics: it is his concentration on the ontological questions, on the problems raised by matter, by force, by power, by time, for thought, that may provide a new direction for a more abstract approach to feminism, the kind of abstraction that is needed to bring about new frames of reference and new kinds of question. This return to ontology is also, I believe, one of the major concerns of Irigaray, particularly in her middle period, in her analyses of Nietzsche and Heidegger, in her work on the elemental, and especially in *An Ethics of Sexual Difference*, on which I will concentrate here.

Irigaray makes it clear that feminism has just barely begun to fathom the intellectual depths of its project. To affirm in full positivity the existence and capacities of (at least) two sexes—the project of sexual difference—is to acknowledge two things: first, the failure of the past to provide a space and time for women as women, with the consequence that all forms of prevailing practices and forms of knowledge, including the most objective of the sciences and the most abstract forms of mathematics and cosmology, represent the interests and perspectives of only one sex. All forms of knowledge are open to the augmentation of their objects, fields, methods and questions through an acknowledgment of their necessary limits, their perspectival emergence in specific rather than universal interests. Second, linked to this recognition, is the necessity, in the future, of providing other ways of knowing, other ontologies and epistemologies that enable the subject's relation to the world, to space and to time, to be conceptualized in different terms. Irigaray makes it clear that a transformation of ontology entails a transformation in the ways in which we understand space and time, which in turn transform our conceptions of matter, subjectivity and politics. Space and time can no longer be understood as neutral or transparent media whose passivity enables the specificity of matter to reveal itself: rather they are active ingredients in the making of matter, and thus in the constitution of objects and subjects. A reconfiguration of the subject will, sooner or later, require that our understanding of space and time themselves undergo dramatic metamorphoses. Irigaray understands this as a becoming beyond the one, beyond the phallic, a becoming in which the all-too-human is understood as the all-too-patriarchal, and the future is beyond recognition, beyond the dualities of the sexes as we know them today and as they existed in the past.

Since Irigaray's work, a feminist future cannot be identified with the attainment of a sameness with men, of the same rights as men and the same access to their conceptual frameworks and systems of value: rather, with the proliferation of alternative and different discourses, knowledges, frames of reference, political investments. The productivity of exchange across boundaries between disparate knowledges may be facilitated and developed on the same model as the interchange between the sexes themselves, the sexes as they will have been from the point of the view of the future, rather than the sexes as they are in the present or have been in the past.

Sexual difference is that which has yet to take place, and thus exists only in virtuality, in and through a future anterior, Irigaray's preferred tense for writing, the only tense that openly addresses the question of the future without pre-empting it in concrete form or in present terms. Sexual difference does not yet exist, and it is possible that it has never existed. The sexes as we know them today have only one model, a singular and universal neutrality. At best, equal participation is formulated. But the idea that sexual difference entails the existence of at least two points of view, sets of interests, perspectives, two types of ideal, two modes of knowledge, has yet to be considered. The only time of sexual difference is that of the future. All the work of sexual difference, its labor of producing alternative knowledges, methods and criteria, has yet to begin. Sexual difference is entirely of the order of the surprise, the encounter with the new, which is why Irigaray invokes the emotion of "wonder" as its most sensible attribute; it is an event yet to occur, an event strangely out of time, for it does not yet have a time; and it is clear that its time may never come.

This is how Irigaray saves herself from the tiresome charges of essentialism and utopianism: by refusing to speculate on what this sexual difference might consist in or how it might manifest itself, in refusing to posit a norm or a form for men or women, in seeing that the future for feminism is that which is to be made rather than foreseen or predicted: "To concern oneself in the present about the future certainly does not consist in programming it in advance but in trying to bring it into existence..." (Irigaray, quoted in Whitford, 14)

Sexual difference implies that there are at least two ways of doing anything, without being able to specify in what ways they may develop or what form they may take. Which means that the production of concepts themselves must provide at least two paths of development, modes or processes, at least two modes of (possibly incommensurable) existence, not in competition with each other to find which is the best, nor in augmentation of each other to provide a more complete picture, but as two singularities that may either conflict with or complement each other, that may be altogether incomparable or simply different. There is no way to judge in advance what forms and paths sexual difference, the perspectives of at least two sexes, may have to offer to concepts, thought, knowledges, except that sexual difference makes and marks a difference everywhere and in everything. Sexual difference entails not only a new epistemologies—new ways of knowing which recognize and affirm the existence of at least two different types of knower, two different ideals for knowledge, criteria of evaluation, and so on. It also entails the existence of an ontology, a world, being, which can no longer be understood as self-identical, but must be understood as bifurcated, as composed of difference. Part of this self-division is the necessary difference central to all of ontology, space and time, which Irigaray places at the heart of a new ontology.

Irigaray affirms that the question of time, and of conceptualizing women's closer alignment with temporality, is crucial to the struggles of sexual difference, insofar as the feminine has remained largely associated with space, place, containment, and inhabitation, while having its becoming, its interiority, its transformations in time, its alignments with the subjective and Godly apprehension of its possible perfection curtailed and contained. One of the most challenging issues facing any future feminism is precisely how to articulate a future in which futurity itself has a feminine form, in which the female subject can see itself projected beyond its present position as other to the one. Which may, ironically, mean that this future feminine may render itself obsolete or the object of profound and even inhuman (or imperceptible) becomings rather than rest itself in the forms of femininity as they have been represented and idealized within sexual indifference, within patriarchy.

> In the beginning there was space and the creation of space, as is said in all theogonies...God would be time itself, lavishing or exteriorizing itself in its action in space, in places.

> Philosophy then affirms the genealogy of the task of the gods or God. Time becomes the *interiority* of the subject itself, and space, its *exteriority* (this problematic is developed by Kant in the *Critique of Pure Reason*). (*Ethics* 7)

Irigaray's understanding of sexuality entails conceptualizing an ontology of becoming, whose central concern is the re-elaboration of time and space, in which time is privileged as a repressed or feminized condition of the world, where temporality must be conceived, not in terms of the (perceptual and practical) privilege of the present, but rather in terms of the preeminence of an undeterminable future. A paradoxical conception of time modeled on an unknowable future. And a paradoxical conception of the relations of subjects and objects based on this paradoxical temporality: a subject that is never what it is, a subject is always in the process of becoming something else, perhaps even a subject becoming beyond subjectivity, which necessarily produces as its correlate and complement an object that is more than an inert, given passivity, but also becomes something else than it was. Time, even more than space, needs to be thought in terms which liberate it from the constraints of the present.

Such an understanding of time as inherently dislocated, bifurcated, is of course not easy to come by. It is rare in the history of Western thought that there has been any consideration of a time beyond or outside of the strictures of counting, calculism and ideally (as science desires), determinism, that is, outside the causal control that the past exerts over the present and future. From Plato to Einstein, from philosophy to physics, the reality of the experience of time, time as an irreversible pull toward the future, time marked by an arrow of directionality that always impels it forward and never backward, has been denied. Time is reduced to formalized representations, to counting, to space and spatialization, which leads many of the most respected physicists and cosmologists to regard the experience of time's irreversibility as mere subjective illusion, beneath which a timeless or unchanging calculability, measure or *ratio* is discernible. Even fewer affirm the positivity of a future not controlled and directed by calculable forces in the present.

Feminist discourses interested in the question of time and its openness to transformation may find themselves in strangely compromising relations with a number of theorists they may have hoped to otherwise avoid, theorists whose unhinging of time may also provide a mode of unhinging subjectivity while nevertheless affirming sexual difference. The strange allies would include, above all, Darwin, who brought the question of indeterminacy to the center of the study of life; Nietzsche, who rendered time the affirmative movement of force, a force that eternally returns to affirm its positive openness, which undermines and complicates every system and every order; Bergson, who makes explicit the bodily and conceptual cost of the mathematization of time and its reduction to spatialization as required by the natural sciences; and finally Deleuze, who, in recognizing all these as predecessors, affirms that time is a multiplicity that nevertheless expresses a fundamental unity, its multiplicity an affirmation of the singularity of the eternal return and of the irreducibility of life to prediction (the basis of Deleuze's opposition to Badiou's valorization of the mathematical, and particularly set theory).

This cluster of theorists may form an uneasy alliance, especially given the self-evident and possibly not misapplied apprehensiveness of feminist theorists to them and what they seem to represent, arguably some of the most misogynist thinkers of their generation. Such, however, are the most productive and complex engagements of contemporary feminist theory—the encounter with what is alien, the meeting with what is outside, with what might otherwise be an irritant, which forces feminism to expand itself to develop and accommodate the new, to actively "evolve", to transform or remake itself. Such feminist theory would engage, not in critique or demolition, not in the defensive hold on already acquired gains, not in the abandonment but in the revitalization of discourses to which they might otherwise seem opposed. This is part of feminism's own self-overcoming, its movement from policing to production.

Such is the scope, at the very least, of a feminist requestioning of the structures of futurity. To adequately begin this questioning means taking on a two-pronged project: on the one side, to address discourses, knowledges, and practices undertaken under the auspices of the hard sciences, including the ways in which time and change are conceptualized in physics, chemistry, astronomy and so on, discourses that analyze the materiality of time, and the time of materiality; and, on the other, to explore the ways in which temporality and change are lived and experienced in cross-cultural and cross-historical terms, the psychic materiality of duration. Neither the material explorations of time undertaken in the natural sciences (time) nor the psychological or phenomenological understanding of the lived experience of time (duration) provide us with a definitive truth, one which supercedes or overrules the truth or force of the other. As Bergson (1988) makes clear, each provides resources whose tension together needs to be explained rather than resolved. Together, they provide us with the parameters of the question of time and becoming: what kind of an understanding of time can be developed in feminism that is able to provide an explanation of the dynamism of the material world, and of the place of living beings within that world in the same language, the same conceptual apparatuses (Deleuze's requirement of the univocity of being, a multiplicity of beings which nonetheless speak in one voice)? How can we use the concept of time to dynamize or revitalize the continuity between the human and the inhuman, in other words, to liberate the becoming-beyond the human? Which is directly linked to the feminist question: how to move beyond the sexes as we know them, and beyond sexuality as it is usually practiced? But also, how to understand this dynamism as always bifurcated and bifurcating, driven primarily by difference (Irigaray's requirement of multiplicity irreducible to the logic of the one)?

Here I can only highlight some key elements of a conception of time in which the future provides the template of temporality: these elements are derived in large part from Deleuze's reanimation of Bergsonism, and of Bergson's peculiar and inventive revitalization of Darwinism, a Darwinism mediated by Nietzsche:

1. Time, or more precisely, duration, is always singular, unique and unrepeatable. Each duration forms a continuity, a single, indivisible whole. Yet, there are many simultaneous durations, which participate in a generalized or cosmological duration, a singular field of discontinuous events. An event occurs only once: it has its own characteristics, which will never occur again, even in repetition. But it occurs alongside of, simultaneous with and in succession to, many other events, whose rhythms are also specific and unique. Duration thus defines qualitative multiplicities, events, singularities;

2. The division of duration—which occurs whenever time is conceptualized as a line (whether straight or curved), counted, divided into before and after, rendered periodic, made the object of the numerical, rendering its analogue continuity into digital or discrete units—transforms its nature, that is to say, reduces it to modes of spatiality. If, as Bergson suggests, space is the field of quantitative differences, of differences of degree, then the counting of time, its linear representation, reduces and extinguishes its qualitative differences and restructures them as quantitative;

3. One of the most significant differences of kind within duration (which is commonly misunderstood as a difference of degree) is the distinction between past and present. The past and the present are not two modalities of the present, the past a receded or former present. The past and the present paradoxically co-exist; they function simultaneously. The whole of the past is contained, in contracted form, in each moment of the present. The past lives in time. The past could never exist if it did not coexist with the present of which it is the past, and thus of every present, as the virtual. Yet the past would be inaccessi-

ble to us altogether if we could gain access to it only through the present and its passing. The only access we have to the past is through a leap into virtuality, through a move into the past itself, given that, for Bergson, the past is outside us and that we are in it rather than it is located in us. The past exists, but it is in a state of latency or virtuality. We must place ourselves in it if we are to have recollections, memory images;

4. If the present is the actuality whose existence is engendered by the virtual past, then the future remains that dimension or modality of time that has no actuality either. The future too is virtual, uncontained by the present but prefigured, rendered potential, through and by the past without the direct mediation or control of the present. The future is that openness of becoming that enables divergence from what exists. Rather than determinism, which necessarily reduces the future to the present, the indeterminacy of the virtual needs to be asserted. The future is that which over-writes or restructures the virtual that is the past. The future that emerges is only one of the lines of virtuality from the past. The past is the condition for infinite futures.

Such an understanding of time as dynamic force, as activity rather than as passive wearing away, erosion, is, I believe, of vital importance for feminist theory: we need an account of time that enables us to have at least partial or mediated access to the resources of the past, those resources consecrated as history and retaining their traces or tracks in the present, which do not tie us to the past in any definitive way or with any particular orientation and which provide us for the very resources by which to supercede the past and the present—the very project of radical politics. The project of radical politics, and thus of a radical feminist politics remains how to envisage and engender a future unlike the present, without being able to specify in advance what such a future entails. It is thus the investment in the power of the leap, by which the actual emerges and produces itself from its virtual resources, that generates the surprise of the new.

I don't want to suggest that there is an easy alignment between Deleuzian and Irigarayan philosophies: like those concept-atoms that constitute Deleuze's understanding of thought, they rub up again each other unevenly, and with jagged edges, and there is no possibility of a smooth or easy fit between them. Each functions as an agitating crystal for the other, creating an alignment that is always uneasy and uncomfortable. Nevertheless, they may offer each other relays, modes of access to other domains and to other modes of action that may be inaccessible without their conjunction or interaction, and without the potentially productive disjunctions they engender. The uneasiness that marks their juxtapositioning—Irigaray's accounts of subjectivity, identity and desire sit uncomfortably with Deleuze's concern with intensities, planes, energies—may prove to be more productive, indeed, more thought-provoking, than any smooth and easy complementarity.

What these two (series) have to offer each other is an expansion rather than a consolidation: Deleuze may enable the Irigarayan concern with the production of sexual difference to understand its need for a reconceptualization of the terms by which time is understood as the mode of actualization of the virtuality the past has for overspilling the present. And Irigaray may enable the Deleuzian focus on becoming to understanding that the becoming-woman of all identity is not just the recognition of micro-sexualities within each subject, but is also the becoming-other of all knowledges and all practices, the becoming-more available to each of the sexes in their own ways.

Why then should feminism turn or perhaps return to concepts like matter, time, space, force, energy—that is to questions usually occupying either the natural sciences or metaphysics—which seems to deflect from its basic occupation with direct changes in the position of women (and men), or of homosexuals (and heterosexuals)? I am not suggesting that all feminists should turn to these rather obscure and abstract reflections on the broad conditions of being and its complication through becoming: clearly this is a project far removed from direct application and from concrete projects aimed at transforming lives. Nevertheless, unless some feminist theorists take the exploration of the implications of sexual difference, and of difference more generally, seriously, and follow these obscure lines where they might lead—however strange—we have no hope of something entirely other, we remained mired in the recognized and the known, mired in the past and the present instead of able to address or at least face the undecidability of the future.

Bibliography

Alain Badiou, 2000, *The Clamour of Being*, trans. Louise Burchell, Minneapolis: University of Minnesota Press.

Henri Bergson, 1988, *Matter and Memory*, trans. NM Paul and WS Palmer, New York: Zone Books.

Gilles Deleuze, 1988, *Bergsonism*, trans. Hugh Tomlinson and Barbara Habberjam, New York: Zone Books.

Luce Irigaray, 1993, *An Ethics of Sexual Difference*, trans. Carolyn Burke and Gillian C. Gill, Ithaca: Cornell University Press.

Margaret Whitford, 1991, *Luce Irigaray. Philosophy in the Feminine*, London and New York: Routledge.

A Difference of Origin

Kristin Sampson

Derrida emphasizes that the form of the question of origin has a history. What are we asking for in such a question about origin? Each time we pose this question within a philosophical context, it presupposes, so it seems, at least that a single point exists: an uncomplicated source of origin (...) a moment or a point, which resists division. A divided origin would, according to such a view, can no longer be an origin. So, all questions concerning origin seem to imply the existence of a single origin.[1] According to Aristotle the pre-Socratic philosophers posed the question of being in relation to the *archê* from which it had been generated.[2] According to such a view, to say what something is, would involve stating its origin, i.e. the one archê from which it was generated, and thus naming one, single origin. This implies the conception of one entity at the back of a line originating many others. According to such a view one could be said to be in possession of identity to the degree that one can name one's original originator—that from which one originates. A certain metaphor of birth could be said to be embedded within this notion of the one original originator generating many others: that of one father generating many children. The problem with such an image of birth is that the role of the mother, or the other, seems to be forgotten. Thus, taking the notion of the one original origin, and considering it in terms of the metaphor of birth that it invokes, it may become visible that this notion involves a certain lack of sexual difference. One solution to the problem of the notion of the one original originator in relation to thinking sexual difference could be to abandon the element of origin altogether, and instead attempt to describe identity in terms of different forms of metaphor, for example in terms of metaphors related to spatiality, e.g. using "a metaphor of the self as a geographical terrain," along the lines suggested by Deleuze and Guattari.[3] A slightly different approach could be to see if the metaphor of birth could be thought in a different way, i.e. in a way in which the notion of the one original origin could be avoided. In this paper I will go

17

back to the *Timaeus* of Plato and take a closer look at how specific metaphors
of birth are displayed as ambiguous and problematic, and see how they make
an impact on a theoretical, philosophical level. I put an emphasis here upon
structural analogies between ambiguities that can be found in the metaphors of
birth and in the philosophical arguments, in an attempt to argue that they are
surrounded by a similar kind of ambiguity. The thought that lies behind my
reading of the *Timaeus* is that a different metaphor of birth could make a different impact on the theoretical, philosophical level of thinking. This is inspired
by Luce Irigaray's emphasis of the necessity of thinking sexual difference as a
radical difference with the feminine and the masculine constituted as mutually
irreducible to each other, where none of them could be posited as the One, i.e.
as a one original originator. The hypothesis that lies behind this is the thought
that a different metaphor of birth, including the notion of sexual difference,
could invoke a different form of ontology.

Being born may be considered the starting point of our human existence.
According to a modern, contemporary view of birth, this is a result of a sexual relation between our parents. In accordance with such a view, this would
normally be considered as having both a mother and a father as progenitors and
originators. Our parents, however, are not considered to be our un-originated
originators. They, in their turn, were once born themselves, and their births are
the result of their parents, our grandparents, of which we have four. But, then
again, our grandparents' births are brought about by their parents, our great-
grandparents, of which we have eight, and so on, almost infinitely, and
assuredly until the number of originators would be enormous and immeasura-
ble. According to such a more modern, contemporary view of birth, it seems
hard indeed to find one original progenitor. In classical Greek Antiquity, on the
other hand, the common view of birth was a different one. The mother's deliv-
ery was considered as a repetition of the father's original act of giving birth
nine months earlier, a view that implies seeing the mother more akin to a recipient functioning as some sort of incubator. A woman's womb was considered
by the ancient Greeks to be something in which the father gave birth, and as
such a passive albeit necessary condition. Numerous examples of comparisons
made between human reproduction on the one hand, and vegetative reproduction on the other, with the mother described as a field in which the father sows
his seed, can be found in the literature previous to Plato, and indicates that this
was the common view of reproduction in ancient Greece. In the tragedies, for
instance in Aeschylus' *Eumenides*, such a view is expressed when Apollo
claims that: "The mother of what is called her child—is no *parent* (*tokeus*) of
it, but nurse only of the young life that is sown in her. The parent is the male,
and she but a stranger, a friend, who, if fate spares his plant, preserves it till
it puts forth."[4] Another famous example can be found in Sophocles' *Antigone*
where Creon, wanting his son Haemon to abandon Antigone and find someone
else to marry, says, "the furrows of others can be ploughed!"[5] Given these veg-

etative images of birth, it is not difficult to conclude that the father is the one true progenitor. If one, as these examples suggest, considers the father to be the real parent of the child, then that seems to imply that a child has only *one* real parent and originator.

The *Timaeus* is the Platonic dialogue in which the birth of cosmos—the *cosmogony*—is described. In this dialogue two versions of the stories about the generation of cosmos are presented. In the first account (*Timaeus* 27d-47e), the generation of cosmos is described as a birth involving only one parent: the father. This first description of the birth of cosmos does not, however, add up, but ends in ambiguities and unresolved difficulties and displacements which necessitates a new beginning, i.e. the second story of cosmogony (*Timaeus* 48a-92c). In this second story, representing a reconsideration of the first account, a feminine figure—a mother—is brought into the picture. But let me take a brief look at the first version first. The description of the generation of cosmos abounds with metaphors related to birth. Timaeus uses expressions like "the father who engendered it [the cosmos] (*ho gennêsas patêr*)," and speaks of the cosmos as "in motion and alive (*zôn*)" (*Timaeus* 37c). The cosmos is generated (*gegonen*), according to Timaeus, and that which is generated (*tô genomenô*) needs something other than itself as its generating cause.[6] The generative cause of cosmos is named the creator (*poiêtên*), father (*patera*), maker (*tektainomenos*) and constructor (*dêmiourgos*) (*Timaeus* 28c-29a). In relation to the metaphor of birth it is the name "father" which carries the most relevance, and in the first story of the birth of cosmos in the *Timaeus* there are thus two main figures present: father and child. According to the metaphor of birth, invoking an image of a father procreating in his own image, the child—cosmos—ought to resemble its progenitor as much as possible. According to Plato, what is generated is secondary in relation to the un-generated model of which it is a copy. An image is less good, less perfect, than that which it imitates. Cosmos is only a copy, an image (*eikona*) of the Eternal being (*Timaeus* 29b). Being implies remaining the same (*tauta*) (*Timaeus* 29a), and the cosmos, being subject to change, is secondary in relation to the un-generated model of which it is a copy. In this sense it is a hierarchic relation that is described in the first story of cosmogony. Since the cosmos is inferior to its father, it differs from him, at least in this respect. Cosmos is not exactly like its father. The vital problem with this dissimilarity, is that there is nothing in the first story which explains, or can explain, it. There is nothing to explain why the difference is there, or what causes it. What is missing is the Other. Cosmos does not—as yet—have a mother.

At *Timaeus* 47e Timaeus realizes that it is necessary to start all over again. This is a turning point in the dialogue. In his first account of the generation of cosmos, Timaeus based his description on a division between being and becoming. He described two kinds of entities: the originating father and the generated cosmos. Now, with the new beginning, Timaeus introduces a third princi-

ple—a *triton genos*, a third kind—in addition to these two. According to the
second story, the first of the three kinds that are present at the birth of cosmos,
i.e. the father, is the model form (*paradeigmatos eidos*). This model form is
"intelligible (*noêton*) and ever uniformly existent (*aei kata tauta on*),"
(*Timaeus* 48e). It is always the same as itself. The second of the three is the
model's copy (*mimêma de paradeigmatos*), i.e. the child cosmos. This is "subject to becoming (*genesin*) and visible (*horaton*)" (*Timaeus* 49a). The third of
the three kinds is at first named Necessity (*anagkê*). With the introduction of
this second parent cosmos seems to have received a mother.[7] In addition to the
name "Necessity" this mother will be called by a variety of names during the
second story of cosmogony, some of which are "receptacle" (*hupodochê*),
"nurse" (*tithênê*) and last, but certainly not least, *chôra* (*Timaeus* 49a, 52b-c).[8]
I will now take a look at the descriptions that are given of this mothering principle. What kind of mother is she, and how is the relation between the two parents structured?

Although the birth of cosmos, according to the second story of cosmogony,
is the result of both a mother and a father, the relation between the two is not
an equal one. In the first story of cosmogony, a hierarchy was displayed
between father and child. In the second story of cosmogony, when the mother
is introduced, a similar hierarchical structure is revealed, but in a slightly different form. In the second story a hierarchical element is embedded also in the
relation between the two parents, with the mother in the subordinate position.
The hierarchical relation between the two parents shows itself in different
ways. One indication is the presentation of Reason as the one controlling and
persuading Necessity: "And inasmuch as Reason was controlling (*archontos*)
Necessity by persuading her (*tô peithein autên*) to conduct to the best end the
most part of the things coming into existence, thus and thereby it came about,
through necessity yielding to intelligent persuasion (*peithous*), that this
Universe of ours was being in this wise constructed at the beginning" (*Timaeus*
48a). The word that is used of the control Reason possesses over Necessity is
archô. This is a word carrying stronger meanings than the English translation
here indicates. In relations involving authority it means to 'lead', 'rule' and
'govern'. When Reason *archei* Necessity, he rules and governs her. Another of
the meanings of *archô* is 'to begin' or 'make a beginning'. This expresses a
connection to the word *archê*. Both of these words display a connection
between being the first, in the sense of constituting a beginning, and being the
one in charge. At *Timaeus* 48a, however, the father—Reason—is described as
the ruling instance also in relation to the second parent, the mother Necessity,
who is thus placed as second, secondary and subordinate in relation to the
father even from the outstart of the second story of cosmogony. From the very
beginning of the second story the birth of cosmos is described as a result of the
father's use of force—the force of persuasion—over the mother. By using persuasion as a means of acquiring power, Reason seems to act similarly to a

sophist. He does not teach Necessity the truth, for instance by dialectic methods. He is no philosopher. The use of metaphors related to rhetoric and force invokes an image more akin to sophistry than philosophy.[9] Neither is there any talk of love in the description of the relation between the parents of cosmos. The closest resemblance the father can be said to have to a lover is that of a persuasive seducer. This is a role Plato elsewhere relates to the sophist, and he leaves neither the sophist nor the seducer much honor.[10]

The inequality between the parents of cosmos shows itself, furthermore, in the description of Necessity as the troublesome factor in the generation of cosmos. It is necessity that imposes imperfection in the cosmos. As Paul Friedländer claims: "Imperfection in the world is due to the power of *Ananke.*"[11] One might rephrase this slightly, according to my interpretation here, and say that imperfection in the world is due to the power of a principle placed in the position of femininity. The reason why necessity was introduced in the first place was that something other than the father was needed to explain the difference between him and his child, i.e. the imperfection of cosmos. Imperfection could be considered to involve a lack of being. If all ideas, for instance, were defined as good, then the notion of e.g. a perfect idea of evil would make no sense, since a perfectly good idea of evil would be a contradiction in terms. Instead, evil could be conceived of as lack of goodness, and given that being was identified with the good, this could mean that evil would involve a lack of being. Similarly with the imperfect cosmos: If the imperfection of cosmos is considered as some lack of being, then the mother, to the degree she represents the cause of the imperfection of cosmos (understood as lack of being), could be seen as related to non-being. Given such an interpretation, reason and necessity appear as ontologically different levels in relation to being and non-being. The father has been called by several different names: demiurge, being, reason, and god. He is a divine cause of the cosmos, related to rationality and permanent, stable being. The mother, on the other hand, seems to have been put into the picture by necessity, to make sense of the lack of perfect rationality and permanence in the child cosmos. Maybe it is not so strange that the first name by which she is called is Necessity. Timaeus calls Necessity an errant cause: "Wherefore if one is to declare how it actually came into being on this wise, he must include also the form of the Errant Cause (*to tês planômenês eidos aitias*), in the way that it really acts" (*Timaeus* 48a). *Plano* means to "make to wander," "lead wandering about," "to lead from the subject," "to lead astray, mislead, deceive."[12] Draped in the guise of an Errant Cause, the mother named Necessity carries at least a certain degree of disorder. That Necessity should contain any amount of random or disorder, such as this wandering and misleading quality implies, may sound surprising, at least if the quality of necessity is understood as the opposite of that which is random. Nevertheless, this might still be seen to make sense. If the mother Necessity in the *Timaeus* is seen as a necessary condition for the birth of cosmos also in the sense that she constitutes that without which the discrepancy between the perfect father and his imperfect child could not be explained, then—as such a necessary condition—necessity does not have to exclude disorder, especially when she is made necessary in order to explain disorder. The mother—necessity—could then be seen as that which leads the child astray, and makes it wander away from the perfect similarity with its true cause and progenitor. Given such an interpretation, it would not be so strange, after all, that necessity and disorderly, misleading wandering is placed together in the figure of the mother of cosmos in the *Timaeus*.

At *Timaeus* 52b the mother is given her most famous name: *chôra*.[13] *Chôra* is presented at 52b in a description of the three kinds, which were identified at 48e-49a. The first being "the self-identical Form, un-generated and indestructible" (*Timaeus* 51e-52a), i.e. the father. The second kind is "that which is named after the former [the father] and similar thereto, an object perceptible by sense, generated" (*Timaeus* 52a), i.e. the cosmos. The third is now named *chôra*. The word *chôra* can be translated in several ways. The two main categories of translation are I) "space," "room," "place" and II) "land," "country."[14]   None of these apply perfectly to *chôra* in the *Timaeus*. Both "space" and "place," for instance, have other, more common, words in Greek: *To kenon* is used of space, i.e. of the empty space, and *topos* is the customary word for place. In the *Timaeus* the word *topos* is used synonymously with *chôra* (*en tini topô*) (*Timaeus* 52c). However, *chôra* cannot be *a* place, or any specific place. She is the place of all places. Since she is depicted as the place of everything born into existence, she is without a place herself.[15] *Chôra* is the soil into which all transient beings of the world of sense perception are sown, but as such she cannot herself be a specific place or any soil that can be perceived by the senses. *Chôra* is the eternal "ever-existing Place (*to tês chôras aei*)." Being eternal, she is there already, before cosmos is born, existing as a pre-condition for the birth of it. Nothing is said of where she comes from. Her origin is left unexplained, but it is stated that she "admits not of destruction," which should imply that she is beyond generation as well, given that destruction and generation presuppose and imply each other. *Chôra* should thus be beyond both birth and death. Instead she "provides room for all that have birth." She is the ultimate receiving principle, the that-in-which (*en hô*) of everything generated and born:

> "(...) we must conceive of three kinds (*genê tritta*),—the Becoming
> (*to gignomenon*), that "Wherein" it becomes (*to en hô gignetai*), and
> the source "Wherefrom" (*to hothen*) the becoming is copied and
> produced (*phuetai*). Moreover, it is proper to liken the Recipient to
> the Mother, the Source to the Father, and what is engendered
> between these two to the Offspring;" (*Timaeus* 50d).

When cosmos is born, it is born from the father and into the mother. Compared to sexual propagation, the cosmos could be considered to be born at the moment of the conception, into the mother as into a womb, and from this it never escapes. Even when a mother is brought into the picture in the second story, the procreation of the father seems to constitute the only birth that is occurring. After the children have been received into the mother, they do not go anywhere else afterwards. They are born into the receiving mother, and stay there. To put it rather bluntly: they are stuck in a pregnancy that never seems to find a further deliverance and release.[16] *Chôra* thus seems like an eternally pregnant mother who carries cosmos as a child she will never give birth to.[17]

Chôra is a core concept in the second story of the generation of cosmos, and she is inherently difficult to get a grip on. Only through a "bastard kind of reasoning" can she be somehow grasped: "We dimly dream and affirm that it is somehow necessary that" *chôra* must be there, Timaeus says (*Timaeus* 52b-c). *Chôra* is the place of everything generated, and in so far as words and meaning are generated, she is the place where they are constituted, too. As such she cannot herself have meaning in the sense that the transient generated *logoi*, of which she is a necessary condition, have meaning. *Chôra* does not have a meaning in the sense of a clearly defined, semantic correlate.[18] Instead she illustrates the limits to what can be said within language. At the same time she represents a necessary condition of any inscription of meaning whatsoever. *Chôra* is thus related to the problem of meaning itself, in a crucial way. Although *chôra* is so hard to translate, and difficult to grasp, she is all the same referred to by a wide variety of names. Immediately after stating the importance of calling her by one single name, Timaeus uses several for her. As mentioned before, the mother is called by a number of different names: "necessity" (*anagkê*), "receptacle" (*hupodochê*), "nurse" (*tithênê*) and *chôra* (*Timaeus* 48a, 49a, 52b-c). There are more: Timaeus mentions her as the bowl (*kratêra*) wherein he blended and mixed the soul of cosmos (*Timaeus* 41d), and as a winnowing basket (*Timaeus* 52e). He also calls her the molding-stuff (*ekmageion*) for everything, comparing her to gold that is molded into many forms and figures (*Timaeus* 50b-c). Being such a molding stuff she is herself formless (*amorphon*) (*Timaeus* 51a).[19] She does not have any clear and definite form of her own. Just as Timaeus is unable to grasp her, he is unable to name her by one and the same name. If a name is something that can be used as a devise to grasp something else, i.e. to grasp it in the grasp of a concept, then the fact that *chôra* is slippery and not possible to hold on to, would make the naming of her by one and the same name difficult. To the degree she does not have a clearly definable meaning, she cannot really hold on to a name either. The numerous names used of the mother, may be considered a sign of how difficult it is to get a firm grasp of *chôra*. Timaeus relates this to the receptive quality of the substance that is to be able to receive all other forms. Timaeus says of her that "if we describe her as a Kind (*eidos*) invisible (*anoraton*) and unshaped (*amor-*

phon), all-receptive (*pandeches*), and in some most perplexing and most baffling way partaking of the intelligible, we shall describe her truly" (*Timaeus* 51a-b). The form—*eidos*—of the receiving mother is to be without form (*amorphon*). This sounds like a contradiction in terms. On the one hand, the mother is obviously necessary as that in which the transient beings accessible to sense perception constitute themselves. On the other hand, the material things are imposed with transience—imperfect permanence and being—by this very mother that they constitute themselves in. The fathers of the material things, i.e. that of which they are lesser copies, are perfect, unchanging and eternal, so they cannot be the cause of imperfection in their imperfect copy-children. Hence it seems that the mother, the in-which where the children are constituted, has to be the cause of imperfection and changeability in the material things. The ambiguity of the mother is that she has to be there, already, so that the transient objects of sense-perception can materialize, but at the same time she represents an obstacle to the achievement of eternal perfection and immortality for the physical objects embedded in her. To the degree this mother is a *something*, with a form or identity of her own, she represents a threat of destruction and imposition of lack. This she does by hindering the copies' complete similarity with their father. According to this image, the ideal mother, or receptacle, ought therefore to be as devoid of any characteristics of her own as possible, "invisible (*anoraton*) and unshaped (*amorphon*)." She seems to be fundamentally ambiguous, possessing a position that implies a paradox in the sense that she is both a necessary condition for the material beings, and represents a threat to their identity and perfection.[20] No wonder she is very hard to grasp.[21]

My interest is related to the specific way in which the ambiguity of *chôra* is displayed as related to the metaphor of birth that is displayed within the *Timaeus*. Far from attempting to dissolve the ambiguities surrounding *chôra*, I attempt to shed some light on the different ways in which it is described and depicted. Rather than ask for solutions, attempting to clarify and dissolve the ambiguities embedded within these metaphorical conceptions, I ask what these ambiguities might mean. Why is this particular pattern of ambiguity put into play, what does it mean, and what does it imply? Why is the feminine figure of *chôra* so hard to grasp? If *chôra* is a necessary pre-condition of everything that is subject to *genesis*, and if *logos* belongs to the realm of the generated, then *chôra* functions as a necessary pre-condition for the imprints of meaning. *Chôra* will then be to meaning what the gold is to the figures made in the gold. The gold into which stamps are being imprinted is not itself an imprint, but the necessary precondition for all the imprints made in it. Likewise, *chôra* into which everything generated is born, is not itself contained within the meaning of a concept, but represents a pre-condition for all the meanings generated in it. According to this metaphorical analogy, an attempt at conceiving of *chôra* as a concept could be seen as akin to an attempt at making a figure representing the gold, in the very gold that is itself to be represented. It would be just as difficult, if not impossible, to define the meaning of *chôra*, as it would be to inscribe the gold into itself. As John Sallis writes: "It [*chôra*] can itself receive, be stamped or impregnated by, all those kinds called paradigms or intelligible *eidê*, but it is not *itself* determined by any of them, cannot itself have any of these determinations, cannot have them as determinations of itself. The ramifications of this utter nondetermination are profound, or rather, abysmal. Suppose that for something to have meaning were defined as its being determined by such a determination. Suppose, further, that for a word to have meaning were defined as its expressing such a determining determination, its signifying the meaning of something. Then it would have to be said that the third kind has no meaning and that the name it is about to be called, the name *chôra*, if it is a name, has no meaning. Both *chôra* and the word *chôra* would be meaningless."[22] Placed as a precondition of the text, of any text, of any meaning whatsoever, *chôra* thus represents a place within the text where the ambiguities of text and meaning are made especially explicit. When Timaeus makes an attempt at grasping her, he is searching for a stable, clear-cut, well-defined meaning, where there is none, at least not in any permanent and steady way. He seems to be performing this search by means of trying out numerous different names and images, in the hope of finding one that fits the meaning, or one that represents a grip—a grasp—on the meaning in question, but, ironically, the abundance of names attributed to *chôra* can be seen as an indication of the fact that there is no one, stable, unchangeable meaning to be found. *Chôra* thus designates a significantly unruly element in the text. It is a name that also seems to demonstrate and make visible that within the realm of generated language, a logic completely devoid of contradiction is unattainable.

In his article on the *Timaeus*, "Khôra",[23] Derrida writes about *chôra* in relation to meaning, emphasizing the necessary contradictory and ambiguous nature of texts. According to Derrida, "[W]hat Plato in the *Timaeus* designates by the name of *khôra* seems to defy that 'logic of noncontradiction of the philosophers (...). The *khôra*, which is neither 'sensible' nor 'intelligible,' belongs to a 'third genus' (*triton genos*, 48a, 52a). One cannot even say of it that it is *neither* this *nor* that or that it is *both* this *and* that. It is not enough to recall that *khôra* names neither this nor that, or, that *khôra* says this and that. The difficulty declared by *Timaeus* is shown in a different way: at times the *khôra* appears to be neither this nor that, at times both this and that, but this alternation between the logic of exclusion and that of participation (...) stems perhaps only from a provisional appearance and from the constraints of rhetoric, even from some incapacity for naming."[24] What Plato's *Timaeus* thus exhibits, according to this view, although it does not speak explicitly of it, is similar to what Jacques Derrida writes about texts in general, i.e. that since they belong to the realm of the generated, they are inherently transient and changing. They do not—and cannot—contain permanent being, but will, being subjected to time, be subjected to transferences and modifications which at least involves a certain degree of transformations of *différance,* to speak in terms of Derrida's own terminology. The text is here like a displaced landscape, constantly being deferred, changed, and different. This textual landscape is seen, not as a stable unchanging ground, but as subjected to disruptions, earthquakes, floods, and uproars.[25] With the passing of time it becomes different even from itself. According to the conception of the text that can be found in Derrida, the task of the reader is to unfold and display the ambiguities in the text. The interpreter cannot acquire any single and solid truth behind the textual weave of the text, if no such unique truth exists. Let me draw the lines back to *chôra* as she appears through the image of the gold at this point. To receive the generated imprints of meaning, the gold needs to be both solid and liquid. Complete lack of liquidity would make it too adamant to receive imprints of any kind, and complete lack of solidity would make the printing akin to writing into floating water. In the first case the print could never even begin its existence; it would be denied being born, so to speak. In the second case the imprint would vanish and die almost at the moment of being generated. In neither case would there be left space for the lasting in-between of generation and dissolution: the in-between of birth and death. That is to say, there would be left no space for the realm of life and meaning. One might perhaps say that according to our own hurried time in history, as well as according to some of the theories of meaning of our time, e.g. Derrida's, it is as if the foundation of meaning—the gold—has come to be considered as akin to gold that has been heated, melted and become more liquid. The gold no longer appears as such a more solid metal as it used to, constituting a place for lasting and durable imprints. Consequently the imprints of meaning seem to be less lasting and durable. Rather, it is the transience and fluidity of the imprints that have become vividly clear.

In neither of the two stories of the birth of cosmos in the *Timaeus* are the feminine and the masculine placed as equally existing entities. In the first story the mother is absent, and in the second story her necessary existence as the that-in-which of the generated beings is displayed as surrounded by profound ambiguities and difficulties. This could be considered a displayal of some of the difficulties involved in a tradition of ontology in search of one original origin. Whereas in Antiquity the father was pictured as the primary originator giving birth at what we would call the conception, we would today, however, usually consider a birth to be the result of a sexual relation between two parents, where both contribute equally to the child, and both the mother and the father would be considered originators of the child. One might perhaps call these two different images of birth, the more modern one and the ancient Greek one, by two different names, describing their different structures: a plural-parent structure and a one-parent structure. If we take the plural-parent structure, with both a mother and a father originating one child, as our point of departure, the image created would contain a different structure than the one-parent structure with the image of one primary parent. According to a plural-parent structure there would necessarily be an increasing amount of ancestors the further back one goes. Thus, according to such an image, a search for a single one—The One—progenitor would not seem very relevant. If one were to start with the notion of a generated human being that was born from the union of (at least) two parents, this picture would seem to open up a scope that would be different from a picture with one singular and original *archê*. According to such a metaphor of birth, one would have one originated child with a vast and incalculable amount of originators behind it, instead of one origin generating many children. There would, according to the image of the plural-parent structure, be hard to imagine *one* first beginning, since the further back one would seek, the more numerous and different the forefathers and foremothers—the numerous *archai*, so to speak—would become, and also the more complicated their intertwining. But still we do exist. We are. And the cause of our being is our becoming, i.e. that someone procreated us, and gave birth to us. Could we not perhaps be considered to have identity and being constituted as a result of becoming, as a result of being generated and born?

Notes

1. Paraphrased from Jacques Derrida in the roundtable discussion at the end of Leonard Lawlor, *Imagination and Chance*, 134-135.

2. Aristotle, *Metaphysics book I*.

3. Tamsin Lorraine, 185 in "Becoming-Imperceptible as a Mode of Self-Presentation" in *Resistance, Flight, Creation*. (Ed. Dorothea Olkowski) Cornell University Press 2000.

4. Aeschylus, *Eumenides* 659-665, in Verrall's translation. Apollo continues with a proof of this theory of reproduction, which deprives the mother of true parenthood, i.e. the birth of Athena (665-670): "And I will show thee a proof of this argument. A father may become such without a mother's aid. Here at my hand is a witness, the Child of Olympian Zeus,—who, even ere she came to light, grew not in a womb, yet is a fairer plant than all the powers of heaven could beget."

5. Sophocles, *Antigone* 569, in Hugh Lloyd-Jones' translation.

6. "that which has come into existence (*tô genomenô*) must necessarily, as we say, have come into existence by reason of some Cause" (*Timaeus* 28c).

7. David Farrell Krell claims that the first turning point in the account of *Timaeus* occurs when he must begin all over again, "because for all his attention to nous he has forgotten its partner, ananke. He has not remembered things concerning women." David Farrell Krell, "Female Parts in *Timaeus*," *Arion: a Quarterly Journal of Classical Culture*, Austin, Texas (1975), 411.

Krell argues that "the resolution of the fundamental ontological problem in

Timaeus, the generation of the visible world (*genesis*) from the Being (*to on*) through model-forms (*paradeigmatos eidos*), requires 'female parts,' and that because Timaeus of Locri insults and degrades all things female his discourse is a resounding, if instrictible, failure" (Krell, ibid., 400). I agree with Krell in his statement about the femininity of *anagkê*, although I disagree with his view that there is nothing Platonic about the *Timaeus*. I further disagree that Timaeus insults and degrades all things female. It is more ambiguous and complex than that. What I would agree with, though, is that "there is ultimately something philosophically unsatisfying about the Locrian's discourse" (Krell, ibid., 405).

8. As David Farrell Krell writes: "now the discourse requires a third kind for which it is difficult to find words. *Timaeus* calls it 'the receptacle and a sort of nurse of all generation' (49a 5-6)" (Krell, ibid., 412).

9. Glenn R. Morrow writes about the relation between necessity and persuasion in *Timaeus* 48a, where we are told that reason (*nous*) persuades necessity (anagkê), and argues that we should not read this too literally, because that would imply a contradiction. For what kind of necessity would be subject to persuasion? Is not the necessary exactly what cannot be persuaded? Glenn R. Morrow, "Necessity and *Persuasion in Plato's Timaeus* (1959)," in R.E. Allen, *Studies in Plato's Metaphysics*. Morrow also points to the strangeness of using a concept like persuasion in relation to natural processes. In Parmenides, *anagkê* functions as a logical necessity, i.e. as something that convinces. Contrary to Morrow I propose to read this passage literally.

10. E.g. the *Phaedrus* 237 b, where Socrates with allusions to the sophist, and would-be-seducer, Lysias, and the beautiful, young boy Phaedrus says: "Now there was once upon a time a boy, or rather a stripling, of great beauty: and he had many lovers. And among these there was one of peculiar craftiness, who was as much in love with the boy as anyone, but had made him believe he was not in love; and once in wooing him, he tried to persuade him of this very thing [of which Lysias has just tried to persuade Phaedrus], that favours ought to be granted rather to the non-lover than to the lover (...)."

11. Paul Friedländer, *Plato*. Vol. 3, chapter XXIX. *Timaeus*, 380.

12. *Liddell and Scott Greek-English Lexicon*. In its passive form—*planaomai*—the word means to wander, stray. Plato uses the passive form of the Necessity that wanders and strays. Krell points out that Plato denominates Necessity as planomenon: "the word that will be used to describe the womb in its hysterical state (91c4)". Krell, ibid., 415. This may be pressing the meaning of the word a bit far, but the word does carry metaphorical meanings related to illusion, deceit and imposture.

13. In recent years *chôra* has received increasing focus and attention. E.g. Derrida has written an article focusing on the ambiguity of *chôra* in the *Timaeus*; Kristeva uses this concept in her own original way, and John Sallis has named his entire book on *Timaeus Chorology*, after this central concept in the dialogue. Already in *Timaeus* 19a Plato puts the word *chôra* into the mouth of Socrates. Jacques Derrida, for one, demonstrates the significance of *chôra* in the *Timaeus* (Derrida, "Khôra," 107). At *Timaeus* 19a *chôra* is used as a denomination of a place for children. Derrida points to another use of the word *chôra* at the beginning of the *Timaeus*, where Socrates speaks of himself as one who is like—or imitates—the poets and the sophists. The exact words he uses

is the tribe of the poets (*poietikon genos*) and the tribe of the sophists (*sophiston genos*) (*Timaeus* 19d-e) (My translation). The sophists were people without a place of their own. They were travelers moving from one place to another. Derrida calls attention to how Socrates in his mimesis of the sophists—i.e. the placeless (and hence being-less?)—places himself in a sort of non-place: "Socrates' strategy itself operates from a sort of non-place" (Derrida, 107. See also 108). This lack of a firmly settled country of belonging may be interesting in relation to *chôra* and the next part of the introduction I wish to look more closely at: the myth of the autochthony of the Athenians. In this myth the identity is closely linked to belonging to a place, and having an origin springing from the earth of the country. The identity or being of somebody comes from being born into a certain land (*chôra*).

14. Liddell and Scott *Greek-English Lexicon*.

15. Attempting to read *chôra* as akin to topos would imply a risk of assimilating the chorology of Plato to the topology of Aristotle. John Sallis warns against "assimilating Plato's chorology to the topology of Aristotle's *Physics*" *Chorology* 115.

16. It may not seem so strange perhaps, that Sara B. Pomeroy wonders, "if Plato believed, as did Apollo in the *Eumenides* (657-61), that only the father is the true parent and the mother only nurses the seed." S.B. Pomeroy "Feminism in Book V of Plato's *Republic*," *Apeiron* (1974), 34. David Farrell Krell also points to Aeschylus' *Eumenides* (657-59) in his paper "Female Parts in *Timaeus*" in *Arion* 1975, 414.

17. The same could be said of the mother-goddess Gê, as she is described in the *Phaedo*, in the great myth of reincarnation.

18. The difficulties involved in translating the word *chôra* can be related to the place of the *chôra* in the constituting and expression of meaning. As John Sallis writes: "To propose a translation of *chôra* would—according to this concept—be to say that both words, *chôra* and its translation, have the same semantic correlate, the same meaning; translation would consist, then, in moving from one word to the other by way of this common meaning. Inasmuch as *chôra* has no meaning—at least not in this classical sense—it is intrinsically untranslatable" John Sallis *Chorology*, 115.

19. Paul Friedländer comments upon the Greek words Timaeus uses to describe this all-receiving chôra. "Tithene is she who suckles an infant (...). *Hypodoche* means reception or entertainment (...)." (Plato, vol. 3, chapter XXIX. *Timaeus*, 370). The word *kratêra* is used at *Timaeus* 41d 4, and at *Timaeus* 50b6 we find *ekmageion* (as at *Timaeus* 50c-2) which can mean "natural recipient of impressions, of imitations of eternal being (50c5) (...) 'mother' (...) *amorphon*." He also states "*Nothos* means illegitimate or baseborn." (413). Paul Friedländer, *Plato*. Vol. 3, chapter XXIX. *Timaeus*.

20. David Farrell Krell emphasizes this problematic and aporetic nature of the receptacle. As he writes about the receptacle described in the *Timaeus*: "Indeed the patrogenic view makes *Timaeus*' own account unintelligible: if the mother is only a container of a seed wholly formed by the male, how can Becoming be other than a perfect image of its father?" Krell, op. cit., 414. And he states this point even more explicitly: "Of all aporias she is the most aporetic" Krell, op. cit., 413.

21. E.g. *Timaeus* 51a.

22. Sallis, *Chorology*, 111. This is a point also Derrida makes. He writes in "Khôra" 117: "But if *khôra* is a receptacle, if it/she gives place to all the stories, ontologic or mythic, that can be recounted on the subject of what she receives and even of what she resembles but which in fact takes place in her, *khôra* herself, so to speak, does

not become the object of any tale, whether true or fabled. A secret without secret remains forever impenetrable on the subject of it/her [à son sujet]. Though it is not a true *logos*, no more is the word on *khôra* a probable myth, either, a story that is reported and in which another story will take place in its turn."
    23. Jacques Derrida, "Khôra" 89-131.
    24. Jacques Derrida, "Khôra" 89.
    25. Jacques Derrida, "Khôra" 126: "The discourse on *khôra* thus plays for philosophy a role analogous to the role which *khôra* 'herself' plays for that which philosophy speaks, namely, the cosmos formed or given form according to the paradigm. (...) Once again, a homology or analogy that is at least formal: in order to think *khôra*, it is necessary to go back to a beginning that is older than the beginning, namely, the birth of the cosmos, just as the origin of the Athenians must be recalled to them from beyond their own memory."

Bibliography

Aeschylus. *The Eumenides*. Translated by A. W. Verrall. Macmillan and co. 1908.

Allen, R.E. *Studies in Plato's Metaphysics*. Routledge & Kegan Paul Ltd, 1965.

Aristotle. *Metaphysics*. Translated by Hugh Tredennick and G. Cyril Armstrong, vol. XVII 1989, vol. XVIII 1990, The Loeb Classical Library. Harvard University Press, 1989.

Derrida, Jacques. *On the Name*. Stanford University Press, 1995.

Friedländer, Paul. *Plato*. Vol. 3. Princeton University Press, 1969.

Grosz, Elizabeth. *Space, Time and Perversion*. Routledge, 1995.

Irigaray, Luce. *Speculum of the Other Woman*. Cornell University Press, 1985.

Krell, David Farrell. "Female Parts in *Timaeus*," *Arion: a Quarterly Journal of Classical Culture*. Austin, Texas: (1975), pp. 400-422.

Kristeva, Julia. *Desire in Language: a Semiotic Approach to Literature and Art* (ed. Leon S. Roudiez). Basil Blackwell, 1980.

———. "The Semiotic Chora Ordering the Drives," *Revolution in Poetic Language*. New York, 1984.

Lawlor, Leonard. *Imagination and Chance*. State University of New York Press, 1993.

Liddell, Henry George and Scott, Robert. *A Greek-English Lexicon*. Clarendon Press, 1994.

Olkowski, Dorothea (ed.). *Resistance, Flight, Creation*. Cornell University Press, 2000.

Plato. *Phaedo*. Translated by Harold North Fowler, Loeb Classical Library, vol. I: "Euthyphro. Apology. Crito. Phaedo. Phaedrus." Harvard University Press, 1990.

————. *Phaedrus*. Translated by Harold North Fowler, Loeb Classical Library, vol. I: "Euthyphro. Apology. Crito. Phaedo. Phaedrus." Harvard University Press, 1990.

————. *Timaeus*. Translated by R. G. Bury, Loeb Classical Library, vol. IX: "Timaeus. Critias. Cleitophon. Menexenus. Epistles." Harvard University Press, 1989.

————. *Timaeus and Critias*. Translated by Desmond Lee. Penguin Classics, 1987.

Pomeroy, Sara B. "Feminism in Book V of Plato's Republic," *Apeiron* (1974).

Sallis, John. *Chorology. On Beginning in Plato's Timaeus*. Indiana University Press, 1999.

Sophocles. *Antigone*. Translated by Hugh Lloyd-Jones, Loeb Classical Library, Harvard University Press, 1994.

From Sexual Difference
to the Way of Breath:
Toward a Feminist Ontology of Ourselves

Johanna Oksala

> Humanity seems past. Philosophies and religions are in a period of
> taking stock. The dominant discipline in the human sciences is now
> history. Sociology, which shares the spotlight with it, is dedicated to
> the description of what already exists. We should be what we are,
> what we have already shown of ourselves. As for the rest, our
> becoming would be prescribed by our genes, or by what has already
> been deciphered of them. Our growth is to have stopped one day.
> We are to have become at best objects of study. Like the whole liv-
> ing world, destroyed little by little by the exploration-exploitation of
> what it is instead of cultivating what it could become. (Irigaray
> 2002, 7)

For many feminist thinkers ontology has become almost a dirty word. As Sally
Haslanger writes (2000, 107), academic feminists, for the most part, view
metaphysics as a dubious intellectual project, certainly irrelevant and probably
worse.[1] Feminist theoreticians from different theoretical frameworks have
argued that ontology masks an effective ideology of oppression by upholding
an immutable hierarchy of beings. The devalued side of such ontological oppositions as mind/body, nature/culture, animal/human has been attached to femininity and this has led to oppressive practices and conceptions about women.
Oppressive regimes justify themselves and eclipse alternative political arrange-
ments by casting their representation of the world as revealing the true structure of reality.[2]

Feminist theory should not, however, respond to the problem ontology
poses by adopting a position of hypocrisy. Not mentioning the word 'ontology'

does not mean that feminist problems concerning it will disappear. If we accept that ontology is a reflection on the nature of existing reality and thereby forms the framework which functions to constrain all our theorizing and thought within the limits it sets, then it also forms a fundamental limit for our efforts to overcome oppressive attitudes and practices. We must therefore face the question of ontology rather than shy away from it: to try to imagine and advocate a different ontology.

The idea of imagining a different ontology is no easy task, however. Ontology is usually not understood as something that we can create, but it is supposed to describe the way the world is and also the way we are as part of it. It thus describes the situation we find ourselves in. This situation moreover forms the context for all our thought and practices. We can only think and act in so far as we find ourselves in an ontological situation. So, if ontology is a description of what there is and what we are, how is it possible to change it? How could we change by our actions something that determines our actions? If ontology describes being, would a different ontology not simply amount to fiction, to a misrepresentation of reality?

To be able to imagine a different ontology presupposes at least two contested philosophical claims. Firstly, it presupposes that we can understand and elucidate the ontology underlying our present thinking. Secondly, we must be able to show that our present ontology is not necessary in any absolute sense. However, while a feminist ontology should satisfy these two requirements, most of us do not want to opt for any form of subjective idealism where the nature of reality is understood as being totally dependent on our individual preferences or political values. One promising possibility for feminist theory would therefore be a historical ontology: the structure of reality changes in history and is therefore different in different historical and cultural epochs.

Hence, before explicitly turning to study the feminist question of imagining a different ontology, I will pave the way for this by a short study of two philosophers—Martin Heidegger and Michel Foucault—who present a radically historical understanding of the ontology underlying our thinking. I will start with Heidegger's thought and particularly with his idea of technology as the domineering form that metaphysics has taken in our age. For Heidegger all philosophy is ontology or metaphysics and it culminates in the development and success of technology.

In the second part I focus my discussion on the ontology of ourselves by taking up Foucault's work on the technologies of the self. Foucault's focus on technologies of the self in his late thinking is a way of inquiring into the practices which constitute our Western understanding of the self. His ontological question concerns our modes of being and the ways they have changed in history. Ultimately both Heidegger and Foucault argue that the question of technology is intimately involved in the current understanding of ourselves, an understanding which they both identify as being in many ways problematic.

I finish by engaging with the thought of Luce Irigaray. Irigaray is arguably the most influential representative of the feminist strategy of imagining a different ontology. Her criticism of the masculine metaphysics of our Western philosophical tradition is a thread that runs through all her works. Her important and recurring argument has been that we need an ontology of two sexes, an ontology founded on being two. For her the question of sexual difference is the question that underlies our most basic ways of thinking and being. It is essentially an ontological question.[3]

The idea of sexual difference as an ontological difference has been met with strong objections among many feminists, however. They have argued that it leads to essentialist views about women and to the granting of a special status to sexual difference in relation to other differences such as race and class. In this paper, however, I will read Irigaray's work in continuum with Heidegger's and Foucault's understanding of a radically historical ontology and argue that this places her ontological claims in a different context. For her, ontology does not describe an immutable order of substances or essences, but rather refers to the historically changing way that reality is revealed to us. The ontological question is thus not: What kind of entities does reality consist of? and her answer to it is not: Men and women. The questions she asks are rather of the type: How is reality revealed to us in this historical epoch? How do we understand ourselves as parts of it? As men and women, as body and soul, as determined by our genes and as objects of study?

I will discuss Irigaray's recent work in particular which takes up the question of ethnic and racial differences. In her book *Between East and West*, Irigaray discusses the question of different races and different traditions alongside the question of sexual difference. She writes that while globalization has forced us to come to terms with the blending of races and traditions which disturb our mental habits, our common laws and our legislative criteria, we are still lacking "a culture of between-sexes, of between-races, of between-traditions" (Irigaray 2002, 139). Rather than emphasizing only sexual difference, she notes more comprehensively that "the generalized mixing in our age" must make us "recognize difference as a fundamental character of the living" (ibid.). Sexual difference is understood as a model for respecting other differences. It is thus a paradigmatic difference rather than one that stands in a hierarchical relationship to other differences.[4]

My aim is thus to show that instead of approaching the question of ontology in terms of essentialist claims about sexual difference, Irigaray's recent work can be read as pointing us towards imagining a different ontology of ourselves based on a fruitful dialogue between Eastern and Western cultural traditions.

The Rule of Technology

For Heidegger, the question of metaphysics is essentially a question of the history of metaphysics.[5] His project is to chart this history and thereby come to an understanding of the metaphysics underlying our age. The central argument is that the history of metaphysics is a forgetting of Being. Since its very beginning in Plato's thought, the aim of metaphysics has been to articulate the truth about all that is and to formulate a general theory of beings enumerating their essences and attributes. It has become ontology, a theory of beings, while Being, irreducible to any totality of beings, has been forgotten. The fact that beings *are* is thus not considered as worth questioning. It arouses no wonder in us, nor do we even understand what it would mean to question Being.

To understand the form that this forgetting and thus metaphysics has taken in our age, we must question technology. This seems at first sight to be a fairly easy task. We talk about technology all the time and spend huge amounts of time and money in researching it. The way Heidegger understands technology, however, makes our usual ways of questioning it irrelevant. He does not understand technology in the sense of technical instruments, machines or mere means of manipulating the environment. For Heidegger, technology is a certain way of revealing of the world. Reality is manifesting itself within technology to the modern man. The question concerning technology is not: What is technology? or How do we best utilize it? but rather, How is reality revealed to us in a historical age dominated by technology? We are thus not posing questions about mobile phones, super-automated spaces or nuclear missiles, but rather about the way the world is in an age when we have such technological advancements at our disposal. The danger that modern technology presents is not a problem to which we should find an effective solution. Instead it is an ontological situation which demands a radical change in the way we understand reality.

Heidegger's central question concerning technology is thus a question about our relationship to Being. He writes that we are questioning concerning technology in order to bring to light our relationship to its essence (Heidegger 1977, 23). Unlike the traditional understanding of essence as the general concept or category that particulars manifest or belong to, Heidegger understands essence very differently. It is not a general category of beings but the mode of their disclosedness, their enduring presence through time. The essence of technology is a certain way that the world shows itself through technology.

Heidegger uses the concept of *das Gestell*, Enframing, to describe the essence, the mode of revealing of modern technology. Under the dominion of Enframing nothing is allowed to appear in any other way except as supply of material to be used, as "standing-reserve." Through modern technology the surrounding world is disclosed as something that is either useful or harmful to us, something that is revealed to us only according to our needs and preferences. Heidegger writes that the river becomes a waterpower supplier or "an object on call for inspection by a tour group ordered there by the vacation industry" (ibid., 16).

This kind of sentences have contributed to readings of Heidegger as a forerunner of ecological movements that are critical of the technological domination of nature. Heidegger's point is not, however, simply to stand up against modern technology. The way he understands technology makes it impossible to be either for or against it. Technology is not something we can choose to take or leave, because what is at issue is our relationship to the surrounding world and the way it shows itself to us. Hence, the ultimate question that concerns us is our way of being. "The threat to man does not come in the first instance from the potentially lethal machines and apparatus of technology. The actual threat has already affected man in his essence" (ibid., 28).

Heidegger's thinking is thus critical, but in a more profound sense than pointing out the problems that modern technology has caused for our environment, socio-economic structures or ways of life. He is trying to show how modern technology has changed the way the world *is* and also ultimately how we *are*. The problem and danger that modern technology poses for Heidegger, and ultimately for the human race, is twofold. Firstly, we can only understand ourselves as interconnected with the world, which provides the horizon for all our understanding of it, including ourselves. When the world is revealed as standing-reserve, also man becomes standing-reserve. Man becomes an object among other objects, to be used, calculated and profited from. Man becomes part of nature, but nature understood not as earth-home but as standing-reserve: mines, power plants and industrialized agriculture.

The main danger that technology poses for Heidegger is not, however, only the fact that man becomes standing reserve. The more serious problem is that this way of being of the world hides a more primordial way. As a consequence man sees himself as the organizer of the world, he sees it as coming from himself.

> ...when destining reigns in the mode of Enframing, it is the supreme danger. This danger attests itself to us in two ways. As soon as what is unconcealed no longer concerns man even as object, but does so, rather, exclusively as standing-reserve, and man in the midst of objectlessness is nothing but the orderer of the standing-reserve, then he comes to the point where he himself will have to be taken as standing-reserve. Meanwhile man, precisely as the one so threatened, exalts himself to the posture of lord of the earth. In this way the impression comes to prevail that everything man encounters exists only insofar as it is his construct. This illusion gives rise in turn to one final delusion: It seems as though man everywhere and always encounters only himself. (Ibid., 26-27)

The danger of modern technology is thus twofold: man becomes standing-reserve, but as the organizer of the world he also becomes the master of it. Yet, while the world seems to be to an ever increasing extent under his control and questions about reality find rational answers, it is more and more apparent that the questions about man himself and human life are still lacking answers.

Hence, despite the strangeness of his terminology, perhaps it is almost too easy to agree with Heidegger. Man's technological domination and destruction of the planet has become fairly common knowledge. Deep-ecologists, for example, have already long argued that we do not need simply more technical solutions, but a profound change at the fundamental level of values and attitudes or else we will soon render our planet uninhabitable by humans.[6] Moreover, the question I posed in the beginning was not whether there are any serious problems facing humanity, but rather, what can we do in the face of them. What can we do about our ontological situation?

In thinking the different modes of Being, Heidegger lays out a fundamentally historical ontology: he argues that the world is revealed in different ways in different epochs. Since Enframing is only one among Being's modes of coming to presence, this means that it changes. But even if we accept that ontology is historical, how should we understand change? If the rule of modern technology determines the way the world is and the way we are as part of it, what can we do about it? What is the role of man?

Heidegger's position seems ambiguous here. On the one hand he makes it clear that man cannot by his actions alone save us from the danger of the epoch of Being coming to presence as Enframing. Because Enframing is a mode of Being itself, this means that technology will never allow itself to be mastered, either positively or negatively, by human doing. "Technology, whose essence is Being itself, will never allow itself to be overcome by men. That would mean, after all, that man was the master of Being" (ibid., 38).

Heidegger answers our question concerning what to do by warning us that perhaps our question already betrays a wrong attitude: thinking that we can devise solutions to all our problems means believing that we are in control of everything. The ideas of control and management of technology are already part of the mindset of Enframing. "Before considering the question that is seemingly always the most immediate one and the only urgent one, What Shall we do? we must ponder this: How must we think?" (ibid., 40).

While thinking is the task Heidegger clearly assigns us, what is not so clear is what exactly he means by it. In his lecture on Nietzsche's metaphysics, the powerful image he gives us of the man who thinks is Nietzsche's madman seeking God in the midst of laughing unbelievers.[7] In thinking we must somehow free ourselves from all those modes of thought which aim at grasping reality through ready-made conceptual schemas. Thinking is something different from the knowing belonging to science which transforms all that is into objects. It is "calm, self-possessed surrender to that which is worthy of questioning" (ibid., 180).[8]

Thinking is thus something that is essentially passive. It means being responsive and open to whatever is manifesting itself to us and letting things emerge as they are. It means wonder at the presencing of things rather than trying to step back from them, to objectify them and to demand that they fit our predetermined conceptual systems. When in thinking we seek to articulate that which is, we do not describe our situation or enumerate the surrounding world of objects, but instead "it is the constellation of Being that is uttering itself to us" (ibid., 42). Thought is a gift of Being.

Man can thus never be the master of Being, but his essence is importantly interconnected with its essence. Man belongs to Being. Any change in its essence requires the cooperation of man. William Lovitt (1977, xxviii) writes that the juxtaposing of the destining of Being and the doing of man is absolutely fundamental for Heidegger's thinking. He is thus not a determinist, even though the destining of Being is an event prior to any act of human willing. Man does forever catch reality up in conceptual systems, but he does this *both* as his own work *and* because the revealing now holding sway brings it about that he should do so.

Heidegger thus grants that there can be a turning: a turning in Being and in humanity. Technology can be surmounted in a way that restores its concealed truth and establishes a different relationship between man and Being. This does not mean that technology can ever be overcome by men or that it will be done away with one day. Rather it can be surmounted from within by understanding its essence and its power. "This restoring surmounting is similar to what happens in the human realm when one gets over grief or pain" (Heidegger 1977, 39). He seems to emphasize by this comparison with healing that it is not an active intending but something more passive. Man in his essence is to be the one who waits, he is "a shepherd of Being" who in thinking must guard the mystery of Being.[9]

An Ontology of Ourselves

Heidegger's historical ontology is clearly echoed in the thought of Foucault. For the latter, a historical study of the different ways of ordering reality is the only way to elucidate our ontological situation. The influence of Heidegger on Foucault's historical ontology can perhaps best be detected in *The Order Of Things*, which relies heavily on Heidegger's antihumanism. Foucault studies the different epistemic structures underlying different historical epochs, which make certain forms of thinking possible.[10]

As far as understanding the changes between the different epistemes, Foucault's position is, however, even more ambiguous than Heidegger's. *The Order of Things* has been strongly criticized for the fact that Foucault offers no explanation as to why the ontological order of things changes at certain points in history or what is the subject's role in instigating these changes.[11] I will not go into the problems of this book here, however. Instead, I will discuss Foucault's late work on technologies of the self, which represents an important contribution to thinking about the role of the subject in actively instigating change.[12]

In Heidegger's thinking, Enframing is not a consequence of our actions because it already determines who we are and what our world is. As George Pattison (2000, 66) explains its hold on us, we are caught up in and defined by Enframing and we do not so much direct it as operate within it or on the basis of it. In so far as we are agents of Enframing, serving it, perpetuating it and ever extending its dominion, we are so on the basis that we are ourselves already framed, already determined in our essence by Enframing. The question about technology thus turns out to be a question of who we ourselves are in our being.

Foucault's late thinking takes up explicitly the question of our modes of being and the ways they have changed in history. Rather than focusing on the relationship we have to the world or beings, the focus is on the relationship we have to ourselves. In a lecture on technologies of the self, Foucault relates his thinking to Heidegger on this point. After presenting a detailed description of the historical changes in the conceptions of the self between Antiquity and Christianity, he notes that he would like to add one final word about the practical significance of this form of analysis. He then, perhaps surprisingly, turns to Heidegger.

> For Heidegger, it was through an increasing obsession with techné as the only way to arrive at an understanding of objects, that the West lost touch with Being. Let's turn the question around and ask which techniques and practices constitute the Western concept of the subject, giving it its characteristic split of truth and error, freedom and constraint. I think that it is here that we will find the real possibility of constructing a history of what we have done and at the same time, a diagnosis of what we are. (Foucault 1997, 179)

For Foucault the theoretical diagnosis of our selves must also have a political dimension. By this he means an analysis that relates to what we are willing to accept in our world. What should we accept, refuse, and change, both in ourselves and in our circumstances? The question thus importantly concerns the possibilities for a change and specifically, for changing ourselves. According to Foucault, this kind of analysis of the possible transformations opens up a possibility for critical philosophy: "Not a critical philosophy that seeks to determine the conditions and the limits of our possible knowledge of the object, but a critical philosophy that seeks the conditions and the indefinite possibilities of transforming the subject, of transforming ourselves" (ibid., 179).

While Heidegger thus seems to hold that human activity can never directly counter the danger posed by modern technology because our being is always partly determined by it, for Foucault the question of ontology becomes, importantly, a political question. One form it takes is a politics of our selves. We are not essentially and eternally anything, but the self is something we must actively create through our practices. The ontology of ourselves must be, perhaps paradoxically, an ontology of becoming. It is a question of transforming ourselves.

This is, however, easier said than done. As Gail Stenstad (2001, 336) writes about Heidegger's thought, to say that we are historical, in other words that what is past shapes the present and in fact shapes us, is so uncontroversial as to be almost trite. To understand the range and depth of that shaping, and to contemplate whether and how we can change is another matter. The idea of transforming ourselves thus seems to open up a host of new, difficult questions lacking definite answers. Who are we now? What do we want to become? By what means can we change? As women, the specific questions that we must consider are: Do we want to be like men, joining them in their technological mastery over nature? Can we envisage an ontological situation that neither involves the subjection of some group of individuals, nor the relentless exploitation of world's resources for technological ends?[13]

Foucault turns to Ancient Greece in his effort to imagine a different ontology of ourselves. According to him, the technologies through which men have tried to change themselves have acquired different forms in different cultures over the centuries, throughout Antiquity and following the transition to Christianity. The main objective of the Greek schools of philosophy did not consist of the teaching of theory. The goal was the transformation of the individual: to give each individual the quality which would permit him to live differently, better, more happily, than other people. Philosophical training thus equipped the individual with a number of techniques which permit him to conduct himself in all circumstances of life without losing mastery of himself (ibid., 184).

Self-examination and confession initially played a very small role in these techniques, but their importance grew during the Roman Empire. The Stoics, for example, practiced the examination of conscience. This examination was, however, still significantly different from the practices of confession that developed with Christianity. The goal of this examination was not the discovery of the truth hidden in the subject, it was to recall the truth forgotten by the subject. The examination would reveal that the subject had forgotten what he ought to have done, that is, to follow a collection of rules of conduct that he had learned. In the Stoic exercise, the sage thus memorizes acts in order to reactivate the fundamental rules (ibid., 186-190).

According to Foucault, a profound change took place with the development of the Christian tradition, as well as with the growing importance of the secular tradition. Technologies of the self adopted the paradoxical position of being the means of deciphering the truth about oneself while at the same time the ultimate aim was self-renunciation, the sacrifice of the self.[14]

In Christianity, there developed a complex technology of the self which maintained the difference between knowledge of being, knowledge of the word, and knowledge of the self. Unlike in Ancient Greece, where knowledge about the cosmic order of the world also meant knowledge about the self, knowledge about the self formed a sphere of its own, and its study required special techniques. It took shape in the constitution of thought as a field of subjective data which were to be interpreted. The role of the interpreter was assumed by continuous verbalization of the most imperceptible movements of thought (ibid., 228).

According to Foucault, what is important to realize is that these Christian practices of discovering and interpreting the self and confessing the truth about it to others have developed into various psycho-therapeutic practices in our secular modern culture. We have become a confessing society. These practices are thus still constitutive of the present ontology of ourselves: the self is understood as something that can be discovered and the truth about it known.

By turning to Ancient Greece Foucault is thus suggesting that rather than understanding the relationship one has to oneself as a relationship of knowledge, we should understand it as a "care" or "concern for oneself." With his explication of Greek technologies of the self he wants to argue further his point that there is no true self that can be deciphered and emancipated, but that the self is something that has been—and must be—created.

> Maybe the problem of the self is not to discover what it is ... Maybe our problem now is that the self is nothing else than the historical correlation of the technology built in our history. Maybe the problem is to change those technologies... And in this case, one of the main political problems nowadays would be, in the strict sense of the word, the politics of ourselves. (Ibid., 230-231)

While the idea of discovering a different relationship to ourselves not based on knowledge resonates strongly with feminist emphasis on more embodied conceptions of the self, it also presents problems for feminist theory. A return to Ancient Greece is impossible, so the model for these practices of the self is a dead culture. We have no living examples of them. Furthermore, Ancient Greek technologies of the self were exclusively practices for free men. There were no technologies of the self for slaves and women. While some commentators have argued that Foucault's practices of the self can be translated to a variety of modern, self-reflective, disciplined and essentially bodily practices such as line-dancing,[15] for example, I would claim that the challenge must lie deeper. I therefore now turn to Luce Irigaray's thought.

An Ontology of Breath

Like Heidegger, also Irigaray demands that we think: disregard all superficial and partial remedies and try to go back to the source from which the danger confronting us is born. What can withstand man's destructive power over the world?

> Has he not, in fact, exhausted the earth, prevailed by his cunning over the wild animal, over the birds and the fishes, subjected to his work the horse and the ox, invented the all-comprehending through speech, and also the government of cities and victory over cosmic storms? Has he not dominated all, or almost all, by his cleverness, only to arrive at nothing? And, surveying from on high the world, his world, does he not find himself finally excluded from it. (Irigaray 2002, 2)

Irigaray is also critical of our ontological understanding of ourselves as masters of the universe. According to her, our Western metaphysics corresponds to a sacrifice of the body and the universe to a coded and codeable knowledge valid in all times and all places. She writes that "in Western philosophy the thought of the world as a living world no longer exists" (ibid., 45).

Like Heidegger and Foucault, Irigaray has also emphasized the crucial role played by the Greeks in the destiny of the West.[16] In her recent book *Between East and West*, however, rather than looking back to Ancient Greece she takes a different route, which I find interesting. Rather than attempting the problematic appropriation of a dead culture dominated by male practices, she turns to the living cultural tradition of India. She does not claim that it can provide us with any simple answers, but suggests that familiarity with it "can put us on or put us back on the way, or, at least, challenge us" (ibid., 48).

In this book Irigaray sketches a different ontology of ourselves based on Eastern teachings which emphasize breath: the human being is made of matter, but also of breath. She claims that we have forgotten the basic importance of breath. We speak of elementary human needs like the need to eat and to drink, but not of the need to breathe, which corresponds nevertheless to our first and most radical need. Breathing also corresponds to the first autonomous gesture of the living human being. To come into the world supposes inhaling and exhaling by oneself. In the uterus we receive oxygen through the mother's blood. That is why we are not yet autonomous, not yet born (ibid., 74).

Irigaray emphasizes the universality of breath by writing that it "is indeed what can be shared by all men and women on this side and beyond differences of culture" (12-13). It is not, however, understood as an inert and universal substance, an Eastern substitute for the immortal soul. Breath is a dynamic principle, which makes it possible to transform ourselves in our fundamental way of being.

"Thanks to the mastery of breath, a surplus of life can be brought to the body, modifying its metabolism, its nature, its inertia. The human being can transfigure it, transsubstantiate it, overcome part of its heaviness. Western man has generally neglected, even forgotten this ability" (ibid., ix).

The ontology of breath corresponds with a concrete, daily practice—yoga. For Irigaray, yoga can awaken or discover worlds and gestures carrying another meaning, another light, another rationality. Learning to breathe, in a conscious and voluntary way, means a second birth. It is equivalent to taking charge of one's life rather than remaining passive at the level of breathing, "bathing in a sort of socio-cultural placenta that passes on to us an already exhaled, already used, not truly pure air" (ibid., 74).

Philosophies present themselves in India as practices which are never complete but always evolving. They are not, furthermore, without intention, as is often presented to us, or as we risk imagining them. Their intention should, however, be understood in a different sense than the one we generally give to this word. Their intention does not aim at an exterior object or project with the objective of appropriation or of possession. Intention has as its objective the constitution of an accomplished interiority that remains tied to and in constant communion with the whole world (ibid., 37-38).

In the West we often believe that the essential part of culture and all that is valuable in it resides in words, texts, or in works of art, and that physical exercise should only help us to dedicate ourselves to this essential. For the masters of the East, the body itself can become spirit through the cultivation of breathing. An Eastern culture often corresponds to becoming cultivated to becoming spiritual through the practice of breathing (ibid., 7-9). The cultivation of the body through breathing is cultivation of the spirit. The divine is not situated in an inaccessible transcendence. It is what I can become (ibid., 43).

So, instead of attempting a radical change in our way of thinking or comprehending reality through some kind of supreme mental effort, such as, for example, phenomenological reduction, the change is achieved through breathing, the cultivation of breath. It is a practice of the self which bridges the gap between body and consciousness, active and passive, immanent and transcendent. The acknowledgment of the central importance of breath thus gives us a different ontology of ourselves free from many of the problematic oppositions of our Western thinking. This is important from the point of view of feminist theory since several feminists have argued that the ontological division between body and consciousness is reflected in our conception of the difference between the sexes. Woman is body, while man is consciousness, mind and spirit.

Perhaps this is the reason why Irigaray assigns the forgotten cultivation of breath as a particularly feminine task in our culture. Rather than reading this as an essentialist claim emphasizing the superior and inherent spiritual wisdom of women, I read it as a historical and cultural, but most of all as a utopian distinction: an ontology of ourselves yet to be.

Irigaray notes that woman, like creator God, engenders with her breath. A woman does it from the inside, without demonstration, without words. Through carrying a child, she shares her life and her breath (ibid., 81). Irigaray's text thus evokes strong, but crucially different images of maternity. In our culture, maternity is often spiritually valorized as a material gift of body, milk and blood. The mother represents matter and the satisfaction of bodily needs, while the father represents the spirit and the word. By emphasizing how the mother engenders through her breath, Irigaray again seeks to destabilize the deep-rooted dichotomy of female body and male spirit: the mother gives her breath to the child and this way engenders life through spirit.

For Irigaray, the highest spirituality for a woman does not, however, lie in becoming a mother. According to her, a woman is capable of rising to a spiritually-higher level from the almost involuntary, daily responsibility of respecting life that sharing and engendering life has bestowed upon her. Her aim can be to become a lover, a spiritual guide. Irigaray does not thus argue that women, by virtue of their biological role in reproduction, are in possession of some spontaneous spiritual wisdom. Her criticism of technological domination and alienation does not amount to a simple call for women to return to the nature or to a more natural way of life. She explicitly writes that "the possibilities of a future for the human species do not reside in a return to a simple natural identity" (ibid., 107). The spiritual journey must be an endless practice, a patient striving.

She ends her essay "The Way of Breath" with a Utopian call, a challenge for women to become more than we are, more than we ever thought we could be. Not just independent and successful, not just equals to men, but guardians of our dying spirituality, instigators of a different future for humanity:

> This passage to another epoch of the reign of spirit depends upon a cultivation of respiration, a cultivation of breathing in and by women. They are the ones who can share with the other, in particular with man, natural life, and spiritual or divine life, if they are capable of transforming their vital breath into spiritual breath. This task is great, yet passionate and beautiful. It is indispensable for the liberation of women themselves and more generally, for a culture of life and of love. It requires patience, perseverance, faithfulness to self and to the other. Women are often lacking these virtues today. But why not acquire them? Out of love of self, out of love for the other? Out of consciousness of the importance of women's spiritual role for the present and the future of humanity. (Ibid., 91)

It is not enough for feminist thinkers to encourage women to be more in control, more confident with technology, masters of all-important knowledge. It is not enough to fight for an equal share of the cake, since this way of posing the problem has already led us astray. The feminist task, most fundamentally, must concern ontology: the way our world is and the way we are as part of it, but also what we can become. It must mean striving for a change at the deepest level of our being. For this change to become possible "demands just one thing: the respect of the natural and spiritual life of the self and the other" (ibid., 12-13).

Notes

1. Haslanger distinguishes two different strands behind feminist's attitude of suspicion. Some have argued that the questions and claims of certain dominant metaphysical theories are male-biased, and recommended less male-biased replacements; whereas others have argued that feminists have good reason to reject the project of metaphysics altogether. Feminist critique of the second sort resists the temptation to engage in any metaphysical theorizing (Haslanger 2000, 108).

2. Cf. Haslanger 2000, 113, 119.

3. See e.g. Irigaray 1993.

4. See also Irigaray 2000.

5. David Carr (1999, 11-12) argues in *Being and Time* that it still seems possible to distinguish between doing ontology and critically discussing its history, but this distinction practically vanishes in Heideggger's later work where the primary way to think about being is to think about the ways it has been thought by others.

6. On Heidegger and deep ecology, see e.g. Foltz 1995.

7. See Heidegger 1977, 112.

8. See also Heidegger 1968.

9. See e.g. Heidegger 1998, 252.

10. Stuart Elden (2001, 1) writes in the opening lines of his recent book, that the affinities between Martin Heidegger and Michel Foucault have been left relatively unexplored. Despite the enormous amount of critical attention that has been given to them separately, only a small amount of text discusses the relationship between them. This is curious, since in an interview given just before his death Foucault claims that his entire philosophical development was determined by Heidegger. More on Foucault's relationship to Heidegger, see e.g. Han 2002, Dreyfus & Rabinow 1982.

11. See e.g. Gutting 1989.

12. Technologies of the self are not separate from technologies of domination, which had been the focus of Foucault's earlier studies. He points out the necessary link between them. Neither do technologies of the self introduce a totally autonomous subject to Foucault's late thinking. As he commented, even if he was interested in the way in which the subject constituted himself or herself in an active fashion by the practices of the self, "these practices are nevertheless not something that the individual invents by himself. They are patterns that he finds in his culture and which are proposed, suggested and imposed on him by his culture, his society and his social group" (Foucault 1988a, 11).

13. Cf. Chanter 1995, 143.

14. In a seminar text, "Technologies of the Self," Foucault claims that the precept "to be concerned with oneself" was the form that technologies of the self followed in Ancient Greece. The other ancient maxim, "Know thyself," was always subordinated to it. With the development of Christianity there was an inversion between the hierarchy of these two principles of antiquity. Knowledge of oneself was understood in Greco-Roman culture as a consequence of taking care of oneself and therefore subordinate to it. In the modern world, it constitutes the fundamental principle. See Foucault 1988b; also Foucault 1985, 1986.

15. See McWhorter 1999, 168-175.

16. For more on Irigaray's relationship to Heidegger, see e.g. Mortensen 1994, Chanter 1995. Both Mortensen and Chanter demonstrate in detail the impact of Heidegger's thought on Irigaray, while acknowledging that she also preserves a critical distance from him.

Bibliography

Carr, David. *The Paradox of Subjectivity. The Self in the Transcendental Tradition.* Oxford: Oxford University Press, 1999.

Chanter, Tina. *Ethics of Eros. Irigaray's Rewriting of the Philosophers.* New York: Routledge, 1995.

Dreyfus, Hubert L. & Rabinow, Paul. *Michel Foucault, Beyond Structuralism and Hermeneutics.* Hemel Hempstead, UK: Harvester Wheatsheaf, 1982.

Elden, Stuart. *Mapping the Present. Heidegger, Foucault and the Project of a Spatial History.* London: Continuum, 2001.

Foltz, Bruce V. *Inhabiting the Earth: Heidegger, Environmental Ethics, and Metaphysics of Nature.* Atlantic Highlands, NJ: Humanities Press, 1995.

Foucault, Michel. *The Order of Things, An Archaeology of Human Sciences.* London: Routledge, 1970.

———. *The Use of Pleasures, The History of Sexuality, Vol. 2.* New York: Pantheon, 1985.

———. *The Care for the Self, The History of Sexuality, Vol. 3.* New York: Pantheon, 1986.

———. *The Final Foucault.* Ed. by James Bernauer and David Rasmussen. Cambridge, A: The MIT Press, 1988a.

———. *Technologies of the Self. A Seminar with Michel Foucault.* Ed. by Luther H. Martin, Huck Gutman and Patrick H. Hutton. Amherst: The University of Massachusetts Press, 1988b.

———. *The Politics of Truth.* New York: Semiotext(e), 1997.

Gutting, Gary. *Michel Foucault's Archaeology of Scientific Reason.* Cambridge, UK: Cambridge University Press, 1989.

Han, Beatrice. *Foucault's Critical Project. Between the Transcendental and the*

Historical. Stanford, CA: Stanford University Press, 2002.

Haslanger, Sally. "Feminism in Metaphysics: Negotiating the Natural." In *The Cambridge Companion to Feminism in Philosophy*, ed. Miranda Fricker and Jennifer Horsnby, 107-127. Cambridge, UK: Cambridge University Press, 2000.

Heideggger, Martin. *What Is Called Thinking?* New York: Harper & Row, 1968.

———. *The Question Concerning Technology and Other Essays*. New York: Harper & Row, 1977.

———. *Pathmarks*. Cambridge, UK: Cambridge University Press, 1998.

Irigaray, Luce. *An Ethics of Sexual Difference*. London: The Athlone Press, 1993.

———. *Democracy Begins between Two*. London: The Athlone Press, 2000.

———. *Between East and West. From Singularity to Community*. New York: Columbia University Press, 2002.

Lovitt, William. "Introduction." In *Martin Heidegger, The Question Concerning Technology and Other Essays*, xiii-xxxix. New York: Harper & Row, 1977.

McWhorter, Ladelle. *Bodies and Pleasures. Foucault and the Politics of Sexual Normalization*. Bloomington: Indiana University Press, 1999.

Mortensen, Ellen. *The Feminine and Nihilism: Luce Irigaray with Nietzsche and Heidegger*. Oslo: Scandinavian University Press, 1994.

Pattison, George. *The Later Heidegger*. London: Routledge, 2000.

Stenstad, Gail. "Revolutionary Thinking." In *Feminist Interpretations of Martin Heidegger*, ed. Nancy J. Holland and Patricia Huntington, 334-351. Pennsylvania: The Pennsylvania University Press, 2001.

"Traces of Otherness"[1]

Lisa Käll

"It is popularly believed that a human being is *either* a man *or* a woman."[2] This quote from Sigmund Freud's *Three Essays on the Theory of Sexuality* calls into question the immediate certainty of the male/female opposition. Freud goes on to tell us that perceptual, common-sense "evidence" is not at all unambiguous but in fact extremely complex. It is the *habit* of making the distinction male/female that leads us to forget that this exclusionary distinction is not primary but, rather, a result of incessant habitual repetition. I shall quickly leave Freud behind, allowing his words to serve only as an introduction, setting the stage and pointing toward a horizon of possibilities. I will follow his claim and explore what it might mean to call into question the immediate certainty of common-sense evidence and to think sexual difference beyond the binary.

Traditionally the "immediate certainty" of the male/female distinction might have lead us to say that while there is a multitude of gender identities, there are only two sexes upon which this multitude of gender identities can be at play. The two sexes are different, distinct and exclusive of one another. As we know, recent feminist discussions have challenged the sex/gender distinction and it has been argued that the category of sex assumed to be a biological fact and therefore natural and unchangeable, is in fact already a gendered category, i.e. subject to the regulatory practices of historical, social and cultural contexts. The what-ness of material reality is not a given but is formed in and through discursive practices. The "multitude" of gender identities turns out to be very limited as it is regulated in a relation of binary opposition. The identity of one gender depends on the exclusion of another and the exclusionary practices constitutive of gender differences reinforce and stabilize specific gender identities which in a binary relation are limited to being only one of two.

Displacing the category of sex and disclosing the naturalness of sex as a carefully staged illusion not only reveal the fundamental instability of the two sexes male and female as well as of their dependence on contingent practices;

49

the very binarism of the relation between the male and female sex is also challenged and displaced. Thus, theoretically space is opened up to understand sexual identity and alterity in terms other than binarism and exclusion. Displacing
the category of sex as a natural, unchangeable fact also challenges the primacy
of a specific configuration of gender identity and the idea that all women,
regardless of cultural and social background and context, are bound together
simply by virtue of being women. However, while we know that there are great
differences within the group designated "woman," we also know that women
have been oppressed, devalued and discriminated against exactly by virtue of
their womanhood and it might be—and has been—argued that since the
exploitation, oppression, and discrimination of women are based on a specific
configuration of sexual difference, they can only be dealt with through that configuration.[3] It might be argued that we as feminists should in fact give primacy to sexual difference and sexual oppression. Should we not in fact fight sexual oppression, discrimination, and exploitation before looking at other injustices?

As post second-wave feminists (such as global, multicultural, and postmodern feminists) have shown, however, oppression—as well as oppressor and
oppressed—cannot be understood in homogenous terms and the fight against
oppression based on an homogeneous understanding does not eliminate but
might actually reiterate and reinforce oppression. It has become quite obvious
that in order to do justice to the multitude of singular identities formed in the
intersections of categories such as race, class, age, gender, etc. we must find
ways of understanding difference in terms beyond binary oppositions. Not only
must we take intersectionality seriously and recognize sex/gender as only one
of many intersectional voices constitutive of identities, we must also deconstruct the dualistic framework which founds difference in terms of negation,
opposition, or complementarity (upholding the illusion of a completely determined wholeness) and which does not understand otherness on its own terms
but only as a variation of, or in negative relation to, selfhood. The obligation
of feminism might thus still be said to be an obligation to sexual difference but
a sexual difference which is overdetermined and kept open "as the space of a
radical uncertainty"[4] and not determined as stable, limited and thereby also limiting.

In order to understand sexual difference (as well as other differences, such
as race, nationality, ethnicity, age, desire, class, weight, etc.) as a space of radical uncertainty and do justice to the richness of identities and identity formation, I will turn to the writings of Maurice Merleau-Ponty and more specifically to the notions of flesh, reversibility and *écart* articulated in his posthumously published unfinished work *The Visible and the Invisible*. I will draw freely
from Merleau-Ponty's writings knowing that my selective reading inevitably
imposes limits and will not even begin to do justice to the richness of his
thought.

The notion of flesh found in Merleau-Ponty's writing resists definition. It is irreducible and described as being "an ultimate notion [and] not the union or compound of two substances, but thinkable by itself."[5] The flesh is neither subject nor object but forms in between, a couple of the two in which each term is the rejoinder of the other.[6] The flesh is that underlying element which unites oppositions through a chiasm or intertwining which breaks down the walls and bridges the gaps which are inherent to and constitutive of binary oppositions. The notion of flesh provides the resources for dichotomizing but the notion is at the same time beyond all attempts of analysis through the categories of subject and object—or any other dualisms—and it resists all attempts at reduction. Merleau-Ponty writes that the flesh cannot be thought of "starting from substances, from body and spirit—for *then it would be the union of contradictories.*"[7]

As that ultimate notion which provides the conditions and grounds for the distinctions between mind and body, subject and object, self and other, the notion of flesh provides the grounds for how difference is constituted and understood. If the flesh—this ultimate, irreducible notion—was to be understood as a "one" in strictly univocal terms, i.e., as an irreducible and absolute unity, we would quite obviously be in trouble trying to theorize about sexual difference. This is however not the case. The flesh is reversible and this reversibility is most clearly made manifest in the notion of touch.[8] With the example of my two hands touching, Merleau-Ponty wants to show that the lived body is capable of so called "double sensations" and that the touching and the touched are reversible. In the phenomenon of touch there is a reversibility in which the touched hand feels itself touching and vice versa; as Merleau-Ponty writes, between "my body touched and my body touching, there is overlapping or encroachment."[9] When I am touching my two hands I can identify the hand touched as the same one that will in a moment be touching.[10]

Reversibility is not however an incessant tossing back and forth between stable notions of touching and touched and must not be understood as a fully determined (nor determinable) closed system which can be viewed from an outside position.[11] It is both impossible and unnecessary to look for otherness and difference outside of reversibility. It must rather be found in the very structure of the notion of flesh itself. The reversibility is characterized by what Merleau-Ponty terms *écart* which is an unrepresentable space of non-coincidence, deviation, difference, and divergence in the ultimate notion of flesh. The flesh is thus not by any means a univocal determinable "one" but is overdetermined, polymorphous, and in continuous movement opening up new gaps and fissures which are made manifest in relations in the phenomenal world. The divergence of reversibility not only marks the gaps and non-coincidence which allow for differentiation between self and other, but it is also what allows me to recognize myself as a temporal self and differentiate myself from what I was—which I may or may not be any longer—and from what I am not yet—which I may or may not become.

The reversibility of touching and being touched reveals the structure of the embodied self as a structure of self-affection and as a structure of movement. As my two hands alternate between touching and being touched in an ambiguous intertwinement in which the touched hand feels itself touching and vice versa, my body appears to me as both subject and object. The underlying unity of my one body does not produce an absolute identity and self-coincidence but, rather, between the touching and the touched there is "a sort of dehiscence [that] opens my body in two".[12] This divergence between the touching and the touched is necessary for the body to be sensible to itself and be able to sense itself, for I cannot touch if I am not distanced from what I am touching and I cannot be touched if I am not distanced from that which touches me.

The reversibility and divergence between my own body as sensing and as sensed, reveal myself as other to myself and thus as fundamentally open to that which is other to me. My intrinsic openness towards the other is revealed to me as the sensing of my own body anticipates the way in which the other can sense my body and the way in which I can sense the other's body. When my left hand touches my right, I experience my right hand as other to my left hand and I can anticipate the way in which the other can touch me and the way I can touch the other. It is in my attempt to grasp my selfhood that I come across this otherness within me which corresponds to the otherness of the external other. My own embodied self-awareness which reveals myself as being other to myself is a presentiment of the external other and my encounter with the other is a revelation of my basic openness. My self is revealed to me as being different from the other but also as being as other to the other as the other is other to the self and therefore I am also revealed as being other to myself. Thus, as I become other to the other I simultaneously become other to myself in so far as the other is an other like myself.[13] My openness to the other renders an openness to myself as other, or to an otherness which is already in myself as an essential part of my being.

The reversibility between touching and being touched—as my right hand touches my left and vice versa—provides a pattern for understanding the relation between self and other. This reversibility not only accounts for the ambiguous intertwinement of two aspects of the same body but is extended to also include the ambiguous intertwinement between self and other who are both part of the same flesh. When I perceive the other—in a handshake, embrace, or gaze—there is a reversibility between the two of us since we are both sensing and sensed in the perception. Here we must ask however, if it is not the case that the anticipation of the other implies the subsuming of one into the other. Is it not in fact so that my handshake, embrace, or gaze shapes the other and fixes the other in relation to my self?

Although the other and I are not one in the way the two aspects of my body form one whole body, Merleau-Ponty claims that the other and I form a system in which there is a transfer of meaning through our different but familiar ways of comporting ourselves toward the world. This transfer of conduct does not risk eliminating the differences between self and other as long as our differences, as well as that which we have in common, are given meaning. Merleau-Ponty writes "my perception of the other is at first sight perception of the gestures and behavior belonging to 'the human species.' But [—-] *if the other person is really another, at a certain stage I must be surprised, disoriented.*"[14] In order for me to interrelate with the other I must recognize the other as radically other to the point where I am disoriented by my experience of the otherness of the other.

The fact that the other and I are not one in the sense that the two aspects of my body are one, implies that there are fundamental differences between touching one's own hand and shaking hands with an other. I cannot experience the other's experience of me and *vice versa*. When I touch my left hand with my right hand, there is an identity between the touching hand and the touched hand and although there is a divergence between my touching hand and my touched hand so that they never quite coincide, they can still be identified as being part of the same body. When I touch the hand of the other there is a limit to my experience due to the fact that the other and I are not the same. In order for me to experience the other's experience of my touch, I would have to be both in the other's body and in my own simultaneously. The self thus never coincides with the other, and therefore never experiences the other's body in the same way as its own body, even though they are both bodies of the same flesh.

This must not be understood as if the otherness I experience in myself is projected onto the other and as if self-objectification consequently is a necessary precondition for the recognition of others as others. Rather, otherness is already inscribed in the flesh, and when I try to grasp my own selfhood I inevitably encounter an otherness which I cannot determine, which transcends any representations I might have or make of it, but, which nevertheless fundamentally is a constitutive part of selfhood. Since reversibility is "a reversibility always imminent and never realized in fact" and the touching and the touched "never reach coincidence",[15] self and other never coincide and the other is never understood as being completely the same as the self. Otherness is irreducible and there is always something of the other which escapes the self. Thus, the reversibility between self and other does allow for an irreducible remainder impossible to determine, forever beyond my grasp.

We know that if alterity is nothing more than a meaning projected upon an immanent object—such as a human body—then that object is not transcendent and not truly other but merely a projection of the self. The otherness of the other would have its origin in the self and that would eliminate all possibilities of understanding the other on its own terms. Merleau-Ponty emphasizes that the perception of other people—the perception and experience of alterity—"is the perception of a freedom which appears through a situation."[16] This clearly suggests that the otherness of the other is a transcendence perceived as transcendent since the freedom of the other is the one thing which always will escape the self and which makes it possible for the other to freely contest the self's projections. The otherness of the other can thus not be understood as a projected meaning for even though I experience the other as another self like myself, I still experience the other as opaque to the categories of my projection and fundamentally resistant to any form of reduction. Merleau-Ponty argues that the other is given to me "precisely in a certain divergence (*écart*) (*originating presentation of the unpresentable*)."[17] My experience of the other is an experience of the other's transcendence which is given to me precisely as transcendent—it is a presentation of the unpresentable as unpresentable. The immediate presentation of the other is thus not a presentation of the other as sameness upon which differences are projected by the self. Quite to the contrary, the other is immediately given as other, as different, as opaque and enigmatic—in short, as ineffable transcendence.

In understanding otherness, both identity and difference must be taken into account. The other must be different from the self in order to be genuinely other and not defined solely by the self in relation to itself. On the other hand, the other must be like the self in order for the self to experience the other as an other self like the self but not the self. There must be a common ground on which the other and the self can experience and communicate with one another (as selves, other to one another) and yet remain opaque and elusive to each other. There must be room for ambiguity to be at play between self and other in order for the other not only to remain other but also to be experienced as other.

As we have seen, Merleau-Ponty's ontology of the flesh must not be understood as a monism and reversibility must not be taken to imply a fixed dualism. The divergence involved in the reversibility when the flesh of the world folds back on itself but never coincides with itself is crucial in understanding Merleau-Ponty's ontology as fundamentally an ontology of ambiguity. The flesh allows for the ambiguous and paradoxical presence of the other in the same, left as a trace in the movement of reversibility.

Understanding sexual difference through the characteristics of the flesh is not an attempt to claim a position outside or beyond sexual difference. It is quite to the contrary a recognition that no such outside position is possible. However, it is an attempt to claim a position beyond sexual difference in terms of binary oppositions, exclusive of one another, a position from within the richness of differences of overdetermined Being. Merleau-Ponty writes that the flesh must be thought as "the concrete emblem of a general *manner* of being"[18] indicating that the reversibility of the flesh does not refer to the what-ness of relations but to the how-ness. What is at stake is thus not the need to recognize a specific configuration or what-ness of difference and otherness but to recognize how the relation between alterity and ipseity is reversible.

To specify and define the what-ness of identities is only possible if there is already a radical, unrecognizable and ungraspable difference at play. As we have seen, the otherness of the other will always and forever escape my grasp and I will experience it precisely as elusive and ungraspable. Identities must be recognized as the more or less temporary solidification of difference and therefore fundamentally fluid and constantly configured and reconfigured. The unrecognizable difference of the other sex must thus be understood in terms other than definable binary categories which are not fundamental, but which are meanings projected in order to overcome the abyss of overdetermination and the elusiveness of otherness.

It is precisely the overcoming of difference by means of reducing it to an immanent meaning constituted by consciousness that Merleau-Ponty rejects. Phenomenal bodies, which are carriers of both ipseity and alterity, transcend their apprehension and in order to take difference seriously and recognize the otherness of the other on its own terms, I must allow the transcendence of the other to transcend any representations I might have of the other.

This understanding of otherness as an essential part of my being does not in any way deny the strength of representations, nor does it deny that sexual difference, in terms of difference between two mutually exclusive categories, is at play and shapes the way reality is conceptualized and human beings categorized. It does however challenge the primacy and fixity of these categories and the conception of them as mutually exclusive. The obvious "evidence" which renders sexual difference as limited to the male/female binarism should certainly be taken seriously. It is "precisely against the background of one's sexed body that gender is produced and created."[19] But, it is also against the background of culturally and socially established gender identities and relations that one's body is materialized and sexed as either male or female. There is an interplay between nature and culture which is just as ambiguous as intertwinement and divergence of reversibility. The male/female distinction is an obvious presence to perception but perception is not in any way neutral and the stabilized what-ness of identities is exactly what needs to be suspended in order for the how-ness, or givenness, of phenomena to appear to the subject. The givenness of things and phenomena to the subject first appears when these things and phenomena have lost their overwhelmingly obvious presence.

I have tried to show that through its *écart*, reversibility does in fact open up space for irreducible, radical otherness and thus, space for the radical uncertainty of sexual difference which recognizes sexual difference as much more enigmatic than the determined male/female binarism would have us believe. In the words of Elizabeth Grosz, "if one takes seriously the problematic of sexual difference, then as mysterious as Woman must be for men, so too must men be for women (and indeed *so too must Woman be for women and Man be for men*)."[20] This ineffable mysteriousness of otherness does not annihilate interrelation between self and other but is rather that which makes me recognize the other as truly other and myself as fundamentally open to the other. It is the reversibility and divergence between the self's body as sensing and sensed, and between the self and the other, which sustain the interrelation and guarantee the non-coincidence between self and other. For, the initial openness to the other in me carries with it an initial separation which is always already there in the very structure of the ultimate notion of flesh.[21] In order not to eliminate interrelation, recognition and respect between self and other, the non-coincidence between the two must be guaranteed through a commonality which escapes grasp.

Notes

1. An earlier version of this paper was presented at the conference "Beyond Parity. Sexual Difference Revisited," University of Bergen, Norway, May 9, 2001. I would like to thank the conference participants, especially Virpi Lethinen, for helpful comments and questions. I am also indebted to Marie Fleming, Saeromi Kim, and Devin Lenda for their comments on earlier drafts.

2. Sigmund Freud, *Three Essays on the Theory of Sexuality*, trans. James Strachey, Standard Edition, volume VII, (London 1953), 141 (italics added).

3. See Luce Irigaray, *Je, Tu, Nous. Toward a Culture of Difference*, trans Alison Martin (London & New York 1993), 12.

4. Diane Elam, *Feminism and Deconstruction. Ms. en Abyme* (London & New York 1994), 26 (italics added).

5. Maurice Merleau-Ponty, *The Visible and the Invisible. Followed by Working Notes*, ed. Claude Lefort, trans. Alphonso Lingis (Evanston 1997), 140.

6. Merleau-Ponty, *The Visible and the Invisible*, 139.

7. Merleau-Ponty, *The Visible and the Invisible*, 147 (italics added).

8. It is in fact so that Merleau-Ponty models all forms of perception and reflection on the reversibility between touching and touched and not that between seeing and seen. "[F]or every reflection is after the model of the reflection of the hand touching by the hand touched, open generality, a prolongation of the body's reserve [—-] hence reflection is not an identification with oneself (thought of seeing or of feeling) but non-difference with self = silent or blind identification." Merleau-Ponty, *The Visible and the Invisible*, 204. Cf also 133, 254.

9. Merleau-Ponty, *The Visible and the Invisible*, 123.

10. Maurice Merleau-Ponty, *Phenomenology of Perception*, trans. Colin Smith (London & New York 1962), 93. This does not mean however that the hand that in a moment will be touching, will be touching in exactly the same way as the hand that is now touching, nor does it mean that the hand that will be touched, will be touched in exactly the same way as the hand that is now touched.

11. Luce Irigaray argues that the reversibility, which characterizes the flesh, constitutes a closed system in which nothing new can be said. "Everything is there and is unceasingly reversible" and there is no "other to keep the world open." I will argue

however, that Merleau-Ponty's notion of reversibility is not quite as limited and limiting as Irigaray claims and that it does leave room for otherness which is radically other to the self. That the flesh as an ultimate notion accounts for everything does not in any way entail that everything has been or even can be spoken or determined. See Luce Irigaray, "The invisible of the Flesh: A Reading of Merleau-Ponty, 'The Intertwining—The Chiasm'" in *An Ethics of Sexual Difference*, trans. Carolyn Burke and Gillian C. Gill (London 1993), 180ff.

12. Merleau-Ponty, *Phenomenology of Perception*, 93; *The Visible and the Invisible*, 123, 147f, 254.

13. Maurice Merleau-Ponty, *The Prose of the World*, ed. Claude Lefort, trans. John O'Neill (Evanston 1973), 85f, 134f; *The Visible and the Invisible*, 139, 224; "The Child's Relations with Others," trans. William Cobb, in *The Primacy of Perception*, ed. James M. Edie (Evanston 1964), 120, 135.

14. Merleau-Ponty, *The Prose of the World*, 142 (italics added).

15. Merleau-Ponty, *The Visible and the Invisible*, 147.

16. Maurice Merleau-Ponty, "The Experience of Others" in *Review of Existential Psychology and Psychiatry* vol 18 (1982-83), 57.

17. Merleau-Ponty, *The Visible and the Invisible*, 203 (italics in original).

18. Merleau-Ponty, *The Visible and the Invisible*, 147 (italics added).

19. Tina Chanter, "Wild Meaning: Luce Irigaray's Reading of Merleau-Ponty" in *Chiasms. Merleau-Ponty's Notion of Flesh*, ed. Fred Evans & Leonard Lawlor (Albany 2000), 224.

20. Elizabeth Grosz, *Volatile Bodies. Toward a Corporeal Feminism* (Bloomington & Indianapolis 1994), 191 (italics added).

21. Merleau-Ponty, *The Visible and the Invisible*, 216.

Bibliography

Chanter, Tina. "Wild Meaning: Luce Irigaray's Reading of Merleau-Ponty" in *Chiasms. Merleau-Ponty's Notion of Flesh*, ed. Fred Evans & Leonard Lawlor (Albany 2000)

Elam, Diane. *Feminism and Deconstruction. Ms. en Abyme* (London & New York 1994)

Freud, Sigmund. *Three Essays on the Theory of Sexuality*, trans. James Strachey, Standard Edition, volume VII. (London 1953)

Grosz, Elizabeth. *Volatile Bodies. Toward a Corporeal Feminism* (Bloomington & Indianapolis 1994)

Irigaray, Luce. "The invisible of the Flesh: A Reading of Merleau-Ponty, 'The Intertwining—The Chiasm'," *An Ethics of Sexual Difference*, trans. Carolyn Burke and Gillian C. Gill (London 1993), 180ff

———. *Je, Tu, Nous. Toward a Culture of Difference*, trans. Alison Martin (London & New York 1993)

Merleau-Ponty, Maurice, "The Child's Relations with Others," trans. William

Cobb, *The Primacy of Perception*, ed. James M. Edie (Evanston 1964)

———. "The Experience of Others," *Review of Existential Psychology and Psychiatry* vol 18 (1982-83)

———. *Phenomenology of Perception*, trans. Colin Smith (London & New York 1962)

———. *The Prose of the World*, ed. Claude Lefort, trans. John O'Neill (Evanston 1973)

———. *The Visible and the Invisible*. Followed by Working Notes, ed. Claude Lefort, trans. Alphonso Lingis (Evanston 1997)

Nietzsche in the Feminine?
Questioning Nietzsche's Will to Power

Ellen Mortensen

If we—as feminists of the 21st century—are to explore Nietzsche's philosoph-
ic legacy, we need to deal with the question of will to power. Albeit the fact
that we now have a substantial feminist scholarship on Nietzsche, few feminist
thinkers have dealt with this question to date. The rationale for this evasion is
that will to power has been too closely associated with the part of Nietzsche's
thought that is deemed most outrageously misogynist and politically suspect. In
the following I will argue that it is important that we grapple with Nietzsche's
thinking on the will to power—not only because it is crucial to any thorough
treatment of his thinking—but also because I believe that it will prove fruitful
to our own pursuits. Our task, as women doing philosophy, is a task of thinking. But thinking is scarce in this day and age, caught as we are in a maelstrom
of technologized theorems, circulating at an ever-faster pace. Today, perhaps
more than ever, we are in dire need of pursuing thinking on an ontological
level. I believe that Nietzsche's notion of will to power may lead us in new
directions in our exploration of the nexus between thinking and freedom, as we
seek alternative ways of thinking new, sexed figurations of being in the world.

In the following treatment of Nietzsche's thinking on the will to power, I
will first give a synoptic exposition of the major figurations through which he
tried to articulate its content, namely the deities Dionysus/Apollo and the poet-
philosopher Zarathustra. I will then try to present—by way of synthesis—some
important conrtibutions to feminist readings of Nietzsche and to assess the mer-
its and limits of these contributions. Finally, I will introduce "Heidegger's
Nietzsche," touching upon important ontological implications of Nietzsche's
legacy. I believe that Heidegger's reading of Nietzsche might open up new
avenues for feminist inquiries of sexual difference in the future, inquiries that
may subvert the current technological imperative in Western thought.

Figurations of Will to Power

The Dionysus-Apollo Duality

Nietzsche first broaches the question of will to power in *The Birth of Tragedy* in 1873. In this in-depth study of Greek tragedy, he launches a fierce attack on German aesthetic philosophy. His startling thesis is that art in the West owes its continuous evolution to a fundamental duality between the Apollonian and the Dionysiac. Nietzsche values art as something sensuous or aesthetic (from the Greek *aisthetikos* = "of sense perception"). The greatness of art, Nietzsche argues, resides in its capacity to touch and affect human beings as sensuous beings, because it enhances their feeling of power. To him Greek mystical doctrines of art are far superior to the doctrines of German idealist and systematic philosophers, precisely because their doctrines develop through plausible embodiments, and not through purely conceptual means.

Nietzsche also challenges Aristotle's claim that all art is fundamentally *mimesis* or imitation, when he states:

> That life is really so tragic would least of all explain the origin of an
> art form— assuming that art is not merely imitation of the reality of
> nature but rather a metaphysical supplement of the reality of nature,
> placed beside it for its overcoming.[1]

The Greeks envision the two art-sponsoring deities, Dionysus and Apollo, as figures that embody the two separate art realms, of intoxication and dream, respectively. To Nietzsche these figures exhibit what he calls "a metaphysical miracle of the Hellenic 'will'."[2] At this juncture, we need to inquire what "the Hellenic will" implies, since we detect in it the seeds of what is later articulated through the notion of "will to power." The "will" of which Nietzsche speaks in *The Birth of Tragedy*, is a transcendent "will" of cosmic proportions, as well as a "will" to transcendence. In the last analysis, the "will" is attributed to that chthonic force through which mythic figures like Dionysus and Apollo come to *be* as embodied figures.

According to Nietzsche, aesthetic embodiments like Dionysus and Apollo appear in the Greek world of antiquity precisely because the Greeks were exceptionally sensitive and healthy. They were healthy to the extent that they were still in touch with their creative as well as their destructive instincts. As such, they were susceptible to the earth's most profound "will," that is, to the "letting-be" of the aesthetic forms that this chthonic force incites to be brought forth. During the Dionysian rites in celebration of the god—usually performed by groups of women—the women experienced the earth's dynamic force in a state of intoxication, a state of mind brought about by wine, rhythm, song and dance.

Nietzsche speaks of the rapture in Dionysian intoxication as "a form-engendering force" which involves both an aesthetic doing and an aesthetic observing.[3] In this ecstatic state, the human body is transported out its own skin and becomes receptive to feel the rhythms of the earth—thus becoming "one" with it. Dionysian intoxication involves a twofold movement; it is both an affirmation and a destruction of the body. In intoxication, the individual experiences an enhancement of its life forces, and as such this is an affirmation. At the same time, the body is in its intoxicated state also subject to *sparagmos*, that is, to dismemberment; it is destroyed as a separate entity, and vanishes as a distinct form. In its disintegrated state, the body in rapture is the most receptive to the earth's form-engendering force.

For these reasons Nietzsche contends intoxication is the most fundamental source of art. And the spirit of music—which most immediately expresses the rhythms of the earth—gives in turn birth to Greek tragedy. This happens at the moment when the figure of Dionysus is coupled with the figure of Apollo. Greek tragedy marks to him the most superior art form brought about by any civilization.

Apollo, the other figure of the duality, embodies the dream. As the figure of the earth's will to individualize, Apollo comes to embody the human capability to imagine forms, that is, to create fictive images. The dream-image is crucial for humans, because it is through this ability that humans may be said to have an individual self, a persona. For Nietzsche, this image is a fictional one, it is the product of an illusion, but as an embodied metaphor, it is attributed with life: For a genuine poet, metaphor is not a rhetorical figure but a vicarious image that he actually beholds in place of a concept. A character is for him not a whole he has composed out of particular traits, picked up here and there, but an obtrusively alive person before his very eyes, distinguished from the otherwise identical vision of a painter only by the fact that it continually goes on living and acting.[4]

Were it not for our Apollonian capacity to dream, we would not be able to establish an aesthetic projection of ourselves, nor of the world, which we inhabit. "We possess art," Nietzsche argues, "lest we perish of the Truth."

However, this impulse to create images is constantly being subjected to the dynamics of the will to power of the earth. In Nietzsche's thought, the subject is not the source of its own image production. By implication, man as artist is not the autonomous or sole creator of any work of art, even though his individual will to power is involved. Rather, the artist must be thought of in terms of a mouthpiece or a medium of the earth's will, much like the epic poet, who merely listens to and echoes the sayings of the muse when he sings.

The tragic dimension of existence occurs, according to Nietzsche, because the Dionysian will does not allow any form of life or any individuation to halt

the dynamism of the earth. To remain frozen in a fixed image—be it of the self
or any other image—is impossible in the face of this cosmic will. All aesthetic
images, like all forms of life, are doomed to be destroyed in time, no matter
how great these appearances might be in their zenith, be they of the king
Oedipus, his daughter Antigone, or an insect. The earth wills new forms to
replace old ones in a never-ending process of meta-morphic gestation. In
Nietzsche's projection of this cosmic will, he insists on the primacy of sensuous materiality—as opposed to abstract spirit—as the groundless ground from
which all beings emerge, blossom, and into which they eventually disappear in
a never-ending cycle of an eternal recurrence of the same.

Zarathustra

It is possible to read *The Birth of Tragedy* as a text which predicts the coming
of the "new" man, who would later appear in the figure of Zarathustra in *Thus
Spoke Zarathustra* (1891).[5] As the "overman," Zarathustra succeeds in overcoming himself in a perpetual process of perishing and self-becoming. The figure of the poet-philosopher speaks of an absolute solipsism, a subjective perspectivism, and the position from which the act of transvaluation is being performed. This singular subjectivity cannot be replicated, not even by itself. Thus
Zarathustra, "the bridge to the future," is a figure that is stretched over an
abyss, without being secured at either end. He is an embodied figure suspended in time, whose essential trait is that he knows that he is a fictive projection
into nothingness.

Zarathustra is a work of art, a perpetual artwork in progress. He is not a
phenomenon, but a subjective value, and therefore cannot be used as a *ratio* or
a measure of anything else, not even himself in his own becoming. In this
sense, he challenges any notion of a stable foundation for systematic thought—
be it science, epistemology, ethics or logic. In addition, he undermines and
destroys any possibility of a predictable future or any reliable intersubjective
structure. In my opinion, this marks the most radical aspect of Nietzsche's
thought, but also perhaps its limit. His figural philosophy undermines the philosophical edifice of the Western metaphysical systems from Socrates up to
Nietzsche's own time. The sensuous body cannot provide any possible ground-
ing for any aesthetic system founded on disinterestedness, nor can it guarantee
a measure for any common ground on which an ethics may be erected, any
more than it can provide any basis for an objective or *a priori* knowledge, given
that there is no stable subjectivity to ground such knowledge.

This is an insight that he reaches in *The Birth of Tragedy*, and which he
develops further in later works, especially in his elaborations on nihilism:

> But science, spurred on by its powerful illusion, speeds irresistibly

toward its limits where optimism, concealed in the essence of logic suffers shipwreck. For the periphery of the circle of science has an infinite number of points; and while there is no telling how the circle could ever be surveyed completely, noble and gifted men nevertheless reach, e'er half their time and inevitably, such boundary points on the periphery from which one gazes into what defies illumination. When they see to their horror how logic coils up at these boundaries and finally bites its own tail—*suddenly the new form of insight breaks through, tragic insight which, merely to be endured, needs art as a protection and remedy.*[6] (My emphasis)

Art then serves as a medicine or a remedy for the loss of this assumed metaphysical security. Art is worth more than truth because it knows that it is a "lying" construction. To Nietzsche, language is fundamentally figural, and therefore more "truthful" than truth. There is accordingly no such thing as a literal language, which guarantees stable meanings. "Truth," he argues, is "an army of metaphors and metonymies," which means that it is always already figural and in the process of deviating from its previous meanings. He ends up subsuming science as well as religion under the auspices of art, when he asks the following question: "Will the net of art, even if it is called religion or science, that is spread over existence be woven even more tightly and delicately, or is it destined to be torn to shreds in the restless, barberous, chaotic whirl that now calls itself 'the present'?"[7]

The Birth of Tragedy also prefigures what would later be formulated under the rubric of nihilism. The following aphorisms in *The Will to Power* articulates what Nietzsche meant by the word nihilism:

§1: Nihilism stands at the door: whence comes this uncanniest of guests?

§2: What does nihilism mean? *That the highest values devaluate themselves.* The aim is lacking; "why?" finds no answer.[8]

Nietzsche senses, long before anyone else, that something eventful had happened in the West, and which he articulates in the dictum: "God is Dead." What he implies by this pronouncement is that all our systems of thought and all our projections of transcendent ideals hitherto, have turned to naught.

No one escapes nihilism, not even Zarathustra. Nihilism constitutes the horizon for all "beings," but it is ambiguous. Nietzsche envisions this ambiguity through different figures. The poet-philosopher Zarathustra is an active or affirmative nihilist. His counterpart is the scholar, a passive or reactive nihilist. Nietzsche abhors all forms of reaction, because in his view they are devoid of any creative impulse. Likewise, he fears the dispersion of passive, reactive nihilism, which for him signals cultural degeneration, due to a powerlessness of the spirit. Nietzsche identifies different manifestations of passive nihilism in his time: German idealism, Schopenhauer, liberal and socialist politics (under which he subsumed all forms of feminist emancipation), institutionalized Christianity and its insipid morality, and a host of other cultural phenomena all come together here. Ultimately, these phenomena contribute to the weakening of power because they, like all reactive forms of nihilism, harbor a *ressentiment* toward the fundamental dynamism of the will to power.

Nietzsche in the Feminine

The feminist scholarship on Nietzsche is already quite impressive, and constitutes one of the most important branches of the Nietzsche reception today. Some of the women philosophers, who have proved important for my own interest in Nietzsche, are Luce Irigaray, Sarah Kofman, Elizabeth Grosz, and Kelly Oliver. They have all been interested in different aspects of Nietzsche's legacy, ranging from questions concerning epistemology and knowledge, ethics, language and metaphor, and ontology.

In *Amante marine: de Friedrich Nietzsche*,[9] Luce Irigaray argues that Nietzsche understands nature as feminine, but that he shies away from probing into this elemental matter in the feminine. According to Irigaray, Nietzsche suffers both from fear of the dark and fear of water, and displays a lack of courage in his evasion of these subterranean, primordial waters. She does, however, attempt to retrieve in her reading of Nietzsche a materiality that the Pre-Socratics heard in their projections of *phusis*. The ancient notion of *phusis* as a primordial ground hides possible figurations of femininity that might still prove to be fruitful to us today. Through these archaic figures, she tries to develop an elemental ontology of sexual difference.

In addition, Irigaray contends that Nietzsche's vision of the "new" man creates a masculine figuration which seeks to expel all traces of femininity. She accuses him of narcissism and of embracing a solipsistic subjectivity in the figure of Zarathustra, who is incapable of dealing with the other, more specifically a feminine other. But Zarathustra is never completely alone, not even at noon, when the sun is in its zenith, because he still casts a shadow. This elemental other follows him wherever he moves, despite his efforts to be alone. Irigaray thus concludes that Nietzschean solipsism cannot escape the existence of the other. From this perspective, she attempts to impose on Nietzsche an ethics of sexual difference that inserts a difference between the one and the other.

I accept Irigaray's view that Nietzsche's thought may open up new avenues to think sexual difference. I have taken issue, however, with Irigaray's reading of Nietzsche in my book *The Feminine and Nihilism: Luce Irigaray with Nietzsche and Heidegger*,[10] because she ends up confounding the ontic and the ontological levels in her projections of an elemental ontology in the feminine. In the final analysis *le féminin* becomes a transvalued value, and as such it does not partake in an ontological problematic, but remains a meditation on sexual difference that operates in the subjective domain.

Despite sharing my skepticism with regard to parts of Irigaray's reading of Nietzsche, Kelly Oliver follows the path of Irigaray's ethical thinking in her book *Womanizing Nietzsche* (1995).[11] She wishes, however, to subvert Irigaray's notion of the feminine and its intimate link to nature, since it is imbued with too many traditional conceptions of the feminine. Instead, Oliver proposes to bring Nietzsche's thought in the neighborhood of a transvalued notion of the "mother," as a founding figure on which she attempts to construct a new inter-subjective ethics.

Oliver introduces some very productive insights into Nietzsche, especially in her dealings with Derrida's reading of the German philosopher *Spurs: The Styles of Nietzsche* (1978),[12] but her efforts to tease out of Nietzsche's text the foundations of an new ethics, seems to me both far-fetched and futile. If we from the legacy of Nietzsche—who sought in all his writings to undermine any ethics or morality—end up founding yet another ethic, then we may have swayed too far from his thinking. In my view, attempts to establish an ethics on a transvaluating subjectivity—even if it evokes Lévinas in the process—is doomed to fail.

Instead, I will argue that we ought to investigate the unorthodox figurations of femininity that Nietzsche actually conjures from the mythic and Pre-Socratic sources he alludes to. In my reading, Nietzsche's notion of cosmic or chthonic will to power in the feminine has little to do with contemporary notions of maternity, which remain steeped in a rhetoric of Christian ideology of *caritas* and its virtues (which Nietzsche despised): care of the other, unselfishness, nurture, etc. Nietzsche's figures of will to power in the feminine suggest something radically other: volatile forces, super-abundance, productivity, fertility and yes, violence. All of the latter attributes are intimately associated with Nietzschean aesthetics, and are related to powers that are crucial to any artistic form-engendering force. As a way of revealing or bringing forth, it is more akin to *poiesis* than to ethics. Like in any "letting-be-in-the-open," this chthonic "bringing forth" is utterly unpredictable and free.

The part of Nietzsche's legacy that intrigues me the most, is that which opens up toward an ontological problematic, because that is where his thinking is most attuned to freedom. Irigaray is one of the few who has pursued this line of questioning. I commend her for raising these questions, even though I take issue with parts her reading. This interest in the ontological implications of Nietzsche is contrary to most other feminist studies of his thought. Feminist theorists, like Butler, Braidotti, Grosz, etc., tend to embrace the subjective dynamism inherent in his thinking, precisely because they value the notion of an empowered feminist subject.

In my view, these appropriations of Nietzsche are too facile and hasty, and might prove to be a dead end. Perspectival subjectivity has attained global dispersion in the age of technology, and serves as the agent for technologized information. Any attempt to subvert this subjective horizon from within a subject position, has a tendency to be swallowed up in technological language. In my latest book, *Touching Thought: Ontology and Sexual Difference* (2002),[13] I take issue with some of the most prolific feminist theorists who skirt the ontological problematic in such a fashion in their theorizing on sexual difference.

Heidegger's Nietzsche

Martin Heidegger spent close to ten years in an attempt to unravel the riddle of Nietzsche's texts. The book that came out of these meditations, and which Derrida refers to as "a mighty tome," is simply entitled *Nietzsche*. Heidegger's reading of Nietzsche is highly controversial, and was violently attacked when it first was released in Germany (1943-46). However, thanks to the readings of Heidegger performed by the French—such as Blanchot, Sartre, Lacan, Derrida and Irigaray—Heidegger's contribution to the Nietzsche scholarship has been reevaluated. Today many scholars, even feminist scholars, express renewed interest in his study of Nietzsche's thinking. What Heidegger does, and which very few other readers do, is to raise the ontological problematic in relation to Nietzsche's texts.

In his book, Heidegger divides Nietzsche's oeuvre into four rubrics of thought. These are: *Will to Power as Art*; *The Eternal Recurrence of the Same*; *Will to Power as Knowledge and as Metaphysics*; and *Nihilism*. I believe, as does Heidegger, that it is in the elaboration of will to power as art that Nietzsche's thinking attains its highest grandeur. It also marks the point at which Nietzsche is most acutely attuned to the question of freedom. In Heidegger's view, Nietzsche ends up subsuming all the other three rubrics of thought under the rubric "will to power as art."

For Heidegger, technology constitutes the highest form of nihilism. Nihilism marks a particular enframing of Being, namely one that announces the ultimate domination of Being by subjectivity. In the age of technology, we are held under the sway of a "subject-object" dichotomy, which again prevents us from thinking ontological difference, that is, the difference between Being and beings. In *The Question Concerning Technology* (1954) Heidegger goes on to argue that the essence of technology is not anything technological. Rather, the essence of technology involves a way of revealing what *is*. In technological enframing, the earth and all other beings are appropriated in terms of their equipmentality—as "standing reserve" or "resources." Our relationship to ourselves, to other human beings, to other objects as well as to the earth on which we dwell—all these things are characterized by instrumentality. As a consequence, we have lost all sense of a true ontological relation to our being-in-the-world.

The Role of the Poet

Nietzsche can be said to demolish the metaphysical edifice that philosophers spent centuries to construe. In its place, he posits art, which functions both as a remedy and a solace for this loss. Zarathustra comes to replace Socrates. But when Nietzsche describes nihilism as the uncanny guest that stands at the door, there is still something familiar in the unfamiliar guest, Heidegger argues. What remains familiar in the unfamiliar is the subjective enframing. Nietzsche neither subverts, nor ends metaphysics; he completes it. Zarathustra transvalues all values hitherto, but in so doing, he still posits values, more specifically from a subjective perspective. What remains familiar with regard to Western metaphysics in Zarathustra's affirmative nihilism is the prolongment of the enframing of being in terms of the "subject-object" opposition.

If Zarathustra were truly a figure embodying freedom from the constraints of Western metaphysical thinking, he would have to explore the nothingness of the poetic language in which he dwells. Nietzsche's will to power as art must therefore be read as a step in the direction of such an inquiry. However, Nietzsche himself stopped short when confronted with the inherent nothingness of language, partly because his projection of will to power as art remained within a subjective framework, even as he sought to find figural expressions of the earth's dynamic will.

It is possible to contend that Nietzsche's will to power as art entails a frantic production of aesthetic forms, "signifying nothing." If that be the case, should not this have been forseen by the prophetic Zarathustra? Heidegger explains this blindness in Nietzsche by his forgetfulness of the question of Being in his pursuit of aesthetics. Thus, he failed to think the ontological difference between Being and beings. The Tübingen philosopher therefore takes it upon himself to complete the thinking that Nietzsche himself left half-complete. By transposing Nietzsche's notion of "will to power as art" into his own ontological questioning, Heidegger attempts to rectify Nietzsche's shortcomings. In so doing, he focuses on the role of the poet. For Heidegger, as for Nietzsche, the poet is a prophetic figure whose importance lies not with "what" he says, but rather "how" he says it. The poet-philosopher Zarathustra opens up language to unpredictable and ambiguous meanings in his act of aesthetic interpretation of himself and the world.

But Heidegger attempts to radicalize Nietzsche's notion of will to power as art when he, among others, claims "language is the house of Being."[14] In order for Being to show itself in language, we have to confront its nothingness, that is, the silence that upholds our ontological *being*. If we remain in the subjective realm, we will not get in touch with our essential connectedness to Being, but will instead get lost in an endless flow of beings, produced by technological language. As objectified beings serving as instruments for other subjective wills, we no longer touch that which constitutes our essential being. We are out of touch with Being.

This is where the role of the poet becomes crucial. Occasionally, poets come to dwell in language in a different way than most of us do in our everydayness. A poet who dwells in language in such a way that she effects an unworking of technologized language, may come in the neighborhood of what Heidegger calls poetic thinking. By confronting that which is truly strange and unfamiliar in language, the poet experiences a mode of Being in language that is truly open or free. Heidegger calls this way of being in language *poietic*, that is, when the poet becomes receptive to the "letting-be-in-the-open" of language. It is important to understand that this mode of being requires that the poet no longer remains in the subjective mode of speaking, but rather loses herself in language in such a way that she opens up to ontological difference. Such an attunement to that which is hidden and silenced in everyday speech, may grant new possibility for new beings to *be*.

And Now?

In Heidegger's view, the task of thinking that lies ahead is to question technology in such a way that the essence of technology may be retrieved in its most fundamental meaning as "a way of revealing." Poetic thinking might still take place today, provided we are able to dwell in language in such a way that we might touch upon that which will bring about new beings. This potential is always already there, hidden in language—even in technological language.

If we now, as women doing philosophy, pay heed to Heidegger's call—not as dutiful daughters, but as women in pursuit of thinking—we may stumble upon some precious insights. These will not be loudly announced and they will not reach the headlines of any webnews, but they might prove insignificantly significant. If I venture to gather some of the threads pursued in my attempt to question Nietzsche's will to power in its relation to the feminine, I am afraid that I shall find myself entangled in "an all-encompassing net of art." Perhaps all I am left with is a path, a movement, and a rhythm that might lead into an as yet unexplored openness. The question of sexual difference still begs an answer in our day and age. Perhaps we should pay heed to Irigaray's contention that it represents *the* question that is given to our age to deal with. Nietzsche's thinking on will to power has opened up new paths for such an inquiry. Is it not high time that we inquire into the groundless ground of his subjective aesthetic projections of the will, by returning to the murky, primordial ground from which all figurations of sexual difference emerges, ontologically speaking? That would, however, transport us into a truly risky terrain, where the *poietic* openness of language is still dangerously free.

Notes

1. Friedrich Nietzsche, *The Birth of Tragedy and The Case of Wagner*, trans. by Walter Kaufmann (New York: Vintage Books, 1976), 140.
2. Friedrich Nietzsche, *The Birth of Tragedy*, 33.
3. Martin Heidegger, *Nietzsche: Vol 1: The Will to Power as Art*, trans. David Farrell Krell (New York: Harper & Row, 1979), 115.
4. Friedrich Nietzsche, *The Birth of Tragedy*, 63.
5. Friedrich Nietzsche, *Thus Spoke Zarathustra* in *The Portable Nietzsche*, trans. & ed. Walter Kaufmann (New York: The Viking Press, 1954).
6. Friedrich Nietzsche, *The Birth of Tragedy*, 97-98.
7. Friedrich Nietzsche, *The Birth of Tragedy*, 98.
8. Friedrich Nietszhe, "European nihilism" in *The Will to Power*, trans. Walter Kaufmann & R. J. Hollingdale (New York: Vintage Books, 1967), 7-9.
9. Luce Irigaray, *Amante marine: de Friedrich Nietzsche* (Paris: Les Editions de Minuit, 1983). *Marine Lover: of Friedrich Nietszche*, trans. Gillian C. Gill (New York: Columbia University Press, 1991).
10. Ellen Mortensen, *The Feminine and Nihilism: Luce Irigaray with Nietzsche and Heidegger* (1994).
11. Kelly Oliver, *Womanizing Nietzsche* (1995).
12. Jacques Derrida, *Spurs: The Styles of Nietzsche* (1978).
13. Ellen Mortensen, *Touching Thought: Ontology and Sexual Difference* (2002).
14. Martin Heidegger, "Letter on Humanism" in *Martin Heidegger: Basic Writings*, trans. Frank A. Capuzzi, ed. David Farrell Krell (New York: Harper & Row, 1977).

Bibliography

Derrida, Jacques. *Spurs: The Styles of Nietzsche*. Trans. Barbara Harlow. (Chicago: Chicago University Press, 1978).

Heidegger, Martin. "Letter on Humanism." In *Martin Heidegger: Basic Writings*. Trans. Frank A. Capuzzi. Ed. David Farrell Krell. (New York: Harper & Row, 1977).

———. Nietzsche: *Vol. 1: The Will to Power as Art; Vol. 2: The Eternal Recurrence of the Same; Vol. 3: Will to Power as Knowledge and as Metaphysics;* and *Vol. 4: Nihilism*. Trans. David Farrell Krell. (New York: Harper & Row, 1979-1986).

Irigaray, Luce. *Amante marine: de Friedrich Nietzsche*. (Paris: Les Editions de

Minuit, 1983).

Mortensen, Ellen. *The Feminine and Nihilism: Luce Irigaray with Nietzsche and Heidegger.* (Oslo: Scandinavian University Press, 1994).

———. *Touching Thought: Ontology and Sexual Difference.* (Lanham, MD: Lexington Books, 2002).

Nietzsche, Friedrich. *The Birth of Tragedy and The Case of Wagner.* Trans. by Walter Kaufmann. (New York: Vintage Books, 1976).

———. "European Nihilism" in *The Will to Power.* Ed. & trans. by Walter Kaufmann (London: Vintage, 1968).

Oliver, Kelly. *Womanizing Nietzsche: Philosophy's Relation to the "Feminine."* (New York: Routledge, 1995).

Matter, Gender and Death in Aristotle

Vigdis Songe-Møller

For a number of years I have been working with the question of the relationship between women—or rather the female—and death in early Greek myths,
in the Pre-Socratics, and in Plato.[1] I have found, perhaps not surprisingly, that
woman, body, sexuality and death form a tight conceptual bundle in texts ranging from Hesiod, through Parmenides to Plato: where one of these concepts
occurs, you quite often find the others.[2] In this essay I shall take a look at
Aristotle and see if this conceptual bundle is present in his thinking too. I
believe it is. There is a tendency in Aristotle's theories for the woman, or the
feminine, to be overlooked, regardless of whether the text is of metaphysical,
biological, ethical or political character. I shall discuss this tendency in the light
of what I see as Aristotle's political ideal: the ideal of the self-sufficient—the
autarch—male citizen. This ideal, I shall suggest, may be interpreted as reflecting a wish to overcome death, or to attain eternity, in some way or other.

I shall start rather indirectly by saying some words about the Greek concept of *arché*, which, in a philosophical context, is usually translated as "principle," or "element." It is supposed that the first Pre-Socratics formulated theories about the *arché* of the world. Aristotle uses the word for what he himself
considers to be the first principles of knowledge, for instance the principle of
non-contradiction (*Met.* 995b8). But he also uses the word in order to denote
the four causes; they are the *archai* behind the existence of any substance, or,
as he also calls them: the *aitiai*. The four causes—the four *aitiai*, the four
archai—are the principles to which a substance owes its existence, or without
which a substance would not have come into being. Without the four causes—
a material cause, a formal cause, an efficient cause and a final cause—Aristotle
says, a substance, an *ousia*, would not come into being. *Aitia* can also mean
"accusation" or "blame" and belongs insofar to juridical language: I can
blame, accuse, the four causes for my existence; as I can accuse my parents for
my existence. If it weren't for them, I would not be, I would not exist; if it

weren't for them, I would not be what I actually am.

It is often useful to see how a philosophical concept is used in a non-philosophical context, or how it was used before it became a philosophical concept. From the beginning, *arché* seems to have had a double meaning, which to my mind is also reflected in the philosophical use of the word. *Arché* means "origin" or "beginning" on the one side, "power" on the other. The verb which belongs to *arché*, namely *archein*, was originally a military expression with the meaning "to lead," i.e. lead soldiers to the battlefield.[3] In this case it is easy to see that the two meanings of *arché*, "beginning" and "power," are connected: the one who goes first and is the leader, is also the one who is in charge, who has the power over the soldiers whom he leads. Beginning and power are thus closely interconnected in the concept of *arché*.

It is therefore hardly surprising that the word *arché* is used in a political context, for instance in the word "monarchy," which means "one power" or "one leader," or "anarchy," which means "no power," "no leader"; or also in the word "autarchy," which means "self-sufficiency," or more precisely, "that which is its own leader, its own origin." I shall say some words about *autarchy*, in order to arrive at my point, my reason for speaking at such length about *arché*.

For Aristotle autarchy was a political ideal, but not *only* a political ideal. It was also what I would call a metapysical ideal. Moreover, it was a biological ideal. Or rather, for Aristotle, politics, metaphysics and biology were ideologically and conceptually so tightly intertwined that it seems appropriate—at least in many cases—to interpret concepts taken from one area with the help of concepts taken from another. In the concept of *autarchy* I see just such an ideological and conceptual combination of politics, metaphysics and biology. Implicit in the concept of *autarchy* is the idea of the ability to maintain one's own existence by oneself alone. And this is the way in which scholars in the field have interpreted *autarchy*.[4] Only the person who is totally independent of anything outside himself is truly self-sufficient. If one were to pursue the concept and the phenomenon of such a radical self-sufficiency to its logical conclusion, which I think Aristotle tries to do, the totally self-sufficient person has to involve his or her own origin. A person, or an organism for that matter—or any thing, any substance—which has its origin in something else, or in someone else, and thus owes its existence to this something else, or to this someone else, is obviously not totally independent from the outer world; it is not entirely self-sufficient, is not entirely autarch. In other words, autarchy is for Aristotle an unattainable—or rather a divine—ideal. Only God is totally self-sufficient and independent; only God is his own origin, his own cause. For Aristotle this means that only God is completely free.

Being one's own *arché* means to be immortal. And this is, I suspect, the utopian ideal for the Aristotalian man, the Aristotalian citizen. If the ideal is to become one's own *arché*, the ideal is to get rid of sexual difference, or: to get rid of man's dependence on woman in order to reproduce himself. In his metaphysics and in his biology, I suspect that Aristotle is trying to get as close as possible to this ideal, insofar as he minimizes the role of the matter in his theory of causes, and the role of the female element in his theory of biological reproduction.

As already mentioned, in his *Metaphysics* Aristotle uses the word *arché* to denote the origin of a thing, i.e. to denote the causes of a thing. For instance, in the first book of the *Metaphysics*, he states that, according to Thales, water is the *arché* (983b19ff.). He goes on to explain that "that from which everything comes into being, is the *arché* of everything" (*Met.* 983b24f.). Interestingly, Aristotle goes on to say: "He [i.e. Thales] came to his conclusion [that water is the *arché* of all things]... from the fact that the sperm [*ta spermata*] of all things have a moist nature; and water is the origin (*arché*) of the nature of moist things." In other words, since the sperm—which for Aristotle is that from which living things grow forth—is moist, it seems reasonable to him that Thales would postulate *water* as the *arché* of everything. Evidently it is quite natural for him to regard the metaphysical principle as closely connected to fertilization and reproduction. For Aristotle *arché* obviously has something to do with reproduction. And this is my point: there is a close connection between Aristotle's speculations on metaphysical causes and biological reproduction. Biological reproduction is, I suggest, the paradigmatic way in which the four causes function when a substance comes into being. This I shall pursue further.

In Book VII of his *Metaphysics*, Aristotle illustrates his concept of cause—*aítion* or *aitía*—which, at least in this context, is obviously used in the same way as he uses *arché*—by looking at the causes for the coming into being and for the existence of a human being. I shall quote a short passage from Aristotle:

> When one inquires into the cause of something, one should, since the "causes" are spoken of in several senses, state all the possible causes. For instance, what is the material cause of man (*anthropos*)? Shall we say "the menstrual fluid" (*ta katamenia*)? What is the moving cause? Shall we say "the seed" (*to sperma*)? The formal cause? His essence (*to ti en einai*). The final cause? His end (*to telos*). But perhaps the latter two are the same. (Aristotle, *Metaphysics*, Book VIII, 1044a33-37)[5]

Aristotle here makes it clear that the causes of a thing are connected to the coming into being of a thing. Every thing, every *ousia*, is to be likened to a child, and the causes of a thing can be understood análogous to sexual reproduction. Sexual difference, here articulated as the difference between seed (*sperma*) and menstrual fluid (*katamenia*), functions as an illustration of ontological principles, or *archai*: woman's contribution to the child which is to be born, is matter, while man's contribution is, as Aristotle says in the paragraph just quoted, the moving cause of a child being born. One might argue that the formal cause also contains both the final and the moving cause: the form determines the goal, and the form gets the thing moving (from within). One might say that there are two determining causes: the formal cause and the material cause. In other words, the two main causes are the masculine and the feminine principles.

Both of these principles must be present in order for a thing—an *ousia*—to come into being and to maintain its existence. This is of course also true for human beings: every man and every woman has both a masculine and a feminine element in themselves. In this respect there is no difference between man and woman: we are both feminine *and* masculine, and insofar as this is the case, Aristotle's theory is no explicit theory of sexual difference. Sexual difference articulates itself only when it comes to sexual reproduction: the difference between man and woman articulates itself in the way man and woman, respectively, participate in sexual reproduction. A woman is the one who contributes with the feminine element—the matter; a man is the one who contributes with the masculine element—the form. Woman also has the masculine element in herself, but this masculinity is irrelevant in her participation in sexual reproduction. In sexual reproduction woman is exclusively female, and man is exclusively male (cf. 729b13ff.).

This Aristotelian theory is not without difficulties. It does not explain why it is necessary to have two sexes. Or rather, why it takes a man *and* a woman in order to reproduce. Why cannot a human being, which, according to Aristotle, has both the masculine and the feminine element in itself, reproduce itself by itself alone, like a plant? Why cannot a human being move its own matter with its own form and thus give life to a new human being? Why has nature differentiated human beings into man and woman? This is a question Aristotle feels obliged to ask, insofar as nature, according to him, makes everything as perfect as possible.

Why has nature differentiated human beings into men and women? Aristotle's answer to this question is ideological. It is better, Aristotle explains, that the superior things in nature are separated from the inferior. Therefore it is better that the formal principle is separated from the material principle. I shall quote from Aristotle's *Generation of Animals*:

> As the first efficient or moving cause, to which belong the definition (*logos*) and form (*eidos*), is better and more divine in its nature than the material on which it works, it is better that the superior principle should be separated from the inferior. Therefore, whenever it is possible and so far as it is possible, the male is separated from the female. For the first principle of the movement, or efficient cause, whereby that which comes into being is male, is better and more divine than the material whereby it is female. (Aristotle, *Generation*

of Animals, II, 1. 732a2-10)[6]

The superiority of the male is here postulated. And this natural hierarchical structure of the universe will be clearer—or "purer"—if men and women in their sexual function are separated. The existence of the two sexes, understood as a separation of the efficient and the material causes, might, in other words, be interpreted as the most adequate expression of nature's hierarchical structure. Still, Aristotle is obviously not totally satisfied with this metaphysical explanation of the sexual differentiation between men and women. That men need women in order to reproduce seems unproblematic: a man cannot bear children. But why do women need men? This is a puzzling point to Aristotle. He poses the question in this way:

> ...the question may be raised why it is that, if indeed the female possesses the same soul and if it is the secretion of the female which is the material of the embryo, she needs the male besides instead of generating entirely from herself? (Aristotle, *Generation of Animals*, II, 5. 741a5-10).[7]

If this were a possibility, if woman could reproduce herself without a male, "the male would," Aristotle says, "exist in vain" (*G.A.* 741b.4-5). But Aristotle right away consoles himself: "Nature does nothing in vain." In other words, there is a purpose in the existence of the male. But what is it? Aristotle is in need of a theory that explains the purpose of male existence.

The purpose of reproduction is clear: individual beings—plants, animals, human beings—cannot last forever as individuals. Their matter is as such a potentiality for non-existence. However, one might say that, according to Aristotle, "everything that exists aims at continued existence."[8] The aim and the reason for reproduction is to overcome individual death. Through reproduction a continuation of the species is made possible. However, it is my thesis that Aristotle is looking for a theory which goes somewhat further: he is looking for a theory, or an explanation, which gives hope to the *individual* man that his child is—or at least comes close to being—his and only his child, i.e. a continuation of *himself*—a continuation of his individual being—and not only of the species. In other words: he is looking for a theory which makes man the one and only origin of his offspring, i.e. a theory that makes man autarch.

Therefore, on the one hand Aristotle needs a theory which makes man into a necessary biological *arché*—this would explain the purpose of male existence; on the other hand he would like a theory which makes him into the one and only *arché*—this would make man totally autarch and give him hope of overcoming individual death. Or at least, Aristotle is in need of a theory that minimizes the obvious role of the female in biological reproduction.

And it is exactly such a theory that Aristotle gives in his biological writings. This theory is well known, and I shall outline it only briefly here. There are, according to Aristotle, two kinds of sperm: the female kind, which he identified as the menstrual blood—the *katamenia*—and the male kind, the male sperm. Both of these kinds Aristotle defines as surplus nutriment: the nutriment which a person does not use, or does not need for growth or for subsistence, becomes the sperm. This explains why young girls and boys do not produce sperm: they need all the nutriment they consume for growth. And it explains why pregnant and nursing women do not produce menstrual blood: all the nutriment which the woman herself does not need is used for the growth of the embryo or for the production of milk.

There is, however, one important difference between the male and female sperm: while the male is able to give life to a material, to *move* the material and make it grow, the female *katamenia* does not have this power. The *katamenia* is also surplus nutriment, but it is imperfect. According to Aristotle: "The female is, as it were, a mutilated male, and the *katamenia* is *sperma*, only not pure. For there is only one thing which *katamenia* does not have, the principle of soul" (Aristotle, *G. A.* 737a25-30). Aristotle compares menstrual blood to a hen's egg, which in itself is only passive matter, without life and movement, but which is impregnated with life and movement through the male sperm.

He also uses the nature-art analogy in order to explain the different roles which the male and the female play in reproduction: a carpenter moves his tools which then move the matter in the same way in which a male moves the *katamenia* with his sperm (*G. A.* 730b13-19). In other words, the sperm is regarded as a tool which forms, or implants, the soul in the *katamenia*, without itself becoming a material part of that which it moves. In the formation of an embryo the male sperm contributes only the human form and soul—the human life—and nothing material. By means of a metaphor—treating the sperm as a kind of tool—Aristotle explains how it is possible for a material thing—the male sperm—to transfer something wholly immaterial—the form or the soul—to another material thing, the *katamenia*. It is for Aristotle not an easy thing to explain. One might regard it as symptomatic that he explains it in this metaphorical way: Aristotle is not particularly fond of metaphorical explanations.

I shall not go into the many problems that Aristotle encounters here: how can he explain that not all the babies born are male? And how can he explain that boys resemble their mothers, not only physically, but also intellectually? Aristotle goes to great lengths in order to explain some of the difficulties that arise from his theory. It does not occur to him that he might change his theory. Evidently he has not come up with the most efficient theory to explain his observations. He has, however, come up with a theory which 1) explains the purpose of male existence; i.e. a theory which explains the biological necessity of the male in the reproduction of an embryo, and 2) makes the male into the substantial and determining *arché*; i.e. a theory which minimizes the role played by the female in biological reproduction and thus minimizes the difference between God and man, or between God and the male. In *De anima* Aristotle says that reproduction, insofar as it produces another living being which resembles oneself, is a way, "in which they (i.e. living beings) may partake in the eternal and divine" (II. 415a25ff.).

I shall comment on these last remarks, which are crucial to my project. To Aristotle, God is perfect life, complete, *life* (*zoé, Met.* XII 1072b26). One might say: *God is life*. And that which is, in a perfect way, will continue to be: God is everlasting life (*Met.* XII, 7, 1072b28). Human, or more generally, organic life is deficient life, insofar as it will not last forever. Organic life contains within itself death as potentiality. The reason, of course, is that every living being—except God—is a composite of form, or soul, and matter. Matter, as Aristotle says in *On Generation and Corruption* (II. 335a24ff.), is the cause of being and not being, i.e. of coming into being and of passing away, or as one might also say: of birth and death. Matter is potential death.

Although every living being—except God—will, because of its matter, necessarily die, death seems to be a problem for Aristotle. Or rather, there seems to be no proper place for death in his biological—and metaphysical—theory. At least: I have not been able to find a proper place for it. "Nature always strives after the better," Aristotle states in *On Generation and Corruption* (336b27f.). And immediately afterwards he says: "Being is better than not-Being" (336b30). Hence, nature will always strive after being. A living being will always strive to keep on living. This insight, which may be said to be "the heart of Aristotle's teleology,"[9] seems to structure Aristotle's own theories.

His biological theories have been described as explanations "of what happens to (a living being) as it develops to maturity and maintains and reproduces itself."[10] As a teleology, Aristotle's theory explains how an organism reaches it individual perfection, i.e. its form, and how it may overcome its individual death, i.e. through reproduction of an individual as like itself as possible. He is not eager to explain why death necessarily occurs in each individual organic life. He does stress that death is a necessity, but still he seems to treat it as an accident, as something which occurs because something has gone wrong, because circumstances are not perfect, or because an accidental obstacle has come in the way (*Met.* 1049a14). If nature were perfect, death would not be a part of it. Or would it? I am not sure. If nature were perfect, what about the female: would she exist according to Aristotle?

I suspect that both the female and matter play an ambiguous part in Aristotle's philosophy, and that this ambiguity has something to do with his teleological thinking, which always strives for being and perfection; i.e. which strives for the divine.

One of the problems with which Aristotle obviously struggles in his work *Generation of Animals*, is to explain why a female is born. On the one hand she is, as Aristotle puts it, "a necessity required by nature, since the race of creatures which are separated into male and female has got to be kept in being" (767b7ff.). On the other hand, she is an accidental product of nature, or, as Aristotle puts it, she is a deviation from nature; "a female is formed," he says, "instead of a male" (ibid.). "Nature has in a way strayed from the generic type." She is, he says, in a way a monstrosity. But what is strange about the female is that she is a necessary monstrosity, she is a necessary deviation from nature. Does nature always strive for the better? The better, of course, would be to stick to the generic type, not to make monstrosities, not to deviate from it. But on the other hand, nature strives to be, rather than not to be. And in order for an animal, or a human being, to be, to continue to be, it has to reproduce itself. And in order to reproduce itself, it needs the female.

The status of the female is therefore ambiguous: as the material principle in reproduction, the female represents death. As necessary for reproduction, she represents life. The female is accidental and necessary. She is death and she is life. She occupies—and this is my thesis—a gap in Aristotle's philosophy which is linked to the gap which death occupies in his teleological thinking.

Notes

1. See my book *Den greske drømmen om kvinnens overflødighet. Essays om myter og filosofi i antikkens Hellas* (Oslo: Cappelen Akademisk Forlag, 1999. English translation: *Philosophy Without Women. The Birth of Sexism in Western Thought*. London: Continuum, 2003) .

2. There are, of course, several Pre-Socratic philosophers who think differently. In Anaximander, Heraclitus, Empedocles and others, there is, I would suggest, at least an *opening* for thinking about woman, or the female, in another way. See my book *Tanker om opprinnelsen. Tidlig gresk filosofi fra Hesiod til Demokrit* (Oslo: Cappelen Akademisk Forlag, 1999).

3. Cf. Charles H. Kahn, *Anaximander and the Origins of Greek Cosmology* (New York: Columbia University Press/London: Oxford University Press, 1960), 233.

4. Cf. Krämer, "Die Grundlegung des Freiheitsbegriffs in der Antike," in J. Simon (red.), *Freiheit. Theoretische und praktische Aspekte des Problems* (Freiburg / München: Verlag Karl Alber, 1977), 259: "Im Begriff der Autarkie liegt … das Moment der Selbsterhaltung, das Vermögen, sich selbst aus sich heraus im Sein zu halten."

5. Cf. Anthony Preus, "Science and Philosophy in Aristotle's *Generation of Animals*," *Journal of the History of Biology*, vol. 3 (1970), no. 1, 1.

6. Cf. Maryanne Cline Horowitz, "Aristotle and Woman," *Journal of the History of Biology*, vol. 9 (1976), no. 2, 193.

7. Cf. Horowitz, 194.

8. Preus, 17.

9. Cf. A. Preus, "Man and Cosmos in Aristotle," in D. Devereux and P. Pellegrin

(eds.), *Biologie, logique et métaphysique chez Aristotle* (Paris: Éditions du CNRS, 1990), 490.

10. John M. Cooper, "Metaphysics in Aristotle's Embryology," in D. Devereux and P. Pellegrin (eds.), *Biologie, logique et métaphysique chez Aristotle* (Paris: Éditions du CNRS, 1990), 55.

Bibliography

Cooper, John M. "Metaphysics in Aristotle's Embryology," in D. Devereux and P. Pellegrin (eds.), *Biologie, logique et métaphysique chez Aristotle* (Paris: Éditions du CNRS, 1990).

Horowitz, Maryanne Cline. "Aristotle and Woman," *Journal of the History of Biology*, Vol. 9 (1976), no. 2.

Kahn, Charles H. *Anaximander and the Origins of Greek Cosmology* (New York: Columbia University Press/London: Oxford University Press, 1960).

Krämer, Hans. "Die Grundlegung des Freiheitsbegriffs in der Antike," in J. Simon (ed.), *Freiheit. Theoretische und praktische Aspekte des Problems* (Freiburg / München: Verlag Karl Alber, 1977).

Preus, Anthony. "Science and Philosophy in Aristotle's *Generation of Animals*," *Journal of the History of Biology*, Vol. 3 (1970), no. 1.

———. "Man and Cosmos in Aristotle," in D. Devereux and P. Pellegrin (eds.), *Biologie, logique et métaphysique chez Aristotle* (Paris: Éditions du CNRS, 1990).

Songe-Møller, Vigdis. *Den greske drømmen om kvinnens overflødighet. Essays om myter og filosofi i antikkens Hellas* (Oslo: Cappelen Akademisk Forlag, 1999. English translation: *Philosophy Without Women. The Birth of Sexism in Western Thought*. London: Continuum, 2003).

———. *Tanker om opprinnelsen. Tidlig gresk filosofi fra Hesiod til Demokrit*. Oslo: Cappelen, 1999.

Secrets and Drive

Jodi Dean

Contemporary conditions of integrated communications media combined with the brutal, intensive, expansion of capital have changed the terms of feminist politics. Feminist theory needs to reorient itself to the new subjectivities and operations of power in technoculture. It has to recognize what it means to operate in cyberia, that is, the world produced through digital interactions. I argue elsewhere that the norm of publicity championed in the enlightenment and now inscribed in various forms in the constitutions of western democracies functions as the ideological form of technoculture.[1] Publicity is to technoculture what liberalism is to capitalism. Here I explain this thesis and draw out the implications it has for feminist theory, generally, and for thinking about gender and sexual difference, more specifically.

Technically Different

I begin with sexual difference. As carried on by Foucauldians and Lacanians, the debate over sexual difference has gotten quite technical. I have nothing to say about these technicalities. I am concerned, however, with the question of feminist politics. Does the notion of sexual difference enable feminist politics or, as Judith Butler suggests, is it ultimately depoliticizing?[2] Is feminist politics thus better served by a more fluid, performative, conception of gender?

It makes sense to approach this question from where we are, that is, from the standpoint of global technoculture's communicative capitalism.[3] In this setting, the symbolic politics of deconstructing and/or reperforming gender has no point. If the operations of power in capitalist technoculture are contingent, fluid, and mobile, then demonstrating that gender is contingent, fluid, and mobile serves rather than confronts capitalism. As Michael Hardt and Antonio Negri argue: "The affirmation of hybridities and the free play of differences

81

across boundaries ... is liberatory only in a context where power poses hierarchy exclusively through essential identities, binary divisions, and stable oppositions."[4] A critique of binary gender is liberatory only in a context where gendered binaries are assumed and enforced. This is not the case today.

More generally, however, the political purchase of the symbolic politics of gender restylization has been over-estimated. That is to say, contemporary technoculture aside, a symbolic approach to gender has political drawbacks. To be sure, I am not endorsing either naturalized sexual difference or strategic essentialism. Rather, I am persuaded by the psychoanalytic account of sexual difference as a failure of symbolization, as a fundamental antagonism in the Real.[5] How this antagonism is manifest in the symbolic is contingent, historically varied, incomplete, contradictory. Locating gender in the symbolic may *seem* to have more readily apparent political applications (pointing out how the subjects of rights are always already masculine, say, or how the feminine is always secondary). Nevertheless, these applications are too limited. On the one hand, gender can be de- and reconstructed in the Symbolic without having effects in the Real. On the other hand, gender restylization can also reinforce and legitimate the symbolic order. Cross-dressing is an age-old practice, and there is still gender. As Lynne Segal notes, "the uncanny strength of conventional sexual and gender binaries is their ability to triumph over repeated attempts, both theoretical and performative, to dismantle and deconstruct them . . . the braided hierarchies of sexuality and gender have a remarkable capacity to thrive precisely on their own contradictions."[6] Slavoj Žižek expresses the same point when he writes that the big Other includes "symbolic norms *and* their codified transgressions."[7]

In fact, yesterday's gender-based critique simply states today's reinvestment with vigor (or a vengeance). "New traditionalist" advertising, for example, relies on images of homemakers and nostalgic evocations of moms baking cookies. To say that these advertisements reinforce traditional images of women is to state the obvious—that is precisely what they want to do! Likewise, to say that sexualized images of women are used to sell consumer items is to surprise no one. Even with regard to pornography to say that some pornography sexually objectifies women is not to make a strong or critical claim—*yes, we know porn makes women sex objects...that's why we like it!*

To bring these two points together, not only does locating sexual difference in language lead to an over-estimation of the political effects of restylization, but it also fails to take into account the viral "recirculation" of sexed, gendered, and sexualized elements, images, memes, or bits of code. This is particularly significant if one accepts Žižek's idea of the contemporary collapse of symbolic efficiency.[8] Today, there is not a coherent, stable, symbolic order. There is not a master signifier holding meaning together and in place. There is a blurring and flow and proliferation of meanings, uncertainties, fears, and possibilities. Indeed, the key attribute of global capitalist technoculture with its flows of capital, information, images, and DNA, is this collapse of symbolic efficiency.[9] Technoculture is characterized by a proliferation of discursive practices, of communicative networks. And this means that there is also and consequently a radical expansion in failures of meaning, inefficiencies of reference, in contacts and conversations in which there are no ways to authorize, validate, or justify a claim.[10] It means that there are all sorts of ways to perform, stylize, and signify gender that will circulate and recombine and mean all sorts of different, difficult to determine, things.

It makes sense, then, to endorse the psychoanalytic argument that sexual difference is Real. Psychoanalysis enables a better account of the persistence of sexual difference in the face of gender restylization and in the networks of technoculture. Sexual difference exceeds gendered performances; we might even say that *it is* that persistent, inexpressible, and unsymbolizable excess. In Joan Copjec's words: it is only where discursive practices falter and not at all where they succeed in producing meaning that sex comes to be."[11]

Sexual difference as and at the faltering of discursive practice appears throughout the history of new communication technologies—and pornography on the Internet is but one example. Communicative media intensify and disperse themselves in part via sexualization, that is, via opportunities to exchange sexual images and sex talk. This is a key aspect of the identity play so prevalent in the MOOs and MUDs of the pre-Web years on the Net. It also appears in satellite imagery: at precisely that point where the images transmitted from space technologies are inassimilable, we find sexualization, more specifically, confrontations with the alien nature of space that in the process evoke sex via references to primal scenes, penetration, birth and reproduction.[12] Communicative opportunities expand and sex erupts. And this eruption marks the faltering of discursive practice. Locating sexual difference in the Real, then, helps the theorization of technoculture in terms beyond gender and beyond communication.

There is more to say about this "faltering." Why, we might ask, should an intensive expansion of communicative opportunities be understood as a faltering of discursive practice? Copjec presents her account of faltering as the site at which sex comes to be via a critique of Butler. Copjec writes:

> ... Butler makes our sexuality something that communicates itself to others. While the fact that communication is a process, and thus ongoing, precludes a complete unfolding of knowledge at any given moment, further knowledge is still placed within the realm of possibility. When, on the contrary, sex is *disjoined* from the signifier, it becomes that which does not communicate itself, that which marks the subject as unknowable.[13]

The intensification of communicative opportunities can be understood as a faltering of discursive practice because of increases in noise, distortion, failed messages, misfires, and unknowability. More communicative opportunities entail more opportunities for uncertainty and an all the more intensive disjoining of sex from the signifier. Who is really sending me these messages? Why are they saying these things? What do they mean? What authority stands behind them? The expansion of communication also expands what is not communicated. It brings with it an incommunicable stain on practices of communication: in cyberspace we are never certain who or what we are communicating with; the other is real and at the same time the other. I imagine to be typing in front of the screen of another computer. My fantasies can run wild. They are no longer hemmed in by symbolic significations (which help hold meaning in place and thereby displace the fantasy structure always already an element of communicative interactions).

Of course, the circulation of sexual difference in faltering communicative processes has little to do with desire. Instead, it is part of the endless repetitive cycling of drive around the failures themselves. This might explain why stories about people who fall in love on the Internet seem so odd, so false: the Net is not a space of desire; it is a pulsing network of drive.

Desire and drive involve two modes of reflexivity or self-relating that are in a closed loop with each other. The subject of desire can never want what it gets; its desire is reflected back into a desire for desire; in desire, *jouissance* is always unattainable. Conversely, in drive, *jouissance* is always attainable; it stains every endeavor, accompanying all our acts, making it impossible to be pure. In drive, everything is tinged with guilty pleasure.[14]

To sum up my argument thus far: I am linking the Real of sexual difference to the circulation of communication in the networks of contemporary technoculture. I am agreeing with Žižek's contention that the collapse of the Symbolic entails the merging of the Real and the Imaginary. And I am suggesting that one place we see these mergings is in the excesses of sexual difference that circulate throughout technocultural networks, not as gender, not as part of a heterosexual or patriarchal matrix, not as desire, but in circuits of drive.

The Public Doesn't Exist

To make this argument more convincing, I turn to my critique of publicity. This critique consists of two, related, points: one, there is no public and, two, continuing to frame democracy in terms of the public is dangerous.

The ideal of the public is a fantasy of unity and wholeness. It is a fantasy that covers over and disavows the fundamental split within the public. Both the fantasy and the split are sustained by the secret. Put somewhat differently, the ideal public of the enlightenment has the form of a disavowal held in place by the secret.

In accounts of the public common to democratic theory, the secret plays a generative role. The norm of publicity depends on a prior conviction that something is hidden and should be revealed. Those to whom it is revealed and from whom it is kept are the public. Disclosure, then, is not simply a way of making something public; it is also a way of making "the" public.

Jeremy Bentham's classic account of the law of publicity is a good example.[15] Here the secret fills out the gap between two competing notions of the public, the public supposed to know and the public supposed to believe. The secret compensates in advance for the public's failure to serve as the unitary subject of democracy. How does this work? Well, Bentham acknowledges that not everyone is able to make a certain and reliable judgment on political matters. With this acknowledgment, he splits the public into the few who know and the many who believe them. For the many to believe that the few know, the few have to have information; the few, in other words, have to insure that a process of disclosure is in place. The secret, then, is the link, the key, the guarantee, the hinge holding together, and yet apart, the public as a whole. Once the secret is uncovered, once the hidden barrier to the realization of an inclusive social body has been revealed, there will be justice and democracy. Or that, at least, is the claim—because, of course, there is no secret beyond the public; this is simply the fantasy that holds the public together.

Interestingly, Bentham refers to publicity as a "system of distrust." The belief of the many, it seems, depends on a prior distrust, a distrust of secrets and those who might keep them. But what about the idea that publicity is a "system"? What makes it run? What mechanisms sustain it? We can answer this question if we break down what Bentham terms "distrust" into two operations—revelation and concealment. Distrust does not operate in only one direction—that of compelling disclosure. It also involves secretization and concealment. For the system to keep running as a system, there has to be this additional operation by which particular contents are constituted as things that are secret and in need of disclosure. It is also important to keep in mind that revelation and concealment are not complementary operations. In any given historical context each side will be invested with particular commitments and expectations.

To conclude this summary of my first claim: the enlightenment norm of publicity posits a fantasy of wholeness that holds together an already split public. Practices of concealment and revelation materialize belief in this fantasy of unity, making the public appear as precisely that subject from whom secrets are kept and in whom a right to know is embedded.

Now, one might say that my claim that the public does not exist is obvious *and* misguided. Of course the public does not really exist; the ideal of the public is regulative; it inspires democratic governance. I have two responses to this, answers that involve the second point in my critique of publicity, the point regarding its danger.

First, as many have observed, one of the dangers of the regulative ideal of the public concerns its reliance on all sorts of exclusions. It hegemonizes particular contents, discourses, and ways of thinking as those proper to the public. It posits a particular notion of the actor, citizen, or subject of the public. It sustains the borders of the nation state. Given all these critiques, it is remarkable that critical theorists continue to invoke a notion of the public.[16] It is as if they are saying, "I know the public doesn't exist, but I believe nevertheless that it exists." Why do they do this?

Perhaps these theorists continue to believe that a public exists because of the way everyday practices, technologies, and institutions materialize the fantasy of the public, making everything run and everyone act *as if* the public really existed. Public opinion polls are one obvious example. Broadcast technologies and technologies that promise everyone a voice similarly materialize the sense that there is a public. To this extent, "public" functions ideologically to secure these technologies and the system of communicative capitalism in which they are embedded and which they intensify and extend.

Some theorists try to escape the problems of the bourgeois notion of public by adding an "s." They speak of *publics*—of subaltern, oppositional, counterpublics, of proletarian, feminist, and black public spheres—as if these proliferating publics could avoid the exclusionary presumptions of a centered, rational, bourgeois public sphere. These counterpublics, however, rely on and reinforce the notion of a dominant public sphere in which they want to be included and recognized. Moreover, they employ a logic of excessive subdivision that repeats within a subset the problems plaguing the larger set. In this context, emphasizing that the public does not exist might function as the opposite of an ironic gesture, as a kind of "taking the system at its word" in order to, if not bring it down, then at least confront the materializing role of the fantasy of publicity.[17]

My second response to the claim for the inspirational potential of the ideal of the public also emphasizes materialization because herein lies the particular danger of the public in cyberia, in the mediated technoculture of global capitalism. What is materialized are the practices of publicity as a system of distrust, the endless drive to know, to find out, to discover the secrets, on the one hand, and the production of contents as secrets in order to reveal them, on the other. In this setting, we do not have to believe in the public, our cameras and screens believe for us: they produce the lure of the undisclosed secret as that which we do not yet know, as that which is but one link or broadcast away. At the same time, confessions and disclosures materialize belief that the audience that hears them, the infosphere or communicative space that receives them, somehow constitutes *the public*. Giving out information, telling the truth, functions here as a kind of lie—it prevents action; it makes action pointless. That is to say, the ideology of publicity suggests that what makes revelation powerful is its impact on action, the way it opens opportunities for engagement and response. In technoculture, however, information is dumped so as to disperse criticism and displace opportunities for contestation. *Oh, the big corporation really is trying to clean up the environment, find workers over six years old, use technologies to help consumers, etc. . .*

One might be tempted to respond to my argument here with a variation of Butler's discussion of identity. In her account of the category "women" as a feminist site of agonistic struggle, Butler asserts that the political efficacy of the category stems from its failure to be descriptive—the identity category "women" is political precisely because of the way it is open to contestation.[18] My argument, however, is not "descriptivist." Of course the term "public" is open; this openness is crucial to its efficacy. But we should ask, efficacious with respect to what? My answer is efficacious with respect to a particular formation of power. The openness of the category of the public is what makes it functional as technocultural ideology. It has political effects that can not be addressed via an appeal to openness precisely because this openness is what functionalizes it for technoculture.

Another response to my rejection of the notion of the public might take up Butler's theorization of contingent exclusion. Butler argues that the failure of the signifier to produce the unity it names is contingent upon specific social exclusions.[19] This argument does not apply to the idea of the public because the failure of "public" to produce the unity it names is a constitutive failure; the public is generated through this failure as its disavowal.

Such a generative failure appears in past and present versions of publicity. In Bentham's account of publicity as a system of distrust, the secret marks the gap holding together the split public. In contemporary technoculture, the secret has become the currency of publicity, the ever circulating lure to search, click, and link as if the only thing missing from realizing democracy were information. Now everyone can know; now everyone has access to the secret. Everyone is included in the public supposed to know, and no one believes. Technologies believe in our stead. In this way, technoculture materializes the belief that the key to democracy can be found in uncovering the secrets. Even if no one really believes, satellites, the Internet, and surveillance cameras believe for us. An externalization of publicity's gap, the secret motivates continued efforts in publicity's behalf.

Now What? Beyond the Public/Private Division

What are the feminist repercussions of my account of publicity and secrecy? The first concerns the public/private distinction. Secrecy as the constitutive exclusion of the public cuts through the public/private distinction. Not only are secrets present already as limits in both spheres, but they are active mechanisms receiving and releasing contents within each sphere, suggesting the prior place of the distinction between the hidden and the visible and, in effect, displacing the very division between public and private.

Feminists, of course, have made great progress by focusing on the public/private distinction. They have demonstrated the masculinity of the public and the femininity of the private. They have drawn out the ways that the very act of dividing the social into two spheres is already part of a masculine logic. Feminist legal theory has produced persuasive versions of this argument by demonstrating how legal boundaries between public and private shift depending on the politics of the situation. There is also interesting feminist work that reverses the argument. For example, Lauren Berlant considers the privatization of the public in an analysis of the sentimentalization of national politics. Her critique of public intimacy highlights how private sexual behavior has become a primary indicator of political activity. More specifically, Berlant takes up the ways that heteronormative, family-based, child-centered, logics of value and meaning organize political possibilities around personal suffering and caring to the exclusion of systematic violence.[20]

I share Berlant's concern with the inadequacies of current imaginings of public life. Yet, the issue, as I see it, is the very concept of the public sphere. Reversing the direction of colonization and arguing that the problem stems from the private's reconstitution of the public rather than the public's reconstitution of the private does not acknowledge cyberia's changed spatialization. It leaves the spatial structure of public and private intact even as the flows it documents suggest a broader, more radical de-spatialization, convergence, and circulation of feeling, imagination, attachment, and power.

Accordingly, I advocate an approach that replaces the normative ideal of a democratic public with a sense of the always partial, limited, and partisan affiliations struggling through and over the political. Grappling with these struggles in technoculture, then, requires an account of the circulation of secrets within a system of distrust. It also entails forgoing arguments about inclusion and exclusion, giving up endeavors to unmask and reveal, and inquiring instead about the technologies, practices, and dynamics of concealment and revelation traversing the social field. Points of inquiry thus have less to do with sites than with practices—of confession and display, on the one hand, and surveillance and dissemination, on the other.

To look at a specific example: in the United States the culture wars of the 1980s and 1990s were often fought through exposing hidden behaviors and desires. Both the right and the left used the shock of revealing or unmasking to support their claims about sex, race, and gender. The events surrounding the Clinton impeachment are a further example—they involved a desperate drive to expose as well as impulses to confess and display. Clearly, an emphasis on telling the secret is particularly effective in an entertainment culture desperate for the sensations that will boost ratings and the stickiness of websites.

Interestingly, Berlant's account of national sentimentality draws out the figure of the infantile citizen in whose name regulatory interventions into the social are mobilized. This vulnerable, dependent subject is the victim in need of protection, the one whose wounds become the ground of attachment. Žižek emphasizes the ideology of victimization as well, arguing that it is the way the Real of Capital exerts its rule.[21] I disagree with both these accounts. The subject of capitalist technoculture, in my view, is fully public, the extreme realization of an ideal of publicity, a literalization of the notion of a citizen in the public sphere. It is the subject making itself an object for everyone else, the celebrity subject that has already exploited and overcome its victim status. This celebrity-citizen—and Berlant discusses this option in an account of the poverty of commercially-mediated mass politics—is now everyone. Or, everyone is now a celebrity because of the opportunities new media provide to make content and the demands they place on us to be content—respond, tell us your opinion, fill out this poll, or sit back while we track your activities on the Web. Qua celebrity, the subject is completely public, out there, accessible, available, in the media sphere, the imaginary/real communicative network of capitalist technoculture. Those excluded by this system, those outside publicity's orbit, fail to register at all. Non-existent, they are the remainders of an unrelenting system preoccupied with celebrity, disclosure, publicity.

What also follows from my critique of publicity is the sense that technoculture is not properly understood as a space of communicative action; communicative exchanges do not create some kind of shared "space." Put too strongly, in cyberia, deliberative democracy is not an option. Paradoxically, the very emphasis on universal or mass communication as the basis of democracy furthers the least democratic aspects of technoculture.

This is true, first, on a mundane and material level: the emphasis on mass communication today furthers the communications industry, the computer industry, the entertainment complex, the whole new media economy. From the first appearance of personal computers as commodities to the development of the "information superhighway" and the World Wide Web, the computer industry has legitimized itself in terms of ideals of democratic participation. Citizens will be better informed. They will have access to important political information. There will be virtual town halls and online discussion fora. This rhetoric has sold the new economy. Like a hegemonic signifier that uses the chain to signify itself, the Net is the currency or system of rules though which the new economy realizes itself. Communication is the means for achieving communication as the end.

Second, not only does the extension of communicative reflection, the exposure of ever more aspects of life to media(ted) surveillance and inquiry, reinforce the primary dynamics of capital in the information age, but it also contributes to the materialization of suspicion and the belief that the secrets are there to be discovered. Networked media bring anything and everything into the discussion. There are always multiple, competing, opinions. A plethora of experts are available for consultation on most any conceivable question. There are always other options, links, and sites. But rather than making people more informed and discussions more rational, the proliferation of competing expert opinions puts us in the horrible position of having to choose even when we lack the criteria for choice. How do we know which expert to believe? In many aspects of contemporary life the wrong choice is potentially disastrous: from individual medical decisions to judgments about product safety to experiments in particle physics, the wrong choice could be deadly. The high stakes often push against making a decision, reinforcing the imperatives of publicity as they command a search for more information. At the same time, they necessitate that no decision will ever be fully informed because new information could emerge exactly after a fateful decision is made—"if only we had known."

Given the reflexivization of everyday life, increases in communicative rationality suggest the radical reconfiguration of the social world. In this world, as Slavoj Žižek writes, "what is increasingly undermined is precisely the symbolic *trust* which persists against all skeptical data."[22] He gives the example of the emergence of "ethical committees" in the context of risk society theory. Like ideal speech situations or mini-versions of Habermasian practical discourses, these committees are supposed to help find ways of making ethical decisions about complex issues like global warming, nuclear energy, cloning, genetic engineering, and similar low probability/high consequence issues. Viewed from a Habermasian perspective, these committees appear as vehicles for the restoration of a disrupted consensus regarding matters of common concern. What Žižek makes clear, however, is that such ethical committees are better understood as symptomatic expressions of the fact of pervasive disagreement, of the fact that there is disagreement even about the ways that disagreements are to be understood, regulated, evaluated, and assessed. In such a setting, new procedures and rules and guidebooks and regulations are not reassuring. Rather, they express the ways that crucial issues remain undecidable.

Now What? The Drive of Communication

There is, of course, another way to talk about the endless cycles of communication, the inescapable loop of reflexivation that characterizes contemporary technoculture, and that it is in terms of the concept of drive. Seyla Benhabib has demonstrated the ways that the critical theory of the early Frankfurt School comes up against a fundamental aporia—the conditions of its own impossibility.[23] Horkheimer and Adorno's response to this aporia was to accept it and to theorize a negative dialectics. Habermas (as well as Benhabib and others) rejected negative dialectics and sought a normative account in a notion of communicative reason. I suggest that discourse ethics does not solve the problem here but repeats it, endlessly, as drive.

Renata Salecl provides an account of drive that aptly describes the aporias of critical theory. She writes:

> The Lacanian term for this "knowledge in the real" that resists symbolization is *drive*, the self-sufficient closed circuit of the deadly compulsion to repeat: the paradox is that which cannot ever be memorized, symbolized by way of its inclusion into the narrative frame, is not some fleeting moment of the past, forever lost, but the very insistence of drive as that which *cannot ever be forgotten* in the first place, since it repeats itself incessantly.[24]

The aporias of critical theory, the foundation that can ground critique, resists symbolization. This resistance compels a circuit of repetition, of never-ending repetitive efforts to symbolize, to include within the symbolic order. In the justification program of discourse ethics, the outcome is always deferred—till the inclusion of everyone and every possibly relevant fact or consideration. Critics of Habermas miss the point when they focus on consensus as the problem in the universalization principle of discourse ethics. The problem is not consensus—it is the endless discursive loop, the way that the discussion itself is the source of satisfaction instead of the norms it is supposed to justify. Discussion, in theories of discursive or deliberative of democracy like Habermas's and in the networks of the information, involves an endless, circulating loop of reflexivity.

Žižek notes that the reversal constitutive of drive relies on a fundamental, constitutive failure, that it relies on "some radically inaccessible X that forever eludes its grasp."[25] Translated into Habermasian, this failure describes the disrupted consensus, the challenge raised to a particular norm, and the unending discussion this failure stimulates.

The horrible paradox is that the endless circulation of discussion results in an even more ultimate frightening silence, a kind of paralysis where there are all sorts of plausible responses, all sorts of information available, but, ultimately, nothing we can say. In discourse ethics proper, decisions are deferred as the conversation moves back and forth into other discursive loops, into other kinds of validating and justifying discussions. Žižek describes drive in terms of a "sudden onset of silence."[26] The break out of language and into silence is, for Žižek, a subjectivization, the subjectivization of drive or the emergence of the subject of drive. This subject cannot talk. It is perverse, not really engaging subjectively at all.

What are some of the other characteristics of the perverse subject of drive? First, the pervert "brings to light, stages, practices the secret fantasies that sustain the predominant public discourse, while the hysterical position precisely displays doubt about whether those secret perverse desires are "really *it.*"[27]

Second, the subject of drive "makes himself seen to the object of his seeing."[28]
The subject makes himself visible to that which had originally attracted his
case. Examples of this reversal from desire to drive can be found in Kjell
Soleim's discussion of the detective making himself visible to the femme fatale
in film noir.[29] We might also think of the move to "home-camming" on the
Internet or display-based television shows such as "Big Brother." Or, we can
say that in television talks shows, the subjects are perverse and the host is hysterical, always asking them "why, why, why..."

Anyway, the point about drive is that instead of simply watching, the subject of drive displays herself, presents herself to be watched. Like a celebrity,
she is certain of the gaze. This makes sense in an entertainment culture in which
cameras, computers, and surveillance condition the practices of everyday life.
In this respect, the gaze is dispersed, not the gaze of an(O)ther subject but the
ever-present watching of cameras, the taping that watches in the stead of the
other.

Now, Zizek presents the subject of drive as the subject of capital or late
capitalist market relations and the subject of desire as the democratic subject.[30]
He argues that, given the collapse of symbolic efficiency—the decline of
Oedipus or the end of patriarchy—the paradigmatic mode of subjectivity is
polymorphous perversity. Political discourse has thus shifted from hysteria to
perversion. For Zizek, this means that a pressing political problem is "how to
hystericize the subject," how to break through drive and inculcate questioning
and lack.

I think the problem should be framed differently. The reflexivization of
communication in the networked economy brings together the hysterical democratic subject and the perverse subject of capitalist entertainment. We can
think about this in terms of the secret: the democratic subject's hysterical questioning is posited in terms of the secret. The secret holds the key to unity, inclu-
sivity, liberation. It is the object-cause of the desire to find the truth of the public. But, now, given networked media, the secret circulates differently. Not
only do subjects display and confess all the time, making themselves available
as the secret to be revealed, but the hysterical quest for the truth, the hysterical question—is that really *it?*—is that around which drive circulates. The subject of technoculture is already hysterical, but she is not a desiring subject so
much as she is a conspiring subject, a subject of conspiracy theory who keeps
making links and looking for answers. She asks questions and tries to uncover
the secret, but not because she believes she will find an answer but because the
technologies and practices believe for her. If drive's logic is, "*I don't want to
do this, nevertheless, I'm doing this*," then the conspiring subject is the one
who makes another link, gets a second or third opinion, reads something else,
asks another question, even when she does not want to—in fact, especially
when she does not want to but nevertheless is compelled to. To hystericize this
subject, to inculcate lack, feeds into the reflexivity of communicative drive.

Now What? The Traffic in Enjoyment

The modern version of publicity as a system of distrust embodies a phallic economy: is not the secret the same as the mystery of woman before the male gaze, the mysterious secret of the feminine? In Žižek's words: "inherent to phallic economy is the reference to some mysterious X which remains forever out of its reach."[31] What does this imply for the postmodern system of publicity, the system where the secret circulates, where the gaze is technological, inter-passive even—the technology gazes for us? This "system" is non-phallic; there is no master signifier, but there is still sexual difference. Like the secret, it circulates, but there is not anything "beyond" it; there is nothing to reveal. It is an eruption of the Real, now circulating through the Real of Capital. Sexual difference does not "mean" anything. It circulates without being reincorporated or refigured into a symbolic frame.

Consider the lingerie company "Victoria's Secret." The company has stores, catalogues, commercials, and a website with beautiful, thin, large-breasted models in fabulous underwear—thongs, push-up bras, teddies, lace and satin. A Foucauldian might read the store in terms of the proliferation of sex in the Victorian age—the real secret of Victorian society was that sex was not repressed; it was incited. The store, then, is a literalization of this fact. A typical psychoanalytic reading would say that the store and the catalogue are really for men. Like the feminine secret, it is simply a production by and for the masculine gaze. Victoria's Secret is for men. In contrast, my reading emphasizes not only that there is no secret—all this fabulous underwear is openly, commercially, broadly circulated so that the secret is functioning not as a lure, but is marking an inversion—but that this is what women want; it is for women—who cares what men think? If men shop there, fine, but the products are for women, women are primary consumers, and many women—enough to support the store—enjoy sexy underwear.

Really, one can not say much about it—is the underwear on the imagery pro- or anti-woman? It is underwear. The store is a store. So again, we are left with the silent circulation of drive.

As incommunicable, can sexual difference inform a feminist politics? We never know if a breast is a powerful sign of the maternal, an object of masculine fantasy, and adorable image for young children, a marker of cancer's rewriting of the female body, or just another body part. Today, the circulating breast, penis, mouth, mask, whip, or high-heeled shoe, is not quilted into or guaranteed by the symbolic order. Emerging at the faltering of discursive practice, sexual difference appears like icons, sound-bites, or memes that travel throughout technocultural networks. It is an obstacle to communication that persists in communicative practices.

Some Lacanians talk about this obstacle in terms of surplus enjoyment, *jouissance*, like surplus value in capitalism. Capitalism is the circulation of value, but always the value of the capitalist Other. Our little enjoyments in shopping and consuming and even producing and saving are always stained by the excess enjoyment of the capitalist who really benefits from our unavoidable participation in the capitalist economy. The capitalist reaps the surplus value or, more precisely, the system is what really enjoys it. Recalling my account of publicity as a system of distrust, we find that the real beneficiary of revealed secrets is not some kind of public who knows—it is the circuit of information itself, the network of screens that runs on the communication of content. The technologies themselves enjoy the surplus, the extra, the secret, incommunicable kernel or obstacle.

Put somewhat differently, the information economy relies on surplus information. The excessive dimension of *jouissance* comes into view when we note the oscillating responses to this sense of information overload. On the one hand, we have the ever-present lament regarding data glut, the uncountable number of websites, the unnavigable and uncatalogable excesses of information on the Net. On the other hand, we see this excess in renewed processes of concealment and revelation: information is privatized, then hacked into; it is considered "private" and then stored on a public debate; it is reclassified, rearranged, and redistributed in different forms. People claim that there is no information. No matter how much is out there, we always have a problem getting what we want. Or, more precisely, getting what we want comes with a price that makes us want something more or something else, something faster, something better, something not slathered in ads. Anyway, accounts of the information economy are marked by an oscillation between too much and not enough.

Accompanying this simultaneous excess and lack of information is a kind of silence, a sense that there is nothing to say. There are always alternative positions and points of view that can be taken into account; there is always another way to look at a problem or an issue. It sometimes seems like, what is the point of saying anything at all, like whatever it is will be not just countered but negated—with an opposing view or a flood of other views or a whole range of other matters, images, and possibilities. Like the oscillation, the silence tells us we are dealing with drive.

If the way beyond drive does not involve hystericizing the subject, then what does it involve? I do not have an answer, but I think the most promising approach takes the obstacle to communication and tries to make it a condition of new possibility. In other words, in the very limits of communication there might be found a way to disrupt a system that relies on communicative circuits, on reflexivization and the extension of discursive networks. Understood in terms of drive, it is clear that the communicative practices of global technoculture inhibit rather than realize their aims. They are extending a brutal capitalist system even as they claim to extend opportunities for democratic participation. In the face of such a system, its falterings, falterings that themselves proliferate as the system intensifies and expands, are opportunities. We might say that in cyberia a broken connection, a missed-link, a failure of relation holds more political potential. The best example of this, of course, is the virus, that communicable element that disrupts communication, that is incommunicative in terms of the system but that relies on the new forms of circulation to spread, mutate, and change.[32] It does not "mean" anything. It is available for different patterns of meaning. Its strength and power stem from this intense combination of incommunicability and communicability, of a communicability that is not communicative.

To conclude, radical politics in technoculture will need to function virally, to disrupt the system by breaking connections and playing up instances of communicative failure. The politics of sexual difference, then, is not simply or even primarily a feminist politics. It is an anti-capitalist politics that recognizes in the circulation of sexed elements the drive of globally networked technoculture.

Notes

1. Jodi Dean, *Publicity's Secret* (Ithaca, NY: Cornell University Press, 2002).

2. See Judith Butler, "Competing Universalities," in *Contingency, Hegemony, Universality*, Judith Butler, Ernesto Laclau, and Slavoj Žižek (London: Verso, 2000) 136-181.

3. For a more developed account of communicative capitalism, see *Publicity's Secret*.

4. Michael Hardt and Antonio Negri, *Empire* (Cambridge, MA: Harvard University Press, 2000) 142.

5. See Joan Copjec's clear and compelling discussion in *Read My Desire: Lacan against the Historicists* (Cambridge, MA: The MIT Press, 1994).

6. Lynne Segal, *Why Feminism?* (New York: Columbia University Press, 1999) 61.

7. Slavoj Žižek, *The Ticklish Subject* (London: Verso, 1999) 264.

8. Žižek develops this account in *The Ticklish Subject*, chapter six.

9. See Jodi Dean, "Feminism in Technoculture," *The Review of Education, Pedagogy, and Cultural Studies* vol. 23, no. 1 (2001) 23-48.

10. See also Jodi Dean, *Aliens in America: Conspiracy Culture from Outerspace to Cyberspace* (Ithaca, NY: Cornell University Press, 1998).

11. Copjec, *Read My Desire*, 204.

12. See Lisa Parks, *Cultures in Orbit: Satellites and Televisuality* (Durham, NC: Duke University Press, 2002).

13. Copjec, *Read My Desire*, 207.

14. This account of desire and drive can be found in Žižek, *The Ticklish Subject*, 290.

15. Jeremy Bentham, "Essay on Political Tactics," chap. 2 "Of Publicity" (1821), in *The Works of Jeremy Bentham*, vol. 2, ed. John Bowring (New York: Russell and

Russell, 1962). A more detailed discussion can be found in *Publicity's Secret*.

16. Craig Calhoun's edited volume, *Habermas and the Public Sphere* (Cambridge, MA: The MIT Press, 1992) brings together a number of these critiques.

17. Slavoj Zizek emphasizes the potentially radical character of taking the system at its word; see, *The Plague of Fantasies* (London: Verso, 1997) 77.

18. Judith Butler, *Bodies that Matter* (New York: Routledge, 1993) 221.

19. Butler, *Bodies that Matter*, 220-221.

20. Lauren Berlant, *The Queen of American Goes to Washington City* (Durham, NC: Duke University Press, 1997).

21. Slavoj Zizek, *The Fragile Absolute* (London: Verso, 2000) 60.

22. Zizek, *The Ticklish Subject*, 332.

23. Seyla Benhabib, "The Critique of Instrumental Reason," in *Mapping Ideology*, ed. Slavoj Zizek (London: Verso, 1994) 85.

24. Renata Salecl, "The Silence of Feminine Jouissance," in *Cogito and the Unconscious*, ed. Slavoj Zizek (Durham, NC: Duke University Press, 1998) 179.

25. Zizek, *The Ticklish Subject*, 304.

26. Zizek, *The Ticklish Subject*, 305.

27. Zizek, *The Ticklish Subject*, 248.

28. Slavoj Zizek, *Tarrying with the Negative* (Durham, NC: Duke University Press, 1993) 196.

29. Kjell Soleim, introduction to his edited volume, *Fatal Women: Essays on Film Noir and Related Matters* (Bergen, Norway: University of Bergen, Centre for Women's and Gender Research, 1999).

30. Zizek, *The Ticklish Subject*, 248.

31. Slavoj Zizek, "Death and the Maiden, or Femininity Between Goodness and Act," in *Fatal Women*, 63-4.

32. Hardt and Negri make a similar point in *Empire*, 56-59.

The Depressed Sex:
Sublimation and Sexual Difference

Kelly Oliver

The discourses of medicine and disease continue to produce and reproduce the meaning of sexual difference. Even while the female body has been excluded from studies in biology and medicine because it is more complicated than the male body, women have been the objects of a medical gaze that renders them passive and docile in a particularly gendered way.[1] Throughout the history of medicine, women's bodies have been pathologized in order to circumscribe, even control, their behavior. In the 19th Century hysteria was the name of the disease associated with women. In significant ways hysteria produced and reproduced stereotypes or ideals of femininity as passive, emotional, irrational and incapable of serious thought or work.[2] In the 20th Century hysteria has been replaced by depression, again a disease associated with women that produces and reproduces the meanings of feminine, woman, mother—that is to say sexual difference.

Femininity as Depression

Depression is diagnosed as a pathological condition, a disease, that according to most studies affects women at rates two or three times the rates of men world-wide. Why is depression disproportionately a female disease? Some studies, never conclusive, link depression to hormone changes and other physical difference between women and men. Few studies, however, consider lifestyle, behavioral, and attitudinal differences imposed in various ways by patriarchal culture and the historical hierarchy of men over women in what is valuable in Western culture. Is it a coincidence that many of the characteristics of stereotypical femininity are also the characteristics of clinical depression? In

97

various ways, lack of activity, passivity, silence, moodiness, irritability, excessive crying, lack of sexual appetite, and nervousness—the very description of the symptoms of depression given by the National Mental Health Association—have been part of our ideas even ideals of femininity for centuries.[3] So is it a surprise that doctors would look for, and find, these characteristics in women more often than in men? In a sense, the female subject is constructed as passive and emotional, then pathologized as depressed, diagnosed as depressed, and finally treated with drugs and electro-shock therapies for mental illness. This is like a case of what Friedrich Nietzsche describes as the philosopher or scientist who hides truth behind a bush and then praises himself when he finds it. Our culture constructs femininity as passive, silent, and without appetites and then identifies an epidemic among women of those very characteristics now pathologized as depression. And as a result millions of women are medicated.

I am not arguing that there is some *Stepford Wives* or *The Handmaid's Tale* type science fiction conspiracy to keep women docile through drugs. Nor, am I denying that there are physiological aspects of depression that should be treated. Rather, I am suggesting that we should extend our critical analysis to the very studies that so powerfully document women's depression and to the social conditions that render women passive, lacking appetites, moody, etc., that is to say depressed.

Several contemporary theorists have analyzed the ways that medical discourses and clinical practices around disease and illness work to reinforce, even create, racial and gendered identities and to legitimate disciplinary and regulatory controls.[4] Particular diseases like anemia, yellow fever, hysteria, depression, schizophrenia, and AIDS are distinguished not only epidemiologically but also by linking them to specific races, genders, sexualities, or places.[5] Identifying these epidemics legitimates intervention and management of these groups in particular. Medical categorizing, surveillance, reporting, regulation, and treatment, not only constructs diseased racial and gendered subjects but also legitimates continued research and treatment that objectifies those subjects and keeps them dependent upon the medical establishment, whose superior knowledge and stature is reinforced against the racialized and sexualized "others" whom they study and treat.

Depression is certainly a gendered disease. The pathologization and treatment of depression affects women more than men. And, through a complex of bio-social factors, depression and its treatment renders women diseased and unable to perform as well as men. Several studies suggest that depression affects performance, especially on the job.[6] These studies conclude that women who are depressed do not perform as well as men (or women who are not depressed). This conclusion is in keeping with stereotypes of emotional and moody women who can't do the job as well as a man can. Some studies have tried to correlate women's depression and "poor performance" to biological changes such as menstruation, pregnancy, and menopause, but none of them are conclusive in their attempts to find a purely biological or hormonal basis for the high rates of depression in women.

There are numerous examples from popular culture, legal discourse, and medical discourse that "explain" poor performance by women and racially and ethnically marked groups with appeals to biological or mental inferiority. Let us take just one seemingly innocent example from the *Seattle Times* newspaper, which ran a story that began: "Biology keeping women awake, study concludes" (October 23, 1998, p. A18). The article said that "A study released...by the National Sleep Foundation shows that three specific biological events—menstruation, pregnancy and menopause—disrupt the sleep of a majority of women and interfere with how well they function during the day." The implication of this study is that women's inferior performance during the day is the result of a biologic fact; this kind of study harkens back to the idea that women are naturally inferior to men, that they just can't cut it in the professional and public world of men. Socially charged issues like menstruation, pregnancy and menopause are reduced to mere biological facts that make women function poorly. The *Times* article tells us that the study was based on interviews with women, that is, women's own perceptions of themselves, their sleep patterns, and how well they perform during the day. In a culture where women internalize sexist ideas about their own inadequacy it should be no surprise that women perceive themselves as unable to function. The irony is that the article also says that women report that their husbands' snoring keeps them awake, which suggests that biology may not be the cause of their sleeplessness and poor performance after all.

It is also curious that some studies find links between depression and race, ethnicity, and social class.[7] Using data from various NIH studies, recent research at the University of Texas Medical Center concludes that the highest rates of major depression are in the lowest social classes and that rates of psychiatric disorders are higher among blacks and Hispanics.[8] And, the National Mental Health Association reports that "the depression rate among African American women is *estimated* to be almost 50% higher than the rate among Caucasian women."[9]

The reason why this is only an "estimate" is that most statistics from various Health organizations are based on the number of cases diagnosed and reported as depression by doctors, a diagnosis that is highest among white women and much higher for whites generally than for blacks. It is interesting that the number of cases diagnosed as schizophrenia, on the other hand, is significantly higher among blacks than whites.[10] While none of these studies address the ways that cultural prejudices inform diagnosis, we need to ask why some categories of mental illness are diagnosed and reported more frequently among women than men and why other categories of mental illness are diagnosed and reported more frequently among blacks than whites. Why are so many women diagnosed as depressed? And, why are blacks disproportionately diagnosed as schizophrenic? In what ways are these diagnoses made through the lens of cultural prejudice?

Just as the link between depression and women can be diagnosed as a symptom of the patriarchal construction of a passive female body, so too the link between schizophrenia and African-Americans can be diagnosed as a symptom of the racist construction of a schizo black body. W.E.B. DuBois poignantly describes the double-consciousness forced on those marked by race in a racist culture. In *The Souls of Black Folk* he says "this double-conscious-ness, this sense of always looking at one's self through the eyes of others, of measuring one's soul by the tape of a world that looks on in amused contempt and pity. One ever feels his twoness,—an American, a Negro; two souls, two thoughts, two unreconciled striving; two warring ideals in one dark body, whose dogged strength alone keeps it from being torn asunder."[11] Fifty years later, Frantz Fanon describes a similar fragmented experience on a train when a child's exclamation "Mama, see the Negro! I'm frightened!" forces him to see himself not only in "a third-person consciousness" but also in triplicate: "In the train it was no longer a question of being aware of my body in the third per-son but in a triple person. In the train I was given not one but two, three places."[12] He describes these three places as one for his body, one for his race, and one for his ancestors.

Forty-five years later, and almost a full Century after DuBois, Patricia Williams again describes the double-consciousness endemic to the fragmented subject of racism: "for black people, the systematic, often nonsensical denial of racial experiences engenders a sense of split identity attending that which is obviously inexpressible; an assimilative tyranny of neutrality as self-erasure. It creates an environment in which one cannot escape the clanging of symbolism of oneself. This is heightened by contrast to all the silent, shifty discomfort of suffering condescension. There's that clunky social box, larger than your body, taking up all that space. You need two chairs at the table, one for you, one for your blackness."[13] A sense of double consciousness and fragmentation is a common theme across decades and throughout writers of African American experience.[14]

There is a connection between this sense of fragmentation or alienation and the imposition of the colonizer's values on the colonized. Elsewhere I have argued that colonization infects the colonized with the white man's super-ego, a cruel and punishing super-ego that displaces "native" taboos and values with the colonizers'.[15] The result is that desire itself becomes split and fragmented and the colonized are forced to identify with the fascinating and terrifying abject excluded by the white super-ego. The introjection of this super-ego nec-essarily creates a sense of double-alienation, which at its extreme can be akin to voices heard by schizophrenics. Like the voices heard by schizophrenics, this perverse super-ego commands self-destruction and undermines the seat of agency.

Fanon's analysis of the role of the radio in the Algerian revolution speaks to the way in which the voices of the colonizers become schizophrenic voices that haunt the colonized. As Fanon describes it, when the radio was introduced into Algeria most of the broadcasts proclaimed French victories and the defeat of guerrilla rebels. These voices were the voices of the enemy, violent and condemning. Fanon notes that as a result in hallucinatory psychoses the voices that were heard were those of the colonizers, hostile voices (1965 88-89). After the introduction of the Voice of Algeria radio broadcasts that focused on accounts of victorious revolutionaries, the voices becomes reassuring and friendly. Fanon's essay "This is the Voice of Algeria" suggests the complex ways in which the white super-ego of the colonizers becomes a hostile voice that haunts the colonized even to the point of hallucinatory voices.

Is it any surprise, then, that the haunting white super-ego of racist culture with its hostile voices is diagnosed as schizophrenia in blacks? Is it a surprise that after racist culture constructs the black subject as fragmented that it also finds higher rates of schizophrenia among African-Americans? If oppression causes depression and schizophrenia, it not only creates pathological subjects who internalize the conditions of their oppression and become more like cultural stereotypes, but also these very categories of disease reinforce racial and gendered identities and hierarchies by linking particular diseases to specific races or genders and thereby legitimating various types of invasive, regulatory practices to manage epidemics. To echo the language of the social sciences, we could say that oppression is a factor in depression.

Sexual Difference and Sublimation

Rather than identify women's or other oppressed people's depression as individual pathology caused by either physical or mental illness, it can be seen as a symptom of the pathology of our culture; the causes of which are social rather than individual. We need to consider reversing the causality between the pathology of women and the pathology of our culture. Turning from the empirical sciences to psychoanalysis, we can gain more insight into how oppression might lead to depression. To this end, I hope to develop a psychoanalytic social theory that does not pathologize individuals but rather diagnoses the relation between social and psychic dynamics. While her lack of social theory limits the usefulness of Julia Kristeva's analysis of depression for feminist theory, her theory can help us begin to formulate an alternative theory of depression that focuses on its social sources.

Kristeva describes depression as a result of a gap between words and affects. When affects or emotions are cut off from means for discharging them, the result is depression. Words and representation more generally have meaning for our lives only when they are charged with affects. If our affects are dis-

connected from our words, then representation seems meaningless and therefore life itself seems meaningless. The charge of bodily drive force in language,
that is to say, the manifestation of affects, makes not only language but life
itself meaningful. Cut off from the life force of the body and affects, language
seems dead, even worthless. In traditional psychoanalytic theory the connection
between representation and affect could be called sublimation. According to
Sigmund Freud's theory, the ability to sublimate drives, and their manifestation
in affects, into representation and artistic practices is the source of human civilization and creativity. Without the ability to sublimate bodily drives and
affects into representation and artistic practices we lose the ability to create
meaning for our own lives. Without the ability to sublimate, we become
depressed and life seems meaningless.

Are women less able to sublimate men? Freud thought so. In *Civilization
and Its Discontents*, he says that "[W]omen soon come into opposition to civilization and display their retarding and restraining influence... The work of civilization has become increasingly the business of men, it confronts them with
ever more difficult tasks and compels them to carry out instinctual sublimations
of which women are little capable."[16] According to Freud, women are not
capable of instinctual sublimations because their anatomy does not permit them
to *act* on those very instincts that must be sublimated in order to become civilized—presumably incest with their mothers and surprisingly....urinating on
fire. Freud identifies control over fire as one of the primary achievements of
primitive man that allowed him to become civilized. In a footnote in
Civilization and Its Discontents, he hazards a conjecture on the origins of civilization as the origins of control over fire:

> The legends that we possess leave no doubt about the originally phal-
> lic view taken of tongues of flame as they shoot upwards. Putting
> out fire by micturating—...was therefore a kind of sexual act with a
> male, an enjoyment of sexual potency in a homosexual competition.
> The first person to renounce this desire and spare the fire was able
> to carry it off with him and subdue it to his own use. By damping
> down the fire of his own sexual excitation, he had tamed the natural
> force of fire. This great cultural conquest was thus the reward for
> his renunciation of instinct. Further, it is as though woman had been
> appointed guardian of the fire which was held captive on the domes-
> tic hearth, because her anatomy made it impossible for her to yield
> to the temptation of this desire.[17]

As I argue elsewhere, "in this theory, civilization begins when man curbs his
desire to display his virility by urinating on phallic flames. Woman cannot sublimate the desire to pee on the fire because she cannot first act on the desire.
We might wonder why Freud doesn't conclude that woman necessarily sublimate this desire since she can't act on it; that her anatomy demands sublima-

tion whereas the male's does not; that in woman, nature has insured sublimation of aggressive instincts and therefore the advancement of the species. In stead, Freud identifies civilization, law, and morality with man's virility and its sublimation, where this sublimation is also described as man's virile act of control over himself."[18]

Given that the overwhelming majority of studies conclude that depression is twice as high for women as for men world-wide and that in some places it may be three times as high,[19] even if we reject Freud's speculations as sexist biologism we are still left with the question: "Are women less able to sublimate than men?" In order to answer this question, we need not only a social theory of depression, but also a social theory of sublimation. Sublimation is facilitated by social supports that provide the language and symbols with which individuals can find and create the meaning of their own experience. We are all born into a world where meaning already exists. We do not choose the meaning of our language and cultural symbols. Rather, every individual must negotiate the language and cultural symbols that her life presents to her in order to find herself there. In other words, every individual finds her own value and the value of her life by virtue of negotiating the various meanings available to her in her culture. As we will see, the ability to put drives and affects into language depends upon the availability of words and symbols not only to discharge those affects but even more importantly to authorize them. While in principle according to psychoanalytic theory any word can discharge any affect, or any affect can become attached to any word, the meanings available to us in our culture make some affects easier to manifest than others. Some affects are encouraged while others are refused. Some individual's or group's experiences are valued while other individual's or group's experiences are not. So, the ability to sublimate—to manifest affects in words or representations—has everything to do with finding socially available meanings that can facilitate the transfer from mute experience to meaningful articulation.

What happens then when the only available meanings for a particular experience are either nonexistent, prohibited, or abject and inhuman? How is sublimation possible for experiences or emotions that can be articulated only through denigration or not at all, experiences that are so profoundly repressed that they are nearly foreclosed from the social? How much of maternal experience and affect can be discharged within patriarchal cultural institutions? How many women are allowed to express the complexity of their feelings and experiences of their bodies, especially sex, menstruation, abortion, motherhood and childbirth? And if they try, will they be shamed and guilty? Where do women find positive social support and rich social symbols for the meanings of their experiences—especially their painful, angry, or frustrated experiences?

This connection between sublimation and available meaning and social support begins to provide a social rather than anatomical explanation for why within patriarchal culture it is possible that women can't sublimate as well as men can. If positive social support is necessary for sublimation—for drives and affects to make their way into symbols and representations—and if within patriarchal societies women don't have loving positive supports within the social, then women would be less able to sublimate. In turn, if women are less able to sublimate—to articulate or discharge their drives and affects—then they will be more depressed. If women can't adequately sublimate their drives into words or creative activities because doing so requires social supports, then they will be less able to interpret their own experiences and find or create meaning, which requires sublimation. Stepping out of the psychoanalytic jargon, if women cannot discharge their affects and experiences in language or artistic activities as easily as men can it is because we don't have the necessary positive social supports for our affects and experiences which remain unspoken, even taboo, within patriarchal cultures. Since these drives and affects must go somewhere, repression and ultimately depression are the only alternatives to sublimation.

The depression or melancholy of oppression, however, has a different dynamic than Freud's notion of melancholy. In "Mourning and Melancholia" Freud describes melancholia as an identification with a lost love object.[20] Freud distinguishes mourning from melancholia. While mourning is a healthy working-through the loss of a loved one, melancholia is a neurotic identification with the lost love in order deny the loss. He says that while in mourning "it is the world which has become poor and empty; in melancholia it is the ego itself." Melancholia, unlike mourning, displays "an extraordinary diminution in self-regard, an impoverishment of ego on a grand scale" (1917 584). This diminution of self-regard that is caused by the subject's identification with the lost love is also hatred toward the lost loved one for abandoning him. More than this, Freud attributes these self-reproaches to the melancholic's guilty delusion that he is to blame for the loss of the loved one (1917 587-8). As Freud describes it, the subject holds onto his love for the lost object through his identification with it. In this way, although he berates the lost object as himself, he refuses to give up the love relation with the lost loved one. Freud maintains that "[I]n this way an object-loss was transformed into an ego-loss and the conflict between the ego and the loved person into a cleavage between the critical activity of the ego and the ego as altered by identification...The narcissistic identification with the object then becomes a substitute for the erotic cathexis, the result of which is that in spite of the conflict with the loved person the love-relation need not be given up" (1917 586-7).

The melancholy of oppression, however, is not Freud's internalization of a lost love, but the internalization of the loss of a loved or lovable self-image.[21] Confronted with abject images of self from the dominant culture, women and mothers suffer from the loss of a lovable image of themselves. Their melancholy is caused by the loss of the self as an active agent and positive force in the world. The oppressed melancholic's wounded ego is not the result of a loss of an other, but the result of a loss of a self. Just as Freud describes the loss of the other as formative of the melancholic's own ego, the loss of a positive self image is formative in the melancholy of oppression. The melancholy of oppression fragments the ego and undermines the sense of agency and thereby renders the ego ineffective and passive. So, if there is no image of womanhood or motherhood that can discharge the affects of women and mothers, if the experience of womanhood or motherhood is a kind of absence within our culture, then the missing woman or mother self becomes the melancholic object for women. Their guilt, self beratement, and depression are the result of a loss of any socially sanctioned discharge of affects.

People who are constantly exposed to negative and denigrated images of themselves cannot help but feel insecure about whether or not they are lovable or can be loved. To feel loved and lovable is possible only if there are positive self-images readily available in our culture. In a culture where women and people of color have been pathologized, abjected, ridiculed, and hated it is difficult for them to avoid some incorporation of self-hatred. The lack of social support can lead to the depressive's feelings of emptiness, incompleteness, and flaws; at the extreme, the lack of social support can lead to the split between words and affects that Kristeva identifies with the depressive position. Within patriarchal cultures where maternal affects are not valued it is no surprise that we lack the social space in which these affects can be articulated or discharged. Women's experience generally, and women's depression more specifically, remain subterranean within dominant discourses. Therefore, the depressed woman has given up on finding the words to discharge or manifest her affects. The silence, especially women's silence, that so often accompanies depression is a socially proscribed silence and its cause. Women's depression can be diagnosed as social melancholy rather than individual pathology, or merely biological chemical imbalance.[22]

In sum, oppression is a factor in depression. The melancholy of oppression results from the double loss of a sense of oneself as an agent and the loss of the sense of oneself as loved or lovable. This double loss is the result of dominant values that represent the targets of discrimination as objects or animals lacking any real human agency and/or as abject or denigrated. Insofar as love and agency are both human activities, and insofar as both agency and love are necessary for a sense of self, let alone a sense of self-worth, stereotypes attack the very sense of self of those oppressed. Lacking socially acceptable words or symbols to discharge affects that have been excluded within dominant culture, marginalized people are not only silenced but also vulnerable to depression, a consequence of the inability to manifest or discharge affects in language. This inability sets up the vicious circle of oppression whereby oppressive stereotypes can become self-fulfilling prophesies insofar as they debilitate their objects through depression, disease, and lowered productivity. If depression is reaching epidemic proportions, especially among young women and mothers, rather than pathologize or biologize women, mothers, or other marginalized people, we need to examine the pathology of our culture.

Notes

1. For examples of feminist critical analysis of medical and biological discourses see Adams, Alice. *Reproducing the Womb*, Ithaca: Cornell University Press, 1994; Corea, Gena. *The Mother Machine: Reproductive Technologies from Artificial Insemination to Artificial Wombs*. New York: Harper & Row, 1985; Holmes, Helen Bequaert and Laura Purdy, (eds.). *Feminist Perspectives in Medical Ethics*. Bloomington: Indiana University Press, 1992; Hubbard, Ruth. *The Politics of Women's Biology*. New Brunswick: Rutgers University Press, 1990; Keller, Evelyn Fox. *Reflections on Gender and Science*. New Haven: Yale University Press, 1985 and *Secrets of Life, Secrets of Death*. New York: Routledge Publishers, 1992; Oliver, Kelly. *Family Values*, New York: Routledge, 1995; and Tuana, Nancy. *The Less Noble Sex*, Bloomington: Indiana University Press, 1993.

2. There are several critical analyses of hysteria, among them Jann Matlock's *Scenes of Seduction: Prostitution, Hysteria and Reading Difference in the Nineteenth Century France*, New York: Columbia University Press, 1993; Sander Gilman et al., *Hysteria Beyond Freud*, Berkeley: University of California Press, 1993; Julia Borossa's *Hysteria*, New York: Totem Books, 2001; and Juliet Mitchell's *Mad Men and Medusas: Reclaiming Hysteria*, New York: Basic Books, 2001.

3. Cf. the National Mental Health Association's description of depression: "persistent sad, anxious or empty mood, loss of interest or pleasure in activities, including sex, restlessness, irritability, or excessive crying, feelings of guilt, worthlessness, helplessness, hopelessness, pessimism, sleeping too much or too little...appetite and/or weight loss or overeating and weight gain, decreased energy, fatigue, feeling slowed down, thoughts of death or suicide...difficulty concentrating, remembering or making decisions..." (July 20, 1998, Website)

4. For example see Benigno Trigo's *Subject of Crisis: Race and Gender as Disease in Latin America* (Hanover: Wesleyan University Press, 2000), Sander Gillman's *Difference and Pathology* (Ithaca: Cornell University Press, 1985) and *Disease and Representation: Images of Illness from Madness to AIDS* (Ithaca: Cornell University Press, 1998), Susan Sontag's *Illness as Metaphor* (New York: Vintage, 1979), Melbourne Tapper's *In the Blood: Sickle Cell Anemia and the Politics of Race* (Philadelphia: University of Pennsylvania Press, 1998), and of course the work of Michel Foucault.

5. This argument is persuasively made by Benigno Trigo in *Subject of Crisis: Race and Gender as Disease in Latin America*; see especially p. 10 and the conclusion (2000).

6. Various studies conclude that depression and other mental risks have physical effects not only on the body by decreasing its tolerance for pain and increasing the likelihood of other illnesses and diseases, but also of decreasing the ability to concentrate and to perform productively. One study finds that "psychological distress... reduces thresholds for pain perception and tolerance (already relatively low in women)" (Winfield 1999). Several studies find that both Chronic Fatigue Syndrome and

Fibromyalgia Syndrome (increased pain) affect predominantly women, many of whom also suffer from depression (Skapinakis et al. 2000; Farmer et al. 1995; Lee et al. 2000). And one Centers for Disease Control study in San Fransisco "found that CFS-like disease was most prevalent among women, among persons with household annual incomes of under $40,000, and among blacks" (Sept 17 1998). The most dramatic result was reported in a study in Spring 2000 in the *American Journal of Psychiatry* which concludes: "Early-onset major depression disorder adversely affected the educational attainment of women but not of men....A randomly selected 21-year-old woman with early-onset major depressive disorder in 1995 could expect future annual earnings that were 12%-18% lower than those of a randomly selected 21-year-old woman whose onset of major depressive disorder occurred after age 21 or not at all. Early-onset major depressive disorder causes substantial human capital loss, particularly for women" (Berndt et al. 2000). And, the August 1997 issue of *American Demographics* reports that "some researchers believe the depression [gender] gap relates to inequities between men and women in numerous areas of adult life, such as pay and authority in the workplace, and the burden of child care and housework at home." Klien "Blue Janes" in *American Demographics* August 1997, Intertec Publishing website.

7. Although its language of "basic personality" may be outdated, although it doesn't attend to gender differences, and although hopefully we have made some progress since 1951, still Kardiner and Ovesey's *The Mark of Oppression: Explorations in the Personality of the American Negro* provides powerful psychological evidence of the effects of racism on the development of the psyche, self-esteem, and agency. Abram Kardiner and Lionel Ovesey's *The Mark of Oppression: Explorations in the Personality of the American Negro*, New York: Meridian Books, 1951.

8. Op. cit., Holzer et al.

9. My emphasis, Discovery.com, National Mental Health Association homepage, May 21 1998.

10. The National Mental Health Association reports that "historically, among health professional, there has been a consistent under-diagnosis of depression in the African American community and an over-diagnosis of schizophrenia" ("Clinical Depression and African Americans," May 21 1998, The National Mental Health Association Website).

11. W.E.B. DuBois, 1903, *The Souls of Black Folk*, New York: New American Library, 1969, 45.

12. Op. cit., Frantz Fanon, 1952, *Black Skin, White Masks*, 110, 112.

13. Patricia Williams, *Seeing a Color-blind Future*. New York: Farrar Straus, 1997, 27.

14. The notion of double alienation that results from oppression is developed in my book *The Colonization of Psychic Space*, Minneapolis, MN: The University of Minnesota Press, 2004.

15. See book *The Colonization of Psychic Space*, University of Minnesota Press.

16. Sigmund Freud, *Civilization and Its Discontents*, Trans. James Strachey, New York: Norton Publishers, 1961, 50.

17. Op. cit. Freud, 1961, 37.

18. Oliver 1997, 166.

19. R. M. Hirschfeld & C. K. Cross, "Epidemiology of Affective Disorders: Psychological Risk Factors", in *Archives of General Psychiatry*, January 1982, vol. 39,

39-46 (finds a 2:1 ratio of women to men); Hiral D. Desai & Michael W. Jann, "Major Depression in Women: A Review of the Literature" in *Journal of American Pharmacology Association*, Jul-Aug 2000, 40:4, 525-37 (reports that "Epidemiologic data from diverse cultures indicate that the lifetime prevalence of major depression is twice as high in women as in men"); John Horgan, *Scientific American*, "Mental Health: Multicultural Studies" November 1996 (reports that "in every country, women were roughly twice as likely as men to suffer from depression"); Susan Nolen-Hoeksema et al., "Explaining the Gender Difference in Depressive Symptoms" in *Journal of Personal and Social Psychology* Nov. 1999 77:5, 1061-72 (reports that "it was hypothesized that women are more vulnerable to depressive symptoms than men because they are more likely to experience chronic negative circumstance"); National Institutes of Health website reports that "In the US nearly twice as many women as men are affected by a depressive disorder each year...According to a recent study by the World Health Organization, the World Bank, and Harvard University, unipolar major depression is the leading cause of disease burden among females ages 5 and older worldwide" ("Women Hold Up Half the Sky" NIH Website, July 9, 1999); M. M. Weissman et al., "Cross-National Epidemiology of Major Depression and Bipolar Disorder" in *Journal of American Medical Association*, July 24/31, 1996, 276: 4, 293-298 (reports that "In every country, the rate of major depression were higher for women than men").

20. Sigmund Freud, 1917, "Mourning and Melancholia" in *The Freud Reader*. Edited by Peter Gay. New York: Norton, 1989.

21. For a discussion of the melancholy of oppression in relation to race and the work of Fanon, see my *Witnessing: Beyond Recognition* (2001 36-7).

22. Although traditionally girls have been socialized to accept dependent and submission roles, and they continue to be socialized to accept instinctual notions of maternity, we can speculate that in adulthood and especially in motherhood, many women are disappointed with their roles as wife and mother and the limitations placed on them by culture and tradition. This could explain why rates of depression are rising fastest among young women 18-24 years old and that world-wide the highest rates of depression are among women 24-34 years old, prime child-rearing years. The results of one study reported just last summer found that "one of every three women between 18 and 24 years of age may be significantly depressed" and that their depression correlates to low-self esteem and negative thinking. Op. cit., Ann Peden et al., 2000. The National Mental Health Association estimates that "the highest overall age of onset is between 25-44, with an increasing rate among those born after 1945, perhaps related to psychosocial factors such as single parenting, changing roles, and stress." Discovery Health. com July 20 1998. And, a National Institutes of Health study concludes that "caregivers are much more likely to suffer from depression than the average person" and caregivers are most likely to be women. NIH publication No 99-4607.

Bibliography

Allison, David and Mark Roberts. 1998. *Disordered Mother or Disordered Diagnosis? Munchausen By Proxy Syndrome*. New York: Analytic Press.
Doane, Mary Ann. 1987. *The Desire to Desire: The Woman's Film of the*

1940s. Bloomington: Indiana University Press.

———. 1991. *Femmes Fatales: Feminism, Film Theory, Psychoanalysis*. New York: Routledge.

DuBois, W.E.B. 1969. *The Souls of Black Folk*. New York: New American Library.

Fanon, Frantz. 1967. *Black Skin White Masks*. Trans. C.L. Markmann. New York: Grove Press.

———. 1965. *A Dying Colonialism*. Trans. Haakon Chevalier. New York: Grove Press.

Fischer, Lucy. 1996. *Cinematernity: Film, Motherhood, Genre*. Princeton, NJ: Princeton University Press.

Freud, Sigmund. 1917. "Mourning and Melancholia." In *The Freud Reader*. Edited by Peter Gay. New York: Norton, 1989.

———. 1961. *Civilization and Its Discontents*. Trans. James Strachey. New York: Norton Publishers.

Kaplan, E. Ann. 1992. *Motherhood and Representation*. New York: Routledge.

Kristeva, Julia. 1987. *Black Sun: Depression and Melancholy*. Trans. Leon Roudiez. New York: Columbia University Press, 1989.

———. 1993. *New Maladies of the Soul*. Trans. Ross Guberman. New York: Columbia University Press, 1995.

———. 1998. *The Portable Kristeva*. Edited by Kelly Oliver. New York: Columbia University Press.

Lee, C.M., and I. H. Gotlib. 1989. "Clinical Status and Emotional Adjustment of Chilren and Depressed Mothers." In American Journal of Psychiatry 146: 478-83.

Oliver, Kelly. 2004. *The Colonization of Psychic Space: A Psychoanalytic Social Theory of Oppression*. Minneapolis, MN: University of Minnesota Press.

———. 1997. *Family Values, Subjects Between Nature and Culture*. New York: Routledge.

———. 2001. *Witnessing: Beyond Recognition*. Minneapolis, MN: University of Minnesota Press.

Skapinakis, Petros, Glyn Lewis, and Howard Meltzer. 2000. "Clarifying the Relationship between Unexplained Chonic Fatigue and Psychiatric Morbidity." In American Journal of Psychiatry 157: 1492-98.

Williams, Patricia J. 1998. *Seeing a Color-Blind Future. The Paradox of Race*. New York: Farrar, Straus and Giroux.

Winfield, JB. 1999. "Pain in Fibromyalgia". In Rheum Dis Clin North Am. 1999 Feb;25(1):55-79.

Out of the National Closet:
Show Me Love

Tiina Rosenberg

The most central and useful theoretical aspect of queer theory is the critique of heteronormativity. In the longer perspective, the minoritising attitude to homosexuality confirms heteronormativity, since it paradoxically presupposes heterosexuality. However, this does not imply that homosexual identity is without meaning. If homosexuality is regarded as an integral part of heteronormativity, as that which defines heterosexuality as normal, it becomes more obvious why claims of a homosexual identity as a category of equal worth do not fundamentally challenge the heteronormative order. In this respect the critical edge of queer theory is poignant. However, many scholars and activists have nevertheless pondered whether or not queer theory is sufficient when analysing power and repression. Identities may be a social construct, but this does not make them less real or necessary in the prevailing political and social reality. The more long-term striving for social justice could, however, benefit from the anti-assimilationist and anti-separatist approach of queer theory. By refusing to minoritise, the majority is challenged, while anti-separatism opens up both categories for greater overlapping and variation.

In the following I will present an example of Swedish heteronormativity, a case study of the reception of the teen movie *Fucking Åmål* (renamed *Show Me Love* for the English-speaking market, due to prohibitions on the use of the oath in the Swedish title) from 1998. In simple terms, heteronormativity is the supposition that everyone is heterosexual, and that the natural way of life is heterosexuality. The term heteronormativity here refers to the institutions, structures, relationships and actions that maintain heterosexuality as a uniform, natural, and all-embracing phenomenon. Heteronormativity is based on the assumption of a binary gender concept and a hegemonic heterosexual norm.

Heteronormativity is actively normative, and anything that does not conform is branded as abnormal and thus is/becomes wrong. The punishment ranges from more concrete, tangible forms, such as imprisonment and violence, to more elusive expressions, such as marginalisation, invisibility, stereotyping, cultural domination and homophobia.[1]

A norm is usually defined as a rule relating to a purpose, an ideal. In practice, norms are social rulebooks that often remain invisible until someone/something breaks them. Normality is the security that comes from the feeling of not deviating, whereas normativity, in the sense of a prescriptive, always involves one or more social and moral imperatives, that is, demands on people to follow rules formulated by others. Normativity is thus the power system that maintains and reinforces norms.

Even if normality is often presented as a statistical average, it is entirely dependent on morally established norms. Heterosexuality may statistically be the most common form of sexual practice, but it is heteronormativity, not heterosexuality in itself, that guarantees its status as a norm by defining and excluding the "abnormal." Thus, an urgent task in queer theory is to identify, describe and analyse the active practices of normalisation that are at work in prevailing norm systems.

A concept such as normativity is intimately linked with an experience of enforcement, which in turn implies repression. Repression, however, is a word that evokes strong reactions, since it is charged with a meaning that appears out of place in an open, democratic social-liberal, albeit fundamentally capitalist, society. Political identity movements such as women's lib and gay liberation gave the term repression a new significance in the '60s and '70s. In this tradition, repression refers to the obstacles and limitations that unfairly affect some people and social groups in society. The feminist legal theoretician Iris Marion Young points out that this is not a case of subjects under a brutal regime, but citizens in a well-meaning, liberal society, and a result of everyday, "normal" rules and behaviour. In this way, repression is a structural phenomenon, rather than the result of the intentions or policies of a handful of individuals. The causes of this structural repression is found, according to Young, in norms, conventions and symbols that are never questioned. They are inherent in the ideas embedded in traditions and institutionalised rules and procedures. Above all, they are found in the social consequences of a general acceptance and adherence to these rules and procedures.[2]

The two guiding principles of heteronormativity are: 1) exclusion of deviation from the norm by a division into the categories us—them; and 2) assimilation by incorporating deviation from the norm. The first principle is in line with the Western tradition of thinking in dichotomies. It describes two parts of a unit that are seen as opposites with the relationship either/or. The dichotomy inevitably leads to a hierarchical order that entails privileges for one category at the expense of the other. The consequence is inequality and social injustices that are legitimised by presenting constructed divisions as being natural. Dichotomies organise existence into two distinct categories, thereby simplifying a complex reality. The dichotomic perspective emphasises the differences between categories, while paying little or no attention to the similarities between the categories, and/or the differences within them.[3]

"Deviant" and queer do not so much signify a particular sort of individual, as a way of underlining and specifying heteronormativity as an excluding and separating practice. The heterosexual norm persists by appearing to be natural and ordinary. Thus, heterosexuality comes across as desirable, while homosexuality is problematic, something that constantly has to be explained. The perception of the deviant as problematic and the norm as natural creates a chasm between "us" and "them," where one's own norm is naturalised and unquestioned.

While the chasm between "us" and "them" is reinforced, the heterosexual norm appropriates deviations. The norm simply takes them over. This appropriation, or incorporation, of deviations into the norm, is an effective way of disarming the deviants politically. It is a form of putative acknowledgement, by which the deviation or deviant is unmentioned and made invisible. By neutralising and making "deviants" invisible they are robbed of their uniqueness.

The second guiding principle of heteronormativity is based on the concept of a universal humanity and uses assimilation as its method. In practice this means that previously excluded groups are to join the dominating culture. According to Iris Marion Young, assimilation therefore always requires that the excluded parties have to join in a game where the rules are set beforehand and the game has already started long ago. On these premises they have to try to assert themselves. This assimilation policy tacitly accepts that the privileged groups are the ones to define the criteria by which everyone is measured. One of the privileges of the dominating groups is that they can pretend that these criteria are not culturally or historically determined. They can blatantly present their norms as being universal and neutral in relation to race, gender, ethnicity and sexuality. But since there are actual differences, the repressed groups often find it difficult to live up to the demands, expectations and norms of the dominating groups. Thus, the existing power relations and hierarchies remain intact.

> Assimilation into the universal and "human" norm allows the privileged groups to ignore the fact that they themselves are merely a group among other social groups. By turning a blind eye to difference they can maintain their cultural domination. The values that express the experiences and intentions of the privileged groups are presented as neutral and good for mankind. Universalism is based on the assumption that everyone can put herself or himself in a form of neutral group position from which they can create or recreate themselves into whatever person they wish to be. If people were left to their own devices, the individual would blossom and no one would

be like anyone else. However, since there is no neutral group consensus of what is good and proper, the strongest groups in practice
define the norm for how everyone should be and behave. According
to such a putatively neutral ideal, the repressed groups will
inevitably be perceived as special and different. The privileged
groups, on the other hand, are normal.

The supposedly normal (read: heteronormative) norms often generate self-
loathing and an internalised derogatory attitude to one's own group.
Assimilation with the prevailing norm requires that queers "fit in," that is, that
they adjust their behaviour, their values and wishes to the norms of the dominating group. However, since the norm does not change, they will, no matter
how hard they try to fit in, be stamped as deviating and different. The assimilation requirement faces the repressed individual with an insoluble dilemma: in
order to participate in society she is forced to adopt an identity she does not
have, and when she tries to do this, she herself and others continuously remind
her of and force her back into the identity she has—but is not permitted to
have.[4]

Example Sweden: The National Coming-Out Process and *Show Me Love*

The new openness with regard to homosexuality in Sweden dates from the
Europride festival in the summer of 1998. However, it is important to remem-
ber that nothing just "happens." Historical phenomena are processes where all
groundbreaking events have a preamble. It is sometimes hard to determine why
something happens at a given time. The national coming-out process was slowly but steadily prepared by bisexual, homosexual and transsexual activists in
collaboration with representatives of various political parties.

     The story of homosexual identity in Sweden is in many ways a success tale
of assimilation policy, where women and men in different political organisations have worked for legal and social equality for homosexuals in relation to
the heterosexual majority. Of the political parties, the Liberals and Left Party
have a particularly solid tradition of working for homosexual and bisexual
rights since the 1970s. The Swedish Federation for Lesbian, Gay, Bisexual and
Transgender Rights (RFSL), which was founded on 21 October 1950, has
played a crucial part. It is one of the oldest still active organisations for bisexuals and homosexuals and the transgender community.[5]

     Assimilationist strategies have worked well in countries such as the
Netherlands and Sweden, where the governments have paid heed to the gay
communities. Homosexuals have, in consequence, managed to move forward
their positions with regard to legislation, which has raised their civil status and

security—something that most homosexuals in the world are without. Homosexuality was decriminalised in Sweden in 1944. In 1979, the National Board of Health and Welfare abolished its classification of homosexuality as a mental disease, and 1987 saw an addition to criminal law prohibiting discrimination against homosexuals (BrB 16:9) and an act on homosexual cohabitation (1987:813). In 1995, it became possible for same sex couples to register partnership. At the time of writing this essay, homosexual parenthood and the right of homosexuals to be considered as adoptive parents, are being debated.

During the post war period, the situation of homosexuals and bisexuals became a legitimate subject in the Swedish parliament. The parliament has also used its influence to improve the legal situation for same sex couples. The process has been gradual, but has, on the whole, led to dramatic changes. However, homosexuals and bisexuals are still marginalised in the political debate. Lesbians and gay men tend to be the object of parliamentary measures, rather than equal parties in public debate. A parallel can be drawn to immigrants, the physically challenged, people living on social welfare and others who are spoken of in the third person.

The big parade with thousands of participants that marched through Stockholm on a gloriously sunny day in August 1998 was a symbolic manifestation of the remarkable changes that have taken place in Sweden. It was not the first time a demonstration for homosexual issues was seen in the city, but Europride 1998 was presented in an entirely different way compared to previous homosexual liberation weeks. Sponsors had been contacted well in advance of the event and there were companies now that were willing to profile themselves as gay-friendly. In addition to the more traditional gay movement, Europride attracted the entire queer society to a rare exhibition of diverse identities. Mass media backing and coverage was extensive and partly managed by a younger generation of journalists.

The new openness also signalled a new confidence among homosexuals. Although this openness had, and still has, Stockholm as its main arena, and thus cannot be termed a national breakthrough, a change had undeniably taken place. Since then, several well known figures have come out and taken on the homosexual identity as part of their public persona. Gay magazines, gay characters in soap operas and docu-soaps, have become commonplace, and gay events are included in the calendars of the mainstream press.

The Europride year 1998 was given the blessing of the Swedish nation especially through an exhibition and a movie. Photographer Elisabeth Ohlson's *Ecce Homo* aroused an outstanding debate about homosexuality that went far beyond the boundaries of aesthetics, demonstrating that a great deal remained to be cleared out of the national closet.[6] The lesbian theme in *Show Me Love*, however, was not discussed to any great extent. This eloquent silence was the subject of my lecture at the annual event Tema Genus (Theme: Gender) at Stockholm University in March 1999, which later resulted in the essay "Det

nya Lukasevangeliet: Om det heteronormativa mottagandet av Fucking Åmål"
("The new gospel according to Lukas: On the heteronormative reception of
Show Me Love"), a reflection on the articles, reviews and interviews written
before and after the film opened on 23 October 1998.[7]

The silence concerning the lesbian theme was one of the most striking
examples of heteronormativity in the late 1990s in Sweden. What is interesting
is the strong imbalance that appeared in the loud disputes around *Ecce Homo*
and the absence of discussion about the lesbian theme in *Show Me Love*. The
journalist Bodil Sjöström formulates this aptly in the leftist journal *Arena*:
"When Jesus is portrayed among homosexuals, a long-awaited discussion tran-
spires. When the combination teenager—woman—lesbian is reflected so ingen-
iously, the cultural competence to interpret this is lacking. And I get yet another lesson in invisibility."[8]

The movie repertoire of 1998 contained other films on the theme of homosexuality: *In & Out, Midnight in the Garden of Good and Evil, The Object of
My Affection, As Good as It Gets, Fire, The Hanging Garden, Hamam, Wilde*
and *Velvet Goldmine* are but a few examples. The number of homosexual characters suddenly rose from around 10% to at least 25%, but most of these were
men.[9] Sadly, lesbian portraits are as scarce now as they were before. In this
respect, *Show Me Love* was a refreshing exception.

Helena Lindblad, film critic in the leading Swedish newspaper *Dagens
Nyheter*, wrote in her January column that 1998 was the year when concepts
such as male and female creativity were turned head over heels: "As we continue to wait for the antiquated inequality of the sexes behind the camera to be
rectified, one can be amazed by the fact that two male directors interpreted
women's experiences with unusual sensitivity. Lukas Moodysson succeeded in
making his teenage heroines Elin and Agnes relevant to practically every
Swede."[10]

Audiences literally stormed into cinemas to see *Show Me Love*. Youth culture is often portrayed from a boys' perspective, but *Show Me Love* focuses on
two charismatic teenage girls, Agnes (Rebecka Liljeberg) and Elin (Alexandra
Dahlström). They belong to different social classes. Agnes comes from a culturally oriented nuclear family. She reads Edith Södergran (Finnish-Swedish
lesbian poet), Jonas Gardell (Swedish gay author, actor and director), Inger
Edelfelt (Swedish author and poet with lesbian and gay themes in her production), and writes poems. In her girl's room with black walls she listens to
Albinoni's melancholy *Adagio*, the saddest music she knows. She is in love
with Elin, she is new in Åmål and has no friends, and is painfully aware of her
status as an outsider. But she is also strong. Young as she is, she has realised
intuitively that she has no choice but to be herself. Agnes is lonely and her well-
meaning parents feel powerless. Clashes constantly arise. "Your daughter is a
vegetarian, and you serve meat on her birthday. Great," Agnes hisses at her
mother who, despite all, arranges a birthday party that Agnes would gladly

have been without.[11]

In Elin's household parties are scarce. And confidential talks between mother and daughter are even scarcer. Her single mother prefers to relax with TV game shows, and Elin's interest in literature is limited to teen magazines. While Agnes has a dark pageboy haircut, large-checked flannel shirts and army trousers, Elin, with her blonde locks, constant low-cut tops and red lips, is both cockier and less confident than Agnes. She longs to get away: "It's all so boring," she exclaims, "I hate my life /.../ I'm gonna stop breathing."[12] She wants to formulate herself but does not know what to aim her rebellion at.

Show Me Love focuses primarily on Elin and her development. The rebellious coming-out-act is, of course, staged by the girls jointly, but Elin is the one who goes through the classical heroic transformation in the film. She is cocky, charismatic and sharp. "Elin is gutsy," Alexandra Dahlström comments her role character, "That's what I like about her."[13] Lukas Moodysson is also delighted with Elin": I love all the characters in the movie, but Elin is, of course, closest to my heart. She and her sister have existed in my mind for a long time."[14] According to critic Nicholas Wennö of *Dagens Nyheter*, the "main character of the film, Elin, is not only an emotional action heroine, but also one of the coolest female portraits ever in Swedish film."[15]

Then how is lesbian Agnes perceived? In reviews she is described as different.[16] "Agnes is different," Rebecka Liljeberg says about her role. "And she wants to be different. I was like that at school, although I didn't have such a hard time as she does. I really like her!"

Reviews and other press material interpret Agnes as being different and defined by her outsidership, while Elin is seen to rebel against her conventional environment. In this rebellion lesbianism is merely one of several alternative means of protest. Agnes *is* lesbian and, as such, static. Elin, on the other hand, was regarded as the dynamic and changeable subject in *Show Me Love*. According to film critic Johan Croneman, Agnes struggles "with her petty-bourgeois parents, her sexuality, her questions about the meaning of life, her outsidership, her incurable loneliness."[17] He also ascribes the actual rebellion to Elin, while Agnes's contribution is limited to the intellectual level. "When they suddenly find one another in the darkness, they fumble about and find where they belong, at least for now."[18]

The lesbian experience and rebellion was something new and different, a welcome change from small-town boredom. Literary critic Åsa Beckman discerned a similarity between Agnes and Elin and the Finnish-Swedish author Monica Fagerholm's 13-year-old heroine Diva from the novel with the same title, who lives in a suburb of Helsinki:

> The only channel for these teenage girls' energy is through sexuality. Diva is not only together with boys and men but also tests girls in the school lavatory. Elin kisses her classmate Agnes and realises

that this is a feeling she has never experienced before. With these lesbian experiences they go beyond exactly those boundaries that they want to transcend. They are both going to break the laws of normality. 'I'm a lesbian. A homosexual,' Elin says tentatively to her mother, who sits calmly watching a game show. Could she have timed her rebellion more exactly?[19]

Critics unanimously praised *Show Me Love* as an excellent portrayal of young people. "A sensitive director is spot on," Nicholas Wennö wrote in *Dagens Nyheter*, adding, "*Show Me Love* is an extreme close-up of the pounding teenage heart, of love and boredom in an ultra-Swedish armpit."[20] Sara Enzell wrote in *Svenska Dagbladet*: "*Show Me Love* is a little master-piece. At last, a teen movie that's credible. No blood, no skinheads, no action. Just a quiet portrayal of being young, in love, insecure and different in a tiny Swedish town."[21]

To be young in the metaphorical small town of Åmål is to be limited to game shows on local TV. "Better than nothing, said the man who saw Åmål," is a popular saying about the town on the North-Western shore of Lake Vänern. "An honour to the town, but an outrage to me, said the man who got lost in Åmål," is another classic saying that asserts Åmål as the small town of small towns.[22] But it could just as well have been Trollhättan, Vänersborg, Uddevalla or Lysekil. Åmål happened to stand godfather to the film about teenage life in a small Swedish community and the nightmare of being forced to remain there. Or, as Elin so aptly puts it: "Why do we have to live in fucking bloody prick-Åmål?"[23] This question was quoted with relish by practically every reviewer and other scribes. The most delighted of these was Jonas Cramby, who exclaimed under the headline "Fucking great" in *Expressen*: "At long last, a Swedish film that is fucking bloody prick-marvellous!"[24] It is perhaps superfluous to point out the discrepancy between the reviewer's choice of words and the negligible relevance of the male sexual organ to the story about Agnes and Elin.

Most critics highlighted the theme of being young in a boring little town as the central subject of *Show Me Love*, while the love affair between Agnes and Elin was described as "odd" and "different." The "different" was turned into a utopian resort without a name. Several critics wrote about the agony of being young and in love in general. Britta Svensson at *Expressen* provides one example of this: "It is so unusual for girls to be portrayed like this that I sit there gulping down every line, every image. It's wonderful to recognise oneself, it's so consoling."[25] Thus far into the text, I start wondering what Britta Svensson has been through, only to find that what she recognised was not "the movie's rather contrived love story, which is more odd." Svensson had noted the invisibility of the girls' world, but it was obviously safest to let the lesbian theme, here called "more odd," remain invisible.

The interesting aspect of the review material is when and how the silence around the lesbian theme is broken. Bo Ludvigsson in *Svenska Dagbladet* was the only film critic who openly discussed the lesbian theme and linked up *Ecce Homo* with *Show Me Love:* "Oh no, we have nothing against homosexuals, as human beings. As long as they live in celibacy," was the ironic introduction to his review.[26] According to Ludvigsson, *Show Me Love* is about love in all its manifestations: between the girls Agnes and Elin, between parents, siblings and friends. He saw *Show Me Love* as a warm, strong and self-assured film about the courage of being human.

A few other reviewers also acknowledged the lesbian love theme in the film. Anders Hansson in *Göteborgs-Posten* writes that Moodysson creates *"a lesbian tension* (my italics) [between the girls] that is a protest against conformity as much as a deeper-lying force. Truly a bold venture, and yet *Show Me Love* ties up all the loose ends into a strong fabric."[27] Jan Aghed wrote in *Sydsvenska Dagbladet* that the film chronicles the girls' "lesbian-tinted relationship which is complicated by Elin's difficulties in coming to terms with her feelings, not to mention the prejudiced and hostile reactions of classmates and adults, as their 'terrible' suspicions are increasingly confirmed."[28]

The lesbian theme is used in *Show Me Love* as a means of heterosexual self-awareness, rather than as a portrayal of lesbian love. The Finnish film researcher Ilona Virtanen, who has written about the reception of *Show Me Love* in Finland, notes that *Show Me Love* belongs to a popular movie tradition which uses lesbianism to express a number of other things.[29] Homosexuality serves as a conductor, and helps to solve various types of problems, while the implication of a potential lesbian identity is ignored. In marketing the film Moodysson toned down the lesbian aspect by emphasising that *Show Me Love* was not primarily a film about homosexuality but about relations between young people, their relationships to their parents and about outsiders.[30] The experience of being different is not linked to a specific homosexual position, neither by the director nor by the critics, and lesbianism is used merely as a symbolic expression of a universal feeling of being an outsider.

The silence around the lesbian theme did not go entirely unnoticed in the press. Karin Thunberg in *Svenska Dagbladet* was baffled. Not by the story of the film, but by the silence about it. That the part that she perceived as the basic theme had remained so hidden and undiscussed: "When you talk to people they say that that was just part of the film and far from the most essential part. There are so many other aspects."[31]

What is perceived as essential and central in a film varies according to the viewer's perspective. The classical queer reading is to interpret more or less famous works so that we see what we have already read/seen in a new, *queer*, light. Often, this type of reading is preoccupied with revealing hidden queer structures and elements which were part of the closet structure. The non-heterosexual elements are plain to those who have the competence to appreciate them, but they are not disturbing to the viewer/reader who does not have the capacity to perceive them.[32]

But whereas a queer reading exposes hidden homoeroticism, the lesbian theme in *Show Me Love* is entirely out in the open. Explicit lesbianism has long been absent from the mainstream film repertoire. And to the extent that lesbian portraits occurred, these were usually negative, in the form of neurotic spinsters, blood-thirsty vampires or pre-Oedipal hostages in complex mother-daughter relationships.[33] Lesbian characters have often been shown as unhappy, lonely and suicidal. The women's and gay movements, changes in attitudes to homosexuality and changes in Hollywood's censorship system have slowly but steadily changed the image of lesbian women in mainstream film.

The film scholar Andrea Weiss points out that lesbian characters have grown more common and are portrayed with greater nuance since the 1960s. In TV serials the number of lesbian parts has increased steadily since the 1980s. *Mad About You, Ellen, Friends* and *Melrose Place* are a few popular examples. Flirting with lesbianism as a possible sexual alternative also occurs. In the popular serial *Ally McBeal* Ally kisses her colleague Ling, only to state that she would probably miss a penis if she entered a lesbian relationship.

The essence of this new attitude is that lesbianism is no longer associated with mental illness or general perversion. It is interesting that the sexual inclination of these lesbian characters is often put down to chance. Where the entire personality of the lesbian woman was formerly explained through her sexuality, homosexuality is no longer given any special significance. The lesbian woman is just a character like the others. Nevertheless, she is formed according to heterosexual patterns, and according to Andrea Weiss, her relationship to homosexual culture, history and identity is cut off. The result is a new form of invisibility.[34]

Since lesbianism is swallowed up by an all-invasive heteronormativity, the fact that hetero/homosexuality does not represent two equal parts of a "common" sexual culture is also obscured. In an article in *Arena*, Bodil Sjöström notes that *Show Me Love* is not an ordinary love story: "For the first time in my life, someone has seen me as a young girl. I am 36. I am conditioned by the phenomenon that *Show Me Love* confirms—I don't exist, above all, I did not exist when I was 14 and didn't understand a-n-y-t-h-i-n-g of what was going on inside me. A film like *Show Me Love* would have saved me many years of agonising outsidership."[35] Film critic Gunnar Rehlin, however, did not accept *Show Me Love* as a gay film, but saw it as a touching movie about first love. Like the small town of Åmål, lesbianism is, in his view, a metaphor for something different, and liberating, in a conservative environment.[36]

What, then, is a lesbian love film? A lesbian love film, or romance, could be said to be a film that focuses, thematises and highlights love affairs between women. The actual narrative technique can vary from heteronormatively conventional love stories to more experimental films. *Show Me Love* is an unusual and yet ordinary love film. It adheres to the conventions of romantic movies with all the habitual obstacles of a love story. The girls storming out of the school toilet is the film's symbolic coming-out scene and serves as a *grand finale*.

Show Me Love has links to other 1990s teen movies on the theme of homosexuality. Hettie Macdonald's film *Beautiful Thing* (1996) is the story of two working-class boys in England who fall in love with each other. The love in this film is a healing force that can cure the boys' outsidership and stop violence. A Norwegian parallel to *Show Me Love* is Svend Wam's film *Sebastian* (1995) which chronicles the teenage Sebastian's coming-out process. Unlike *Show Me Love*, *Sebastian* was never an international success. *Show Me Love* was overtly promoted in Berlin, Paris, London and New York as a lesbian film under the title *Show Me Love*, and was presented with the Gay & Lesbian Teddy Award at the Berlin Film Festival in 1999.

Coming-out films focus on the process whereby homosexuality falls into place, the instant when things finally feel right. In a piece in *Dagens Nyheter* Jessica Kempe sees Moodysson's film as a powerful and frantic defence of shackled desires: "It is not until frustrated Elin, who desperately tries to find relief from her secret desires by washing down painkillers with soft-drink, meets her true and much more aware other half, that she can come to rest. Not until the girls have embraced can they rise from their bodies and start talking about school and career dreams. Without a body there is no rational thought," Kempe wrote.[37]

In *Show Me Love* the lesbian theme is presented immediately in the opening scene set in Agnes's room. She is writing on her computer. One by one, the letters appear on the screen:

> My secret list of wishes:
> 1. That I don't have to have a party.
> 2. That Elin will look at me.
> 3. That Elin will fall in love with me.
> I LOVE ELIN!!!!!!!!!!!!!!!!!!!!!!!

> When Elin finally arrives at Agnes's disastrous birthday party with her sister, Jessica asks her:

> *Jessica:*
> Have you heard that she's a lesbian?
> *Elin:*
> What? Really? (Shouts to Agnes) Agnes? Is it true that you're...

> *Jessica puts her hand over Elin's mouth.*[38]

Elin muses for a while, then concludes that being a lesbian is cool, and that she's going to be one too. This is a provocation, rather than a considered standpoint. The sisters make a bet that Elin will kiss Agnes, and she does. Further on in the film, Elin asks Agnes if it is true that she is a lesbian. The question takes Agnes by surprise, but Elin explains loyally that she understands: "Because if you are I can understand that, because all boys are such bloody creeps. I think I might become a lesbian too."[39] Elin gets more and more curious and asks Agnes if she's been with many girls.

Eventually, the time comes for the kiss that is not part of a bet. Elin jauntily tells her mother that she is going to be a lesbian, but then pretends it was just a joke. Meanwhile, Agnes lies in her bed, listening to Albinoni, leafing through school photos and masturbating. In her diary she writes about her unhappy love for Elin:

> Why am I so stupid? Why do I love Elin?
> I hate her but love her at the same time.
> I love her so my heart almost breaks.
> But no one has hurt me as deeply as she has.
> She spits and tramples on me, and yet I love her.[40]

Agnes's little brother Oskar contributes to the discussion about lesbianism by asking the mother what *lesbian* means. The mother's reply is pedagogical and tolerant. But Oskar has more questions: "Do they have to go to hospital?"[41] Mother chuckles and says that there's *absolutely* nothing wrong with being lesbian. Her tolerant facade shatters when Oskar adds that Kalle says Agnes is a lesbian: "Agnes? That's nonsense... Of course she isn't."[42] Then events take their course. The girls leave the school lavatory together and come out.

Show Me Love came as a surprise to everyone. It was refreshing and unexpected to be confronted by a teen movie where the lesbian theme is central and totally obvious. Lukas Moodysson's discerning portrayal of Agnes and Elin is also a reminder of all the lesbian life and love stories that remain untold. The absence of discussion around *Show Me Love* proves just how excluded and unnamed lesbian identity is.

With regard to the absent discussion on lesbianism, journalist Birgitta Tollan-Driesel wrote an angry piece in the feminist magazine *Bang:*

> But in *Show Me Love* there are no subtle Sapphic signals, invisible to the unreceptive heterosexual soul of critics. No, here the love of women is quite open and obvious. I don't believe the film would forfeit its audience if the critics revealed that the main theme and red thread is a passionate lesbian love story. /.../ If the critics' censorship is due to not having noticed the strong lesbian dimension of *Show Me Love*, then they must have slept through the performance. No, another sad—historically tainted—truth probably lies behind this. And, horror of horrors, what if film critics today are at the tail-end of the discourse, and more lesbophobic than the audience![43]

The silence Tollan-Driesel refers to here is historic as part of the epistemology of the closet. The silence of the critics can only be regarded as a form of non-seeing, the cultural gaze that automatically weeds out homosexuality. This silence consists partly of an inability, and partly of an unwillingness, to discuss homosexuality in general and lesbianism in particular. It contributes towards not articulating homosexuality, and also to heterosexualise everything and everyone. And when the specifically lesbian element is removed from *Show Me Love*—even though we can see it with our own eyes—it is hard to draw any conclusion other than that lesbo/homophobia has not in any way receded.

The reception of *Show Me Love* is a school example of heteronormativity. To notice lesbianism would therefore have been tantamount to acknowledging an already discredited difference. To reinforce invisibility with silence is to deny that the homosexual community is part of our culture. Critics whose job is to question the gaze of others would benefit by reflecting on their own heteronormative gaze once in a while.

Lukas Moodysson emphasised in several interviews that he wants to influence and, if possible, change those who see his films. "I may be naive, but I believe you should have that ambition when making a film. If, for instance, I could get 10% of one Christian Democrat with prejudices against homosexuals, I'm pleased," he says in an interview in *Sydsvenska Dagbladet.* Despite playing down the importance of the lesbian theme in *Show Me Love,* Moodysson was still convinced that his own open attitude to homosexuality was not shared by all: "I wanted to make a film about love and about perceiving oneself to be different. I tried different constellations and the film eventually came to be about two girls who fall in love with one another. I saw it as a completely innocuous film that no one would be incensed by. But now [refers to *Ecce Homo*—my comment] when I hear what certain Christian Democrats, who have even been elected into parliament, say about homosexuals, I guess I've done a good deed. I wish it were possible to be different in a small community, but it's still difficult."[44]

Happy endings are an essential ingredient in the new gospel according to Luke: "I believe people have forgotten that one of the tasks of art is to give comfort and guidance. This has been replaced by provocation when we try to state some kind of truth. Rise and fall are easy to describe. But happy endings are the hardest thing to get right." says Moodysson.[45] In *Svenska Dagbladet* Bo Ludvigsson thanked Moodysson for making *Show Me Love* such a courageous film that dares to have a happy ending where the girls don't get stoned to death.[46]

In *Dagens Nyheter* Åsa Beckman describes the situation that many of us who saw *Show Me Love* recognise. It was a rich mixture of street festival, lovingness and comfort that made this visit to the cinema so unforgettable:

When I see *Show Me Love* at one of Stockholm's largest cinemas it
is filled with noisy teenagers, mostly girls. This is exactly the sort
of audience that immediately makes a, well, lower-middle-aged person think "oh no," because you know that there will be hysterical
laughs in the wrong place. But when Agnes and Elin make their way
through the crowd, everyone stands up and cheers victoriously. It is
as though the movie succeeds in describing the longing for expansion and liberation that the teenage girls in the audience are feeling
right now. To all of them, Diva would say: "When is a girl the most
beautiful? A girl is most beautiful at 13. When is the revolution? The
revolution is this year."[47]

On 23 October 1998, *Expressen* raised its glass for the film: "Are there things
you'd like to do but don't dare? See *Show Me Love*. Afterwards nothing feels
impossible."

Notes

1. Lauren Berlant & Michael Warner, "Sex in Public," in Simon During (ed.), *The
Cultural Studies Reader*, London & New York: Routledge 2000, 355; Stevi Jackson,
Heterosexuality in Question, London: SAGE Publications, 1999, 176; Raia Prokhovnik,
Rational Woman—A Feminist Critique of Dichotomy, London: Routledge, 1999, p. 129.
My notion of heteronormativity is based on the collective body of work on compulsory
heterosexuality in lesbian feminist thought, Lesbian and Gays Studies and queer theory.
    2. Iris Marion Young, *Justice and the Politics of Difference*, Princeton, NJ:
Princeton University Press, 1990.
    3. Prokhovnik (1999), 25. The guiding principles of heteronormativity resemble
the categories identified by the historian Yvonne Hirdman as the gender system.
According to Hirdman, the gender system rests on the logic of separation *(segregation)*
and the primacy of the male norm *(hierarchisation)*. Hirdman's notion of gender system
has been extremely influential in Sweden, but what Hirdman has done is simply an over-
taking of Gayle Rubin's concept of a sex/gender system already in 1975, in her article
"The Traffic in Women: Notes on the 'Political Economy' of Sex." In addition to defining the sex/gender system, she also presented a theory on the origin of female repression and formulated a radical feminist critique of Marxism. Hirdman does not, however, talk about sexuality, only of gender.
    4. Young (1990).
    5. Stig-Åke Petersson, "En svensk homorörelse växer fram: RFSL 1950-2000"
(The emergence of a Swedish gay movement), in Martin Andreasson (ed.), *Homo i
folkhemmet: Homo- och bisexuella i Sverige 1950-2000*, (*Homo in the Swedish 'People's
Home': Homosexuals and Bisexuals in Sweden 1950-2000*) Gothenburg: Anamma,
2000, 11.
    6. Elisabeth Ohlson, *Ecce Homo: Photographs 1996-1998*, Malmö: Föreningen
Ecce Homo, 1998; Gabriella Ahlström, *Ecce Homo: Berättelsen om en utställning*,

(Ecce Homo: The story of an exhibition), Stockholm: Bonnier, 1999.

7. Tiina Rosenberg, "Det nya Lukas-evangeliet. Om det heteronormativa mottagandet av *Fucking Åmål,*" ("The new gospel according to Lukas: On the heteronormative reception of *Show Me Love*"), in *Lambda Nordica,* Vol 6 no. 4 (2000).

8. Bodil Sjöström, "Varför har ingen sagt något?"("Why didn't anyone tell me?"), *Arena* no. 1/1999.

9. In addition to films, the number of homosexual characters in TV serials, especially in the USA, rose to some 23% in 1998.

10. Helena Lindblad, *Dagens Nyheter,* 5/1 1999.

11. Lukas Moodysson, *Fucking Åmål. Manuskript ("Show Me Love.* Script"), Stockholm: Bokförlaget DN, 1998, 29.

12. Moodysson (1998), 20.

13. Eva Redvall, "Ung, kär och udda i Fucking Åmål" ("Young, in love and odd in *Show Me Love"), Sydsvenska Dagbladet,* 17/10 1998.

14. Nicholas Wennö, "Lågbudget blev storsuccé. Fucking Åmål. Kritiker och publik jublar åt Lukas Moodyssons regidebut" ("From budget to blockbuster. Critics and audiences celebrate Lukas Moodysson's debut film"), *Dagens Nyheter,* 24/19 1998.

15. Wennö, ibid.

16. Jonas Cramby, "Fucking Great," *Expressen,* 23/10 1998.

17. Johan Croneman, "Längtan bort förlamar och frigör. Lukas Moodyssons film *Fucking Åmål* beskriver tonårslivet på en liten ort utan att fastna i schabloner" ("The longing to get away paralyses and liberates. Lukas Moodysson's film *Show Me Love* describes small-town teenage life without getting stuck in stereotypes"), *Dagens Nyheter,* 23/10 1998.

18. Croneman, ibid.

19. Åsa Beckman, "Tonårstjejerna är för stora för omgivningen" ("Teenage girls too big for their environment"), *Dagens Nyheter,* 2/11 1999.

20. Nicholas Wennö, "Lågbudget blev storsuccé. Fucking Åmål. Kritiker och publik jublar åt Lukas Moodyssons regidebut ("From budget to block-buster. *Show Me Love.* Critics and audiences celebrate Lukas Moodysson's debut film"), *Dagens Nyheter,* 24/19 1998.

21. Sara Enzell, "Fucking Åmål. Ung, osäker, annorlunda: man längtar efter att allt ska förändras," ("*Show Me Love.* Young, insecure, different: the longing for everything to change"), *Svenska Dagbladet,* 16/10 1998. Anette Kullenberg in *Aftonbladet* (4/11 1998) presents an unexpected perspective, not to say a side discourse, when she points out that there is not a single immigrant boy in this movie. This is a point that no other critic has even mentioned.

22. Denizens of Åmål were mightily upset when they heard that a film called *Fucking Åmål* was being made. Local politicians criticised the tax-funded Film i Väst for allowing the film team to use their premises for a production that would "bring disgrace on the metropolis in the county of Dalsland," as the local paper *Provinstidningen i Dalsland* put it. "Filmen *Fucking Åmål* upprör Åmålbor" ("The film *Show Me Love* angers Åmål inhabitants"), *Sydsvenska Dagbladet*/TT, 25/4 1998.

23. Moodysson (1998), 20-29.

24. Jonas Cramby, "Fucking Great," *Expressen,* 23/10 1998.

25. Britta Svensson, "Om helvetet att vara ung" ("On the agony of being young"), *Expressen* 16/10 1998.

26. Bo Ludvigsson, "Starkt och modigt om att finna sitt liv" ("Strong and coura-geous about finding one's life"), *Svenska Dagbladet*, 23/10 1998.

27. Anders Hansson, "Ett storverk med äkthet. Moodyssons dialog är en fröjd att lyssna till i biosalongen" ("A sincere masterpiece. Moodysson's dialogue is a joy to lis-ten to in the cinema"), *Göteborgs-Posten*, 23/10 1998.

28. Jan Aghed, "Känslig tonårsskildring i svensk småstadstristess" ("Sensitive teenage portrayal in Swedish small-town torpor"), *Sydsvenska Dagbladet*, 23/10 1998.

29. Ilona Virtanen, "Fucking Åmål—lesboelokuva joka makuun" (*"Show Me Love*—a lesbian film to suit all tastes), *Lähikuva*, no. 2-3 / 1999, 81.

30. Annika Gustafsson, "Hem till byn" ("Home to the village"), *Sydsvenska Dagbladet, Dygnet runt supplement*, 16-22/10 1998.

31. Karin Thunberg, "Vart tog det lesbiska vägen?" ("Where did lesbianism go?"), *Svenska Dagbladet*, 12/12 1998.

32. See Alexander Doty, *Making Things Perfectly Queer. Interpreting Mass Culture*, Minneapolis & London: University of Minnesota Press, 1993; Tiina Rosenberg, *Byxbegär (Desiring Pants)*, Gothenburg: Anamma, 2000.

33. Andrea Weiss, *Vampires and Violets. Lesbians in Film*, London: Jonathan Cape, 1992, 51 f.

34. Weiss (1992), 63 f.

35. Bodil Sjöström, "Varför har ingen sagt något?" ("Why didn't anyone tell me?"), *Arena*, no. 1/1999.

36. Gunnar Rehlin, *Variety*, 26/10 1998.

37. Jessica Kempe, "Striphårig Slösa får revansch i Fucking Åmål" ("Lanky spendthrift gets her own back in *Show Me Love"*), *Dagens Nyheter*, 16/2 1999.

38. Moodysson (1998), 59.

39. Moodysson (1998), 79.

40. Moodysson (1998), 123.

41. Moodysson (1998), 131.

42. Moodysson (1998), 132.

43. Birgitta Tollan-Driesel, "Tystnadens historia" ("The history of silence"), *Bang* no. 1/1999.

44. Annika Gustafsson, "Hem till byn" ("Home to the Village"), *Sydsvenska Dagbladet, Dygnet runt supplement*, 16-22/10 1998.

45. Anders Hansson, "Det nya Lukas-evangeliet" ("The new gospel according to Lukas"), *Göteborgs-Posten*, 6/2 1999.

46. Bo Ludvigsson, "Starkt och modigt om att finna sitt liv" ("Strong and coura-geous about finding one's life").

Bibliography

Aghed, Jan. "Känslig tonårsskildring i svensk småstadstristess" ("Sensitive teenage portrayal in Swedish small-town torpor"), Sydsvenska Dagbladet, 23.10.1998

Ahlström, Gabriella. *Ecce Homo: Berättelsen om en utställning (Ecce Homo:*

The story of an exhibition), Stockholm: Bonnier, 1999

Beckman, Åsa. "Tonårstjejerna är för stora för omgivningen" ("Teenage girls too big for their environment"), *Dagens Nyheter*, 2.11.1999

Berlant, Lauren & Warner, Michael. "Sex in Public," in Simon During (ed.), *The Cultural Studies Reader*, London & New York: Routledge, 2000

Cramby, Jonas. "Fucking Great," *Expressen*, 23.10.1998

Croneman, Johan. "Längtan bort förlamar och frigör. Lukas Moodyssons film Fucking Åmål beskriver tonårslivet på en liten ort utan att fastna i schabloner" ("The longing to get away paralyses and liberates. Lukas Moodysson's film *Show Me Love* describes small-town teenage life without getting stuck in stereotypes"), *Dagens Nyheter*, 23.10.1998

Doty, Alexander. *Making Things Perfectly Queer. Interpreting Mass Culture*, Minneapolis & London: University of Minnesota Press, 1993

Enzell, Sara. "Fucking Åmål. Ung, osäker, annorlunda: man längtar efter att allt ska förändras" (*"Show Me Love*. Young, insecure, different: the longing for everything to change"), *Svenska Dagbladet*, 16.10.1998

Gustafsson, Annika. "Hem till byn" ("Home to the village"), *Sydsvenska Dagbladet*, Dygnet runt supplement, 16-22.10.1998

Hansson, Anders. "Det nya Lukas-evangeliet" ("The new gospel according to Lukas"), *Göteborgs-Posten*, 6.2.1999

———. "Ett storverk med äkthet. Moodyssons dialog är en fröjd att lyssna till i biosalongen" ("A sincere masterpiece. Moodysson's dialogue is a joy to listen to in the cinema"), *Göteborgs-Posten*, 23.10.1998

Jackson, Stevi. *Heterosexuality in Question*, London: SAGE Publications, 1999

Kempe, Jessica, "Strihårig Slösa får revansch i Fucking Åmål" ("Lanky spendthrift gets her own back in *Show Me Love*"), *Dagens Nyheter*, 16.2.1999

Ludvigsson, Bo. "Starkt och modigt om att finna sitt liv" ("Strong and courageous about finding one's life"), *Svenska Dagbladet*, 23.10.1998

Moodysson, Lukas. *Fucking Åmål. Manuskript* (*Show Me Love. Script*), Stockholm: Bokförlaget DN, 1998

Ohlson, Elisabeth. *Ecce Homo: Photographs 1996-1998*, Malmö: Föreningen Ecce Homo, 1998

Petersson, Stig-Åke. "En svensk homorörelse växer fram: RFSL 1950-2000" ("The emergence of a Swedish gay movement"), in Martin Andreasson (ed.), *Homo i folkhemmet: Homo-och bisexuella i Sverige 1950-2000* (*Homo in the Swedish 'People's Home': Homosexuals and Bisexuals in Sweden 1950-2000*), Gothenburg: Anamma, 2000

Prokhovnik, Raia. *Rational Woman–A Feminist Critique of Dichotomy*, London: Routledge, 1999

Redvall, Eva. "Ung, kär och udda i Fucking Åmål" ("Young, in love and odd in *Show Me Love*"), *Sydsvenska Dagbladet*, 17.10.1998

Rosenberg, Tiina. *Byxbegär* (*Desiring Pants*), Gothenburg: Anamma, 2000

————. "Det nya Lukas-evangeliet. Om det heteronormativa mottagandet av Fucking Åmål" ("The new gospel according to Lukas: On the heteronormative reception of *Show Me Love*"), in *Lambda Nordica*, Vol 6, no. 4, 2000

————. *Queerfeministisk agenda* (*Queer Feminist Agenda*), Stockholm: Atlas, 2002

Sjöström, Bodil. "Varför har ingen sagt något?"("Why didn't anyone tell me?"), *Arena* no. 1, 1999

Svensson, Britta, "Om helvetet att vara ung" ("On the agony of being young"), *Expressen*, 16.10.1998

Thunberg, Karin. "Vart tog det lesbiska vägen?" ("Where did lesbianism go?"), *Svenska Dagbladet*, 12.12.1998

Tollan-Driesel, Birgitta, "Tystnadens historia" ("The history of silence"), *Bang* no. 1, 1999

Andrea Weiss. *Vampires and Violets. Lesbians in Film*, London: Jonathan Cape, 1992

Wennö, Nicholas. "Lågbudget blev storsuccé? Fucking Åmål. Kritiker och publik jublar? Lukas Moodyssons regidebut" ("From budget to blockbuster. Critics and audiences celebrate Lukas Moodysson's debut film"), *Dagens Nyheter*, 24/10 1998

Virtanen, Ilona. "Fucking Åmål—lesboelokuva joka makuun" (*"Show Me Love*-a lesbian film to suit all tastes), *Lähikuva*, nr 2-3 / 1999, 81.

Gustafsson, Annika. "Hem till byn" ("Home to the village"), *Sydsvenska Dagbladet*, Dygnet runt supplement, 16-22.10.1998

Young, Iris Marion. *Justice and the Politics of Difference*, Princeton, NJ: Princeton University Press, 1990

Differences that Matter?
Or: What Is Feminist Critique?

Cathrine Egeland

"Sexual difference"—a disturbing notion indeed. At worst it seems to be an essentialist conceptual framework supporting dubious arguments in favour of different versions of biological determinism and heterosexism. At best sexual difference is a rather confusing term; is sexual difference the natural, given bedrock of femininity and masculinity, a symbolic distribution, a discursive construction or a contingent, cultural code for heterosexuality? Following Luce Irigaray (1993 [1984]) I understand sexual difference as a decisive, unresolved issue for our time—that is, as an unsettled *question* as opposed to a settled fact. In this article I want to explore some of the conditions for the question of sexual difference to be posed as a decisive, unresolved issue for feminism understood as critique precisely of any essentialist conceptual framework that seems to support biological determinism and heterosexism.

Sexual Difference as the Question for Our Times
– and for Feminism

In feminist theory the notion of sexual difference has often been associated with French-speaking theorists like Luce Irigaray, Hélène Cixous, Julia Kristeva and Catherine Clément who, in different styles and from different positions in psychoanalysis, linguistics, philosophy and literature, have emphasized "the feminine" as a de/constructive tool to be used against the phallogocentrism of Western thought. This is especially clear in the works of Irigaray, who, in *An Ethics of Sexual Difference* describes sexual difference as one of, if not *the* major, philosophical issue of our age. Indeed: "Sexual difference is probably the issue in our time which could be our 'salvation' if we thought it through.

But whether I turn to philosophy, to science, or to religion, I find this underlying issue still cries out in vain for our attention" (Irigaray 1993 [1984]: 5).
The issue of sexual difference does not refer to an anatomical fact but to a question. Furthermore, the question of sexual difference is not a question of what
sexual difference really *is*; the sexual indifference inherent in the phallogocentrism of Western philosophy makes sexual difference unrepresentable and
unspeakable outside the narrow frameworks of essentialism. The question of
sexual difference is not a question among other more or less interesting questions, but a question that marks our time; a question that marks modernity by
calling our attention to the horizon of worlds, to the horizon of language in a
time of inevitable, disturbing irresolution and dissymmetry. For Irigaray language is a house of being where men, not women, are able to dwell. The notion
of dwelling is borrowed from Heidegger. Irigaray employs it in order to indicate the sexual, social and discursive homelessness of women: "Some [mascu-
line] creators of worlds, constructors of temples, builders of houses; others
[feminine] guardians of a *phuein* making its resources available, prior to any
culture" (Irigaray 1983: 120).[1]

Reading Irigaray through Foucauldian lenses I consider her notion of sexual difference both intriguing and promising because it challenges and undermines our hopes and dreams of freedom and sexual symmetry within the frameworks of phallogocentric discourse, understood as a specific libidinal and political economy. Even though Irigaray insists on the ontological (not biological)
basis of sexual difference as an ultimate horizon—parallel to death—for the
human being, thereby making her project incompatible with that of Foucault's,
I nevertheless find their projects to be united in their disruptive interventions in
philosophy. I will discuss the importance of intervention in philosophy towards
the end of the essay. For the time being I will only suggest that while Foucault
is quite evasive when it comes to the question of sexual difference, Irigaray
describes her de/constructive rereadings of the philosophical canon in terms
that most certainly find their resonance in the works of Foucault:

> Whence the necessity of "reopening" the figures of philosophical
> discourse—idea, substance, subject, transcendental subjectivity,
> absolute knowledge—in order to pry out of them what they have bor-
> rowed that is feminine, from the feminine, to make them "render
> up" and give back what they owe the feminine. This may be done in
> various ways, along various "paths"; moreover, at minimum sever-
> al of these must be pursued. One way is to interrogate the conditions
> under which systematicity itself is possible: what the coherence of
> the discursive utterance conceals of the conditions under which it is
> produced, whatever it may say about these conditions in discourse
> (Irigaray 1985 [1977]: 74-75).

The question of sexual difference is also a question for feminism.[2] This may sound self-evident—is there a more obvious question for feminism than the question of sexual difference? But it is far from self-evident; during the 1980s the notion of sexual difference seemed to cause a double discursive homelessness for some feminists. They refused to dwell in what apparently was a house visited by the spectre of essentialism inherent in French feminist thought. Strange as it perhaps may seem—since "woman" in the works of for instance Irigaray is described as "not yet" and sexual difference as an unresolved question as opposed to a given, natural fact—the apparent essentialism attached to the notion of sexual difference led many feminists to apply the term gender as the "proper" object of inquiry for feminism (as opposed to for instance queer, gay and lesbian studies that supposedly have sex and sexuality—but not sexual difference—as their proper object).

The uncertainty and uneasiness associated with the notion of sexual difference involves the question of what feminism is or ought to be. Not all feminists are ready or able to detach the notion of sexual difference from essentialism; not all feminists are ready or able to accept sexual difference as a critical, subversive, feminist tool since it does not entail the possibility of symmetry through emancipation. There seems to be a general agreement that feminism—in one way or the other—is critique, but not how feminism is critique and what critique altogether is. For instance, Seyla Benhabib and Drucilla Cornell, the editors of the important collection *Feminism as Critique* from 1987, associated feminism with critique in a Marxist sense while desisting from giving the term an unequivocal definition. Instead they traced the decisive elements of feminism as critique in the movement from the first phase of feminists' deconstruction of patriarchal thought to the emergence of theoretical reconstruction in contemporary feminism. Throughout the 1990s the notion of feminism as critique has prevailed even though the Marxist concept of critique has been hijacked by the Foucauldian understanding of "critique" (in quotation marks) as always being immanent to the relations of power it adjudicates.[3]

I understand the notion of feminism as critique as dependent on rather dim, but ideologically effective notions of what feminism is and ought to be. In what follows I will therefore take a closer look at the question of feminism by probing into texts by Judith Butler, Seyla Benhabib and Toril Moi before returning to feminism as critique and the question of sexual difference. Let me start by following the traces of gender in feminist theory.

Gender as a Ghostbuster

Though not originally a feminist concept ("gender" is primarily a term developed in and derived from biology, linguistics and psychology) and most certainly rooted in Anglo-American languages, "gender" has made and still does make sense to many feminists as a useful conceptual opposition to "sex," where sex refers to biological sexual differences and gender to the discursive, cultural and social interpretation or construction of these differences.

In her famous essay "The Traffic in Women" from 1975, Gayle Rubin states that:

> Hunger is hunger, but what counts as food is culturally determined and obtained. Every society has some form of organized economic activity. Sex is sex, but what counts as sex is equally culturally determined and obtained. Every society also has a sex/gender-system—a set of arrangements by which the biological raw material of human sex and procreation is shaped by human, social intervention and satisfied in a conventional manner, no matter how bizarre some of the conventions may be (Rubin 1975: 165).

Rubin employed a distinction between sex and gender in order to avoid biological determinism. For Rubin, the object of interest was gender, not sex. Sex is just the more or less inert biological raw material of human procreation. Gender, however, is the oppressive social norms resulting from an unjust social process of production.

In contemporary feminist theory gender "...primarily fulfills the function of challenging the universalistic tendency of critical language and of the systems of knowledge and scientific discourse at large" (Braidotti 1994: 152). This function is clearly an important one. It is equally worth noting the relative institutional success that "gender studies" have enjoyed in Academia. In a critical passage about the adoption and application of the term gender in feminist theory Rosi Braidotti (1994) argues that the application of gender and the development and spreading of gender studies have resulted in a shift of focus away from the feminist agenda toward an attention to the social construction of differences between the sexes. The result might at worst be a slimming down of the political agenda caused by what seems to be an assumption of a new symmetry between the sexes expressed for instance in a renewed interest in men and "men's studies" and a drying up of whatever was left of "feminist studies."

Gender Acts

The application of the term "gender" in feminist theory has also been problematized from the vantage point of a presumed distinction between sex and gender. The obvious problems involved in this distinction has been analysed and criticized in different ways for the last two decades and reached a well-known and well-discussed summit in the early 1990s when Judith Butler in *Gender Trouble* (1990) presented the following argument:

> Gender ought not to be conceived merely as the cultural
> inscription of meaning on a pregiven sex (a juridical concep-
> tion); gender must also designate the very apparatus of pro-
> duction whereby the sexes themselves are established. As a
> result, gender is not to culture as sex is to nature; gender is
> also the discursive/cultural means by which "sexed nature" or
> "a natural sex" is produced and established as "prediscur-
> sive," prior to culture, a politically neutral surface *on which*
> culture acts (Butler 1990: 7).

Since there is no essence of which gender is an interpretation or expression,
Butler (in a Nietzchean sense) argues there is no gender behind or underlying
the act of gender; gender *is* the various acts of gender. Gender is thus not a
given, but a regulatory ideal, a construction that constantly conceals its supposed genesis through repetitions of specific *"gender acts."* Gender then, is not
a locus of agency, but a constituted social temporality; the "doer" is regularly
produced and reproduced in and through the deed.

This understanding of gender has given rise to many interesting research
projects—both in the humanities and in the social sciences—focusing on the
ways different gender acts operate in culture and society and how, for instance,
the very notions of masculinity and femininity are constituted as elements in
strategies that disguise the performative character of gender, thus concealing
possible ways of undermining the restricting conceptual framework of male
domination and compulsory (hetero)sexuality.

This, perhaps surprising, regeneration of gender, resulting from the deconstruction of the distinction between sex and gender did not, however, entail a
decrease in the interest of sexual difference. Inspired by the works of Irigaray
and Gilles Deleuze, Rosi Braidotti (1994) argues for a productive nexus
between feminist nomadism and sexual difference—one that is irreducible to
biology and to culture, one that resists the phallogocentric definition of woman
as a non-man. Emphasising the important symbolic status of sexual difference
Braidotti insists on mimetic repetition and consumption of monstrous differences, differences that allow for a feminism commited to the affirmation of
post-Woman women. The irreducibility of sexual difference should not to be
understood as an essentialist claim. At the same time, Braidotti, however,
emphasises, with Irigaray and Gayatri Spivak, that feminists cannot afford not
to be essentialist confronted with the reductionist sexual indifference of
Western phallogocentrism. Thus, according to Braidotti, transformation:
"...can only be achieved through de-essentialized embodiment or strategically
re-essentialized embodiment: by working through the multilayered structures of
one's embodied self" (Braidotti 1994: 171).

From a somewhat different theoretical position Butler (2001) likewise
draws on Irigaray's claim that sexual difference is an important question for our

times. Referring to the debates concerning the theoretical priority of gender to
sexual difference and of sexual difference to gender, Butler suggests that these
debates are cross-cut by the problem that sexual difference poses, namely, the
seemingly eternal question of where the biological, the psychic, the discursive
and the social begin and end, and how they interact. According to Butler:

> ...sexual difference is the site where a question concerning the rela-
> tion of the biological to the cultural is posed and reposed, where it
> must and can be posed, but where it cannot, strictly speaking, be
> answered. Understood as a border concept, sexual difference has
> psychic, somatic, and social dimensions that are never quite col-
> lapsible into one another but are not for that reason ultimately dis-
> tinct (Butler 2001: 427).

The Retreat from Utopia

Throughout the 1990s Butler and other feminist theorists, in part inspired by
the works of Michel Foucault and Jacques Derrida, nevertheless felt the need
to defend their positions as real feminists engaged in the task of qualifying and
securing a critical agency, which they apparently deemed crucial in order for
feminist political action to take place. The problem for feminist politics is that
it is necessarily associated with a subject—the category of women—a "we"
whose interests is to be expressed and represented in theory and emancipatory
politics. Originally centered on the problematic relation between feminism and
postmodernism, the collection *Feminist Contentions* from 1995 serves as a
symptomatic instance of the debate concerning feminist theory in the 1990s.
Feminist Contentions reflects some of the important tension between what I
would call postmodernist interventionism and critical theory, as developed by
the Frankfurt School. Consider for instance this worried passage from Seyla
Benhabib's contribution to the collection, where she, on the one hand, admits
that subjectivity is structured by language and by the codes of intelligible narratives available in our culture, but on the other hand concludes as follows:

> We can concede all that, but nevertheless we must still argue that we
> are not merely extensions of our histories, that vis-à-vis our own sto-
> ries we are in the position of author and character at once. The sit-
> uated and gendered subject is heteronomously determined but still
> strives towards autonomy. I want to ask how in fact the very proj-
> ect of female emancipation would even be thinkable without such a
> regulative principle on agency, autonomy and selfhood? (Benhabib
> 1995: 21)

This is indeed a problem because what Benhabib here raises as a problem
touches the very core of feminism, namely the question: What is *feminism* with-

out a subject in the category of women?

Already in *Gender Trouble* Butler adressed this problem by questioning the way agency is usually associated with the existence and viability of a relatively stable subject and hence broached the foundationalist tendencies inherent in feminist political theorizing. What she wanted to undermine in *Gender Trouble* was the foundationalist logic of identity politics inherent in feminism, not feminist politics:

> The critical task for feminism is not to establish a point of view outside of constructed identities; that conceit is the construction of an epistemological model that would disavow its own cultural location and, hence, promote itself as a global subject; a position that deploys precisely the imperialist strategies that feminism ought to criticize. The critical task is, rather, to locate strategies of subversive repetition enabled by those constructions, to affirm the local possibilities of intervention through participating in precisely those practices of repetition that constitute identity and, therefore present the immanent possibility of contesting them (Butler 1990: 147).

According to Benhabib, however, there is hardly any critical task left for a feminism contaminated by postmodernism; postmodernism has produced a veritable "retreat from utopia" within feminism (Benhabib 1995: 30). This is the result of what Benhabib interprets as a strong version of postmodernism commited to three theses that Butler and other feminists flirting with postmodernism cannot avoid: the death of Man, understood as the dissolution of the autonomous subject; the death of History, understood as the renunciation of "grand narratives," including the epistemological interest in historical narrative accompanying the hopes, dreams and aspirations of struggling historical actors, and finally; the death of Metaphysics, understood as the rejection of transcendent, ultimate instances from where institutions and practices can be criticised and diagnosed. These three proclamations of death implied in the strong version of postmodernism undermine the feminist emancipatory endeavour by deconstructing the commitment to women's agency and the possibility of critique—i.e. the possibility of examining present conditions from the standpoint and perspective of feminist utopian visions.

Benhabib's critique of what she interprets to be an undermining of the feminist emancipatory endeavour inherent in for instance Butler's deconstruction of the category of women as the locus of feminist agency, is a relatively common one. In part it rests on a problematic notion of feminism as a necessarily emancipatory endeavour, implying the possibility of sexual symmetry. I will return to this. In part Benhabib's critique rests on a misunderstanding or misrepresentation of the implications of deconstruction. Since this has been thoroughly debated throughout the 1990s I will only indicate a few of the main points of discussion here. What Benhabib seems to forget or ignore is that Butler's and other feminists' deconstruction of the foundationalist logic of identity politics inherent in feminism deals with the question of legitimation; somewhat akin to Bourdieu. Butler argues for instance that claims to legitimacy result from authoritative speech acts that are simultaneously dependent on, constituting and reproducing authority. Rather than rejecting and resisting the existence of authority, deconstruction discloses the processes of legitimation and the possibilities of renegotiation inherent in them. Or to use the words of the Butler from the mid-1990s:

> To take the construction of the subject as a political problematic is not the same as doing away with the subject; to deconstruct the subject is not to negate or throw away the concept; on the contrary, deconstruction implies only that we suspend all commitments to that to which the term, "the subject" refers, and that we consider the linguistic functions it serves in the consolidation and concealment of authority. To deconstruct is not to negate or to dismiss, but to call into question, and, perhaps more importantly, to open up a term, like the subject, to a reusage or redeployment that previously has not been authorized (Butler 1995a: 49).

So the deconstruction of the category of women as the locus of feminist emancipation does not necessarily imply a dismissal of the category of women as an important tool in political struggles. What is contested is the category's status as the ontological premise for political action. Thus Benhabib's worry is only justified in so far as one assumes that agency presupposes a subject and that deconstruction of the subject consequently undermines the possibility of agency.

Feminist Theory in an Ordinary Mode

A far more interesting critique of Butler and other feminist theorists working within the theoretical frameworks of postmodernist interventionism was presented in Toril Moi's eminent study *What Is a Woman?* from 1999. I will dwell upon Moi's critique for a moment because it seems to presume a certain notion of feminism and of feminism as critique that expels the question of sexual difference from feminism. This may perhaps sound strange and surprising since Moi in her introduction to *What Is a Woman?* states that she is trying to work out a theory of the sexually different body (Moi 1999: 4). For this purpose, however, Moi considers Butler's and other "poststructuralists"[4] deconstruction of the distinction between sex and gender theoreticist—i.e. haunted by the belief that theoretical correctness can guarantee political correctness (Moi 1999: 59). The deconstruction of this distinction is simply superfluous and irrelevant for the production of knowledge or understanding of what it means to be a man or a woman situated in a concrete, historical society. Why?

According to Moi, the hopes and aspirations of Simone de Beauvoir, Gayle Rubin, and poststructuralist feminists like Judith Butler do not appear to be politically different; all feminists want a society relieved of repressive norms of social and sexual behaviour. However, it seems like the poststructuralist feminists have completely forgotten that the distinction between sex and gender had a specific (political) function, namely that of avoiding biological determinism. Instead they have been caught up in utterly useless theoretical reflections concerning realism, nominalism, materiality, power and discourse resulting in an almost scientist understanding of sex and an idealist understanding of gender, obscuring the positive political objectives that the poststructuralists share with non-poststructuralists like Simone de Beauvoir and Gayle Rubin. Far from theoreticism, Moi argues that "What we need today more than ever is a feminism commited to seeking justice and equality for women, in the most ordinary sense of the word. Only such a feminism will be able to grasp the complexity of women's concrete, everyday concern" (Moi 1999: 9). And as for the positive political objectives, Simone de Beauvoir "...achieved them first, and with considerably greater philosophical elegance, clarity, and wit" (Moi 1999: 59).

While I do not intend to question the importance of Simone de Beauvoir's contribution to philosophy and feminist theory—nor her elegance, clarity and wit for that matter—I find it necessary to question one of the main premises of Moi's critique of Butler and other poststructuralists, namely the presupposition that emancipation is a naturally universal—hence also feminist—objective. According to Moi, when poststructuralists "prefer" to think in terms of subversion—as in "strategies of subversive repetition" (Butler 1990: 147)—instead of in terms of juridical emancipation and liberation, they complicate the feminist project by introducing terms utterly superfluous to the positive objectives already described and achieved by, for instance, Simone de Beauvoir. So what Moi tries to contest in her discussion of the poststructuralists' deconstruction of the sex-gender distinction is not the assumed shared political objectives of the theorists in question, but rather the theoreticism of poststructuralist thought, which Moi believes obscures these objectives. This argument must be understood in light of what kind of enterprise theoretical and philosophical writing can be, according to Moi. Reading Beauvoir through the lenses of ordinary language philosophy as this is unfolded in the works by Ludwig Wittgenstein and Stanley Cavell Moi argues for a feminism released from metaphysical images "...and so return our words to the sphere of the ordinary, that is to say the sphere in which our political and personal struggles actually take place" (Moi 1999: 120).

Therapy

The unfortunate feminists struck by theoreticism are held captive in their own theoretical framework and what they need, as far as Moi is concerned, is Wittgensteinian, philosophical therapy (Moi 1999: 119-120). What seems to attract Moi's attention to Wittgenstein—(in his struggle with the paradoxical limit of philosophical justification) may perhaps be summed up in the following reflection from *Philosophical Investigations*:

> We must do away with all *explanation*, and description alone must take its place. And this description gets its light, that is to say its purpose, from the philosophical problems. These are, of course, not empirical problems; they are solved, rather, by looking into the workings of our language, and that in such a way as to make us recognize those workings: *despite of* an urge to misunderstand them. The problems are solved, not by giving new information, but by arranging what we have always known. Philosophy is a battle against the bewitchment of our intelligence by means of language (Wittgenstein 1991 [1958]: § 109).

Philosophical problems arise when "language *goes on holiday*" (Wittgenstein 1991 [1958]: § 38)—that is, when language stops working for us, as Moi correctly points out. When language goes on holiday, we end up in a linguistic fog where we try to find answers to muddled questions. The solution to this problem is not to find the right answer, but to liberate oneself from the problem by realizing that it is the way in which the problem is posed that is the (real) problem. So the role of philosophy is to produce diagnoses and be therapeutic in order to liberate us from confusing quasi-problems. In a similar line of thought Toril Moi seems to think that feminism is in danger of being bewitched (sic.) by the theoreticism of poststructuralists like Judith Butler, and she therefore prescribes Wittgensteinian therapy for the patient.

It is, of course, quite tempting to follow up and question this slightly paternalizing tone and the somewhat unpleasant picture of the unruly daughter of (real) Feminism lying on the couch of the Philosopher giving her proper therapy. This is not what I want to question, however; Moi may even be justified in asking for some clarity in feminist theory. The problem is rather, as I have already mentioned, that Moi, like Seyla Benhabib, seems to presuppose an understanding of emancipation as a naturally universal—hence feminist—objective and freedom as a universal value. Consequently, deconstruction and subversion are, at worst, regarded as theoreticist obstacles on the road to freedom, or, at best, as something like means to this end, thus ignoring the incompatibility inherent in the relation between Beauvoir's "feminism of freedom" and postmodernist interventionism as it is found in the works of Irigaray, Foucault and Butler.

The Master's Tools

According to Moi the poststructuralists try to avoid emancipation and liberation and prefer to think instead in terms of subversion. The reason for this is, as Moi points out, the immanence of power:

> Since we cannot escape power, we can only undermine it from within. For this reason they [the poststructuralist theoretists of sex and gender—ce] have often invoked the male drag artist as a particularly subversive figure. By parodying dominant gender norms, he shows them up as conventional and artificial, and thus enables us to maintain a critical or ironic distance to them. Unlike Gayle Rubin, poststructuralists do not explicitly dream of a society without gender; rather, they seem to hope that greater freedom or justice or happiness will arise when we are able freely to mix and match socially normative concepts of masculinity and femininity as we like. Perhaps the idea is that this will eventually so weaken the impact of the dominant social norms that gender might ultimately wither away after all (Moi 1999: 58).

This is a quite surprising interpretation of the reasons that might be given for the employment of strategic subversion as part of a feminist theoretical framework. In an essay discussing the relations between sexual politics and psychoanalytical theory in Freud's *Dora*, Moi makes the following argument regarding the possibilities of resistance towards patriarchal ideology and phallocentric epistemology:

> The attack upon phallocentrism must come from within, since there can be no outside, no space where true femininity, untainted by patriarchy, can be kept intact for us to discover. We can only destroy the mythical and mystifying constructions of patriarchy by using its own weapons. We have no others (Moi 1999: 347).

If the attack upon phallocentrism must come from within, if we have no other tools at hand than "the master's" tools, then how can feminism be anything but subversive?

I share the view held by most poststructuralists that emancipation is a problematic Enlightenment notion presupposing an alienated or oppressed subject that has to be liberated from oppressive conditions, institutions and norms. In the context of feminism understood as an emancipatory, critical endeavour I furthermore consider freedom to be a specific, regulatory ideal—that is a self-explanatory anchoring point of discourses producing and reproducing their own historical objects. As an ideal, freedom is the anchoring point of discourses producing and reproducing the cultural, social and political logic of capitalism. Emancipation is thus already a part of phallogocentric discourse understood as a specific libidinal and political economy resting on ideals like freedom, equality and fraternity.

Preferring subversion to emancipation is not a theoreticist detour to freedom. Preferring subversion to emancipation indicates a monstrous, fundamental break with freedom as a self-explanatory ideal producing, reproducing and legitimating the cultural, social and political logic of capitalism. What in my eyes seems to be at stake in Toril Moi's and Seyla Benhabib's critique of postmodernist interventionism is a reluctance to associate feminism with this break. Even if Moi wants to return our words to the sphere of the ordinary emphasising that "there can be no outside, no space where true femininity, untainted by patriarchy, can be kept intact for us to discover," she still seems to except human transcendence and freedom from the implications of this insight, describing them as "fundamental, universal values." One could interpret this as an indication of the difficulties inherent in any attempt to detach a concept like freedom from its (obscure and obscuring) metaphysical connotations in order to return it to the sphere of the ordinary. More important, however, is it to consider whether or not values like human transcendence and freedom can be conceived of as "untainted" by phallogocentrism at all. If the answer is no, as I believe Moi would argue, it is hard to understand why she regards subversion to be a theoreticist detour to freedom. Again, I repeat the question: How can feminism be anything but subversive?

What the critique of postmodernist interventionism and the reluctance to associate feminism with a break with freedom as a self-explanatory ideal indicates is that there is a continuous struggle over the meaning of feminism among feminist theoretists. To be more precise: There is a continuous struggle over the meaning of feminism as critique and it is particularly evident in the encounter between postmodernist interventionism and critical theory as it is understood by feminists theorists influenced by the Frankfurt School.

Feminism as Critique and the Question of Sexual Difference

Traditionally, critique of philosophy and science is often exercised as immanent critique or as dialectical critique. Immanent critique attempts to be in accordance with the criteria limiting the object of critique while dialectical critique is supposed to originate from something other than, or the negation of, the object of critique. As an alternative to these different forms of critique, intervention suggests itself as a possible approach.

Within feminist theory the term intervention has become rather popular, primarily as a way of indicating a recognition of the death of Metaphysics, understood as the rejection of transcendent, ultimate instances from where institutions and practices can be criticised and the renunciation of "grand narratives." However, what intervention more precisely can be said to be is not particularly clear. It seems like intervention more often than not is regarded as a self-explanatory and in itself destabilising component in critiques of philosophy and science.

A fine account of critique as intervention can be found in the Norwegian philosopher Arild Utaker's twenty-five year old essay discussing the implications of the works of Gaston Bachelard, Louis Althusser and Foucault for the critique of science (Utaker 1984 [1979]). Utaker here explains critique as intervention as a form of critique interfering with or doing something to the object of critique. This may be done by describing the object of critique in ways that cannot be limited by the criteria defining the object. Critique as intervention is thus neither immanent nor dialectic; critique as intervention displaces the place of critique from the standpoint to the effects of critique (Utaker 1984 [1979]: 9). Critique as intervention may thus be understood as strategies aimed at unfolding, describing and combining elements of knowledge that may have critical effects. This kind of critique would of course not be able to draw a clear line between science and ideology or between what is Inside or Outside of the defined limits of scientific production of knowledge. Rather, the intervention would unfold and describe the way in which the Inside and the Outside of science is produced and reproduced. This strategy would in particular challenge the traditional line drawn between "science" and "society," where society is regarded as something "out there" which either influences science or in one way or the other benefits from the scientific production of knowledge. Accordingly, critique as intervention does not promise any emancipation, only the possibility of subversive effects.

While much of contemporary feminist theory—including contributions from theorists like Seyla Benhabib and Toril Moi—somehow seems to echo critical theory by balancing between immanent[5] and dialectical critique of philosophy and science presupposing an understanding of feminism as a critical, emancipatory endeavour, Irigaray—again read through Foucauldian lenses—seems to articulate a critique of philosophy that may be described in terms of intervention. Her de/constructive rereadings of the philosophical canon do not unfold in accordance with authoritative readings, nor do they originate from a position outside phallogocentrism—the position of "the feminine." Instead Irigaray strategically blurs the line drawn between what is inside and what is outside of phallogocentrism, thus clearing a space for subversive critical effects. Understanding the question of sexual difference not as a question belonging to the sphere of the ordinary—the sphere "in which our political and personal struggles actually take place" (Moi 1999: 120)—but as a question that calls our attention to the horizon of this sphere, I thus find Irigaray's interventions monstrously promising[6] for the future of feminism as critique.

Notes

1. Cf. Whitford (1991: 156). As Margaret Whitford remarks *phuein* means "to grow," "to engender." *Phusis*—"nature"/ "matter"—is derived from *phuein*.

2. In her remarkable essay "What is ethical feminism?" Drucilla Cornell (1995) elaborates her visions for feminism through readings of Lacan, Derrida and Wittgenstein. In this paper I address similar questions concerning the paradoxes implied in the feminist project. Philosophically and theoretically my approach has a somewhat different point of departure though I focus on problems related to the understanding of feminism as critique.

3. See for instance Butler (1995).

4. Moi employs the term "poststructuralist" to refer to Anglo-American critics discussing the sex/gender distinction from a poststructuralist perspective. In what follows I employ poststructuralist refering to Moi's understanding of the term. Otherwise I have come to the conviction that this term actually is best avoided because it more often than not leads to misunderstandings and problematic attempts to join together theoretical and methodological frameworks, concepts and subject matters that may perhaps not be compatible.

5. Seyla Benhabib explores the notion of immanent critique in *Critique, Norm and Utopia* (1986). Toril Moi discusses the concept of critique in relation to the possibility of appropriating Pierre Bourdieu's sociology of culture for feminist purposes: "Neither 'appropriation' nor 'critique' rely on the idea of a transcendental vantage point from which to scrutinize the theory formation in question. Unlike the Enlightenment concept of 'criticism', the concept of 'critique' as used here is immanent and dialectical. My proposal of 'appropriation' and 'critique' as key feminist activities is intended to contest the idea that feminists are doomed to be victimized by what is sometimes called 'male' theory" (Moi 1999: 265). My conception of immanent critique differs from that of Benhabib and Moi.

6. I am indebted to Donna Haraway's and Rosi Braidotti's reconstructions of the notion of monster as a powerful feminist tool.

Bibliography

Benhabib, Seyla. 1986. *Critique, Norm and Utopia*. New York: Colombia University Press.

———. 1995. "Feminism and postmodernism." In S. Benhabib, J. Butler, D. Cornell & N. Fraser: *Feminist Contentions—A Philosophical Exchange*. New York & London: Routledge.

Benhabib, Seyla & Drucilla Cornell (eds.). 1987. *Feminism as Critique: On the Politics of Gender*. Minneapolis: University of Minnesota Press.

Braidotti, Rosi. 1991. *Patterns of Dissonance. A Study of Women in Contemporary Philosophy*. Cambridge & Oxford: Polity Press.

————. 1994. *Nomadic Subjects. Embodiment and Sexual Difference in Contemporary Feminist Theory*. New York, Columbia University Press.

————. 1996. "Signs of wonder and traces of doubt. On teratology and embodies Differences." In Nina Lykke & Rosi Braidotti (eds.): *Between Monsters, Goddesses and Cyborgs*. London: Zed Books.

————. 2001. "Becoming—Woman: Rethinking the positivity of difference." In E. Bronfen & M. Kavka (eds.): *Feminist Consequences. Theory for the New Century*. New York: Columbia University Press.

Butler, Judith. 1990. *Gender Trouble: Feminism and the Subversion of Identity*. New York: Routledge.

————. 1993. *Bodies That Matter: On the Discursive Limits of 'Sex'*. New York: Routledge.

————. 1995a. "Contingent foundations. Feminism and the question of "postmodernism." In S. Benhabib, J. Butler, D. Cornell & N. Fraser: *Feminist Contentions—A Philosophical Exchange*. New York & London: Routledge.

————. 1995b. "For a careful reading." In S. Benhabib, J. Butler, D. Cornell & N. Fraser: *Feminist Contentions—A Philosophical Exchange*. New York & London: Routledge.

————. 2001. "The end of sexual difference?" In E. Bronfen & M. Kavka (eds.): *Feminist Consequences. Theory for the New Century*. New York: Columbia University Press.

Cornell, Drucilla. 1995. "What is ethical feminism?" In S. Benhabib, J. Butler, D. Cornell & N. Fraser: *Feminist Contentions—A Philosophical Exchange*, Routledge, New York & London.

Rubin, Gail. 1975. "The Traffic in Women: Notes on the 'Political Economy' of Sex." In *Toward an Anthropology of Women*. Rayna R. Reiter, ed. New York. Monthly Review Press, pp 157-210.

Irigaray, Luce. 1983. *L'Oubli de l'air chez Martin Heidegger*. Paris: Minuit.

————. 1985 [1977]. *This Sex which Is Not One*. New York: Cornell University Press.

————. 1993 [1984]. *An Ethics of Sexual Difference*. New York: Cornell University Press.

Moi, Toril. 1999. *What is a Woman? And Other Essays*. New York: Oxford University Press.

Utaker, Arild. 1984. "Fra filosofikritikk til vitenskapskritikk. Bachelard, Althusser, Michel Foucault" [From critique of philosophy to critique of science]. In *Kunnskapens makt. En innledning til Michel Foucault* [The power of knowledge. An introduction to Michel Foucault], University of Bergen.

Whitford, Margaret. 1991. *Luce Irigaray. Philosophy in the Feminine*. London

& New York: Routledge.
Wittgenstein, Ludwig. 1991 [1958]. *Philosophical Investigations.* Oxford: Basil Blackwell.

"Through Desire and Love":
Simone de Beauvoir on the Possibilities of
Sexual Desire[1]

Sara Heinämaa

The philosophical core of Simone de Beauvoir's *The Second Sex* (*Le deuxième sexe* 1949) is the argument that the humanistic tradition has failed in its attempt to theorize the general structures of human existence. This is due to the neglect of women's experiences and due to the focus on the functions of the male body. Beauvoir starts her treatise by stating:

> He [man] sees his body as a direct and normal connection with the world, which he believes he apprehends in its objectivity, whereas he regards the body of woman as weighed down by everything peculiar to it, as an obstacle, a prison (Beauvoir DSI 15/15).

At the very end of the book, she summarizes:

> There is a whole region of human experience which the male deliberately chooses to ignore because he fails to *think* [*penser*] about it: this experience woman *lives* (Beauvoir DSII 501/622).

Beauvoir argues that if we study women's lived experiences [*expérience vécue*, *Erlebnis*] about their own bodies and the bodies of others, we come to realize that traditional accounts of the self-other relation are seriously defective. Especially two forms of feminine experience can teach us about the possibilities and necessities of human existence. These are the experiences of pregnancy and erotic desire. In both cases women's ways of experiencing their own bodies and the bodies of others confuse the traditional account that presents living bodies as tools or instruments for well-defined ends (Beauvoir DSI 485/609).

I have argued elsewhere (2003, 2004b) that Beauvoir's discussion of pregnancy and motherhood includes a radical problematization of the traditional philosophical account of embodiment. In this paper, I want to focus on Beauvoir's discussion of feminine desire. My aim is to show that also in the case of desire, Beauvoir's analysis calls into question the traditional understanding of embodiment and its implications on femininity.

Attractive and Repulsive Bodies

Beauvoir's descriptions of feminine desire and love apply two classical distinctions: the distinction between *active* and *passive*, and the distinction between *attractive* and *repulsive*.[2] These concepts dominated the existential phenomenological accounts of affection and perception that Beauvoir took as her starting point. Her main sources were two contemporary investigations into embodiment, Sartre's *Being and Nothingness (L'être et le néant* 1943) and Merleau-Ponty's *Phenomenology of Perception (Phénoménologie de la perception* 1945).[3] However, to realize the full strength of her critical inquiries, we need to go further back in the phenomenological tradition. Sartre as well as Merleau-Ponty based their discussion of corporeality on Edmund Husserl's comprehensive account of the living body. This is the source from which we need to start in order to get to the core of Beauvoir's feminist critique.

In his phenomenology of embodiment,[4] Husserl emphasizes that perceived objects (objects given in sense-perception) are not neutral but attract our attention and move us in many different ways. We see things with tempting and inviting qualities, colorful things, for example, that arrest and capture our attention and make us turn toward them. We also perceive unpleasant things that drive us away, make us turn and move further away: harsh voices, sharp smells, restless movements, bright light. So we are not indifferent to the things that we encounter in perception but are clearly influenced by them; they stir us, prod us, pull us, and provoke us.

Husserl uses the concepts of affective [*affektiv*] and receptive [*rezeptiv*] to characterize this level of perception. Following him, we can say that perceived objects actively affect us, and whenever we react or reply to their "calls," we relate to them passively. Husserl argues that such active objects are necessarily part of our experience as human beings, despite the fact that all experienced realities result from the constitutive activity of transcendental consciousness.[5] To understand this, one needs to distinguish between two levels of activity. On the one hand, the positing acts of consciousness constitute all reality and all being that can be perceived; on the other hand, most objects of sense-perception are constituted as active, such that they can move us, attract us and repel us. Husserl explains this duality in the following way:

> Therefore we find, as *the originally and specifically subjective, the ego in the proper sense*, the ego of "freedom," the attending, considering, comparing, distinguishing, judging, valuing, attracted, repulsed, inclined, disinclined, desiring, and willing ego: the ego in any sense is *"active"* and *takes a position*. This, however, is only one side. Opposed to the active ego stands the *passive*, and the ego is always passive at the same time whenever it is active, in the sense of being affected as well as being receptive [...] (Husserl IdII §54 213/225, cf. §25 105/112, appendix XII §2 335–336/346–347).

Husserl's own examples are familiar from everyday situations. He describes how the stale air in a room makes him rise and open a window, how a ball approaching fast from above makes his arm rise to hit it, and how his fingers reach for tempting food (Husserl IdII §55 216–218/228). What is operative in all these cases is not a causal relation between the external object and my own physical body, but the motivational force that the perceived and sensed object has on my body as I experience and live it. Husserl states: "[t]he object stimulates me in virtue of its experienced properties and not its physicalistic ones" (IdII §55 217/228). His argument is that the conceptual framework of motivation covers the whole field of sensibly given things. It includes natural things, such as trees and flowers, and cultural things, such as tools and utensils, but also human faces and bodies as they are given to us prior to natural scientific abstractions.[6]

On the basis of Husserl's concepts and distinctions, Sartre and Merleau-Ponty developed an argument to the effect that the original objects of our experience are not theoretical objects, and not even practical instruments, but affective things that move, attract and repulse our bodies (e.g. Sartre EN 649–651/769–771, Merleau-Ponty PP 235–242/203–209, 371–373/321–323, cf. Beauvoir DSII 155/399). We do not see a table, for example, primarily as a structure of wood fiber, cells, or molecules, nor do we perceive it merely as a support for objects close at hand. The perceived table is not given as a theoretical object of natural sciences nor as a practical object of everyday affairs. Primarily, we see the table as an attractive thing which invites our bodies to move in certain ways: we slide our hand on its smooth cool surface, as if it "demanded those movements of convergence that will endow it with its 'true' aspect" (Merleau-Ponty PP 367/318).[7] Merleau-Ponty explains how the phenomenological method discloses a more fundamental level of experience, behind or below theoretical life:

> The perceiving subject ceases to be an "acosmic" thinking subject, and action, feeling and will remain to be explored as original ways of positing an object, since "an object looks attractive or repulsive before it looks black or blue, circular or square" (Merleau-Ponty PP 32/24).[8]

Merleau-Ponty uses the concepts of communication and dialogue to characterize the relation that we have to the primary objects of perception. He argues
that the world and its different things "invite" us, "call" us, and "appeal" to
us, motivating different actions and movements (Merleau-Ponty 123/106,
161/139, 368–370/319–321). His aim is not to postulate animal spirits or natural forces to explain behavior but to provide an unprejudiced description of the
fundamental level of experience free from theoretical and practical assumptions:

> The visual thing [*la chose visuelle*] (the moon's pale face) or the tac-
> tile thing (my skull as I can feel it when I touch it), which stays the
> same for us through a series of experiences, is neither a *quale* effec-
> tively subsisting, nor the notion or the consciousness of such an
> objective property, but what is discovered or taken up by our gaze
> or by our movement, a question to which these things provide an
> exact answer (Merleau-Ponty 366–367/317).

Affectivity—the attractive and repulsive value of things—is not added to perceptual things retrospectively but is constituted together with their very presence, their being (Sartre EN 650–652/770–772, Merleau-Ponty PP
235–242/203–209, 369–371/321). Valueless theoretical objects are abstractions
having a constitutive basis in primary affective objects. This means that the idea
of a perception that would present the material object as pure extension and
form, free of all affectivity, is a theoretical construct.

   Merleau-Ponty offers more diverse examples of affective perception and
its object than Husserl.[9] He describes a whole "life-world" with objects composed of smells, sounds, flavors, colors, values of light, spatial patterns and
figures, and he studies the systems of movements and postures that correspond
to these affective objects. From the point of view of Beauvoir's reflections on
sexuality and eroticism, it is crucial to notice that Merleau-Ponty argues that
the center of the life-world is the desiring and sensing living body. The most
original objects of affective perception are two bodies touching one another:
one's own body and the body of the other.[10]

   In a psychological framework of ontogeny, such an argument would
hardly be surprising for it is part of our post-Freudian understanding of the
human psyche. However, Merleau-Ponty does not present the claim as an
empirical thesis about the psychological development of human individuals. He
means it as a statement about constitutive primacy. He argues that all experience and all objects of experience —including objects of theoretical knowledge
—are constituted on the basis of affective perception. We can abstract away
affective qualities, but a merely material body without anything that moves the
perceiver is merely a construct of thought. It is not anything that any perceiv-

er (finite or infinite) could see, hear, touch, or smell (Merleau-Ponty 249-250/215, cf. Husserl IdII §18g 85-86/89-91).

Phenomenology of Perception includes a whole chapter that deals with the sexuality of the living body. Sexuality and sexual relations are not thematized here in the interest of understanding reproduction or the economic relations between the sexes. The aim is not to develop a theory of sex or sexuality nor to criticize sexual practices. The focus of the investigation is, and stays, on perception throughout the book: Merleau-Ponty analyzes erotic life in order to illuminate the basic structures of perceptual experience and it objects:

> Let us try to see how a thing or a being begins to exist for us through desire and love. We shall thereby come to understand better how things and beings can exist in general (Merleau-Ponty 180/154).

The idea is that living bodies are given to us as centers of signification. They "breathe life" into the material environment, they "animate" it, and thus create whole systems of expressive and affective relations, in which material things are internally bound together (Merleau-Ponty 235/203). This means that in order to understand the nature of any perceptual object—natural or cultural, animal or human—we need to focus our phenomenological investigations on the relation between two living sensing bodies. The original and paradigmatic case of affective perception for Merleau-Ponty is the bodily relation between two desiring subjects: two corporeal selves touch and look at one another and experience each other as both separate and connected (Merleau-Ponty 180-183/155-157 401/348).

Merleau-Ponty and Sartre follow Husserl also in focusing on two types of affection. They argue that in primary perception we encounter attractive things to which we respond by approaching, reaching, and grasping; and on the other hand, we experience repulsive things that make us dissociate and turn, draw, and move further away. This duality of attractive and repulsive objects corresponds to the duality of our own movements: we move toward things and away from them, we stay near to things and distance ourselves from them, we grasp and reject, possess and refute.

The duality of oppositional directions and movements has been established as an integral part of the contemporary phenomenology of embodiment. For example, Donn Welton, a well-known Husserl scholar, characterizes the movements of living bodies with the following pairs: approaching and distancing, grasping and repelling, penetrating and resisting (Welton 1999 43). The list is natural in reflecting the main directions that structure our perceptual experience and motor activity: our life is full of situations in which we identify two alternative directions and two alternative movements.[11] However, in *The Second Sex*, Beauvoir argues that human life also involves original modes of experience that do not fall into such categories. Most interestingly, she claims that for a woman the object of desire is not simply given as attractive but is fundamentally ambivalent. Correspondingly, women do not feel that their own bodies are simply pulled towards objects of desire; they also experience a simultaneous distancing effect. So both the character of the object and one's own movement is experienced as ambiguous or indefinite.

According to Beauvoir, this is not just typical of women's erotic life but characterizes their basic relations to all things: "instead of being interested solely in the grasp [*prise*] of things, she adheres to their signification, she catches their singular profiles, their unexpected metamorphoses" (Beauvoir DSII 135/384, translation modified). Thus understood, women's erotic experiences condense and express the specificity of their ways of relating to the sensible world (Beauvoir DSII 209/437). To understand the radical nature of this thesis and to explicate its implications, I will study more carefully the descriptions and analyses that Beauvoir offers of women's eroticism.

Between Attraction and Repulsion

In the beginning of *The Second Sex*, Beauvoir thematizes a special mode of bodily experience characteristic to woman's desire. She writers: "we should regard as originally given this type of call [*appel*], at the same time urgent and frightening, which is female desire: it is the indissoluble synthesis of attraction and repulsion that characterizes it" (Beauvoir DSI 92/81).

We can find similar passages in all the main chapters of *The Second Sex*.[12] These accounts have often been neglected as theoretically insignificant; most commentators assume or argue that they merely reflect Beauvoir's personal history and her personal problems with sexuality or else capture the cultural attitudes characteristic of her time.[13] I challenge this view by arguing that her aims were philosophical and that she struggled to conceptualize the features that distinguish feminine desire, or women's desire, from the forms of experience that male thinkers have privileged in their philosophical and psychological theories of eroticism. If my reading is correct, or at least is in the right direction, then Beauvoir's discussion of feminine desire would not just reflect her personal life or her contemporary cultural forms of experience, but would contribute to our understanding of human embodiment in general.

It is worth emphasizing that Beauvoir speaks about a "synthesis" in which attraction and repulsion are inseparably intertwined. By this she means that the object of desire is not given to the woman as simply attractive but appears at the same time also as repulsive. The ambiguity, obscurity, or vagueness of women's bodily expressions and verbal accounts of desire do not stem from indistinction in which desire is confused with other emotional experiences—fear or anxiety, for example, as Freud and Adler suggest. Rather, the object of desire, as it appears to the desiring subject, is genuinely and essentially ambivalent (Beauvoir DSI 92/81).

Beauvoir argues that in the feminine body, desire is expressed as a subtle, almost unnoticed bodily movement, which does not decide between two "options," does not grasp its object or reject it, does not approach the object or take distance from it, but holds its position and oscillates between two directions:

> There is a surge [*élan*] in her which unceasingly ebbs and flows: the ebb creates the spell [*envoûtement*] that keeps the desire alive. But it is easy to destroy the equilibrium between ardour and abandon (Beauvoir DSII 156-157/399-400, cf. 181-182/415-416).

An inattentive observer may confuse this specific way of moving to stagnation or immobility, because the body does not change place, does not move to this or that location. Despite its seeming modesty, the movement is intense and shakes the whole body. According to Beauvoir, this is evident to the woman as well as to the other person who recognizes her desire and is able to respond to it.

In the same way as other phenomenologists, Beauvoir sees desire as always passive in that the desiring subject experiences the desired object as motivating the movement of his or her own body (Beauvoir DSII 156/399). But unlike her contemporary phenomenologists, Beauvoir argues that feminine desire is specific and complex in two interrelated ways: the feminine body moves in two directions and, correlatively, the desired object is given as ambivalent, both attractive and repulsive. Beauvoir claims that this ambiguity or ambivalence is not secondary or derivative but an original way of experiencing. In other words, feminine desire is not derived from some other, more basic, mode of desiring by any emotional addition or subtraction. The withdrawal is not due to any motivation external to desire, but desire itself is dual: the approaching movement toward the object is possible only because of the withdrawing counter movement. And conversely, the withdrawal is not an expression of rejection or negation but makes possible a new approaching which again turns into a new withdrawal.

If Beauvoir's analysis is correct, then the result is not just important to women but is significant for any theory of desire. We need to question all accounts that posit pure attraction as the basis or core of different forms of desire. We also need to problematize the notion that the movements of approaching and grasping are the paradigmatic expressions or manifestations of human desire. Sartre's early accounts of erotic experiences, for example, prove problematic.

In *Being and Nothingness*, Sartre conceptualizes and analyzes our erotic lives through the distinction between one-directional desire and the opposite experience of "sexual horror" [*horreur sexuelle*]. In the Sartrean framework, each erotic experience is understood as a modification of one of these two basic attitudes. An experience involving not just a mixture of attraction and repulsion, but a genuine synthesis of them or an intermediate between them, would be impossible. Beauvoir's discussion of feminine desire urges us to abandon this conceptual framework.

Also the Freudian theory of femininity proves inadequate. Beauvoir points out that it is based on the definition of libido as a one-directional drive or energy flow, and argues that feminine desire cannot be described adequately by such concepts. The object of desire as well as the desiring body are given in ways that transcend the simple concepts of libido. Beauvoir illuminates this explanatory difficulty by comparing feminine experience to color perception: attempts to adjust feminine desire into the Freudian framework with auxiliary concepts, such as "passive libido," are equally hopeless as attempts to explain the experience of green by the existence of yellow and blue light. Feminine desire, in the same sense as the perception of green, is an original and non-reducible form of experience with its own object, and should not be analyzed as a modification or mixture of some other form of desiring (Beauvoir DSI 93/81).

We have two alternatives in interpreting Beauvoir's analyses of feminine desire. We can either assume that the same complexity or ambiguity can also be found in men's erotic lives and that the idea of one-directional desire is an abstraction based on explanatory and practical interests. The other option is to argue that human experience includes two different types of desire, the masculine and the feminine, with different intentional structures, different types of objects, and different bodily expressions. Beauvoir's own argument in *The Second Sex* is, as explained, for sexual difference. In the following, I will first focus on this argument, but then widen the perspective by looking into Beauvoir's fictional works. We will see that her novels confuse her initial account of sexual difference and offer a more nuanced view of feminine eroticism.

Beauvoir develops her account of the specificity of feminine desire in *The Second Sex* in chapters dealing with sexual maturation. She emphasizes the difference between feminine and masculine experience and argues that feminine desire differs from masculine desire by its subject-object relation and by its non-practical character.

According to Beauvoir, masculine desire is structured by ends and means. This type of desire has a well-defined endpoint and outcome in orgasm, and all forms of excitement are given in it as phases that lead to the goal. Also the subject-object relation is dominated by this teleology: one's own body and the desired body of the other are given as means that contribute to the reaching of orgasm:

[...] with penis, hands, mouth, with his whole body, man reaches out

toward his partner, but he himself remains the centre of this activity, as the subject does in general in relation to the object that he per-
ceives and the instruments that he manipulates; he projects himself
toward the other without losing his autonomy; the feminine flesh is
for him a prey, and in it he captures the [same] qualities that his sen-
suality claims of all objects (Beauvoir DSII 147/393).

So what is characteristic to masculine desire, in Beauvoir's account, is the practical intentionality of means and ends. The analysis is ethically neutral: The
masculine mode of desiring can be realized egoistically but also in an altruistic
way: the self may be totally immersed in the attempt to reach his own orgasm,
but he may also be devoted to the satisfaction of the other, to her orgasm. In
both cases the goal of orgasm—own and/or other—dominates perception, motil-
ity, and bodily expression. Beauvoir's philosophical interest is not in judging
any form of love or sex. She claims, however, that we can find a different
mode of desiring, if we attend to the expressions, movements, and postures of
women's bodies.

Beauvoir argues that it is a mistake to conceptualize feminine eroticism
as a modification of "masculine activity," as its opposite, complement or
reverse. Feminine desire is not pure passivity. It has its own form of intentionality differing from the practical directedness of means and ends.

Orgasm is certainly also part of enjoyment in the case of women, but it
is not the primary form of enjoyment and it is not experienced as the goal to
which other forms of enjoyment contribute. We should not make the mistake
of thinking that it follows from this that women merely submit or adapt themselves to the demands of others. Nor should we conclude that feminine desire
is dominated by autoeroticism or auto-affection. In love-making, woman acts
and actively accommodates her movement to the movements of her lover. Her
activity, however, is not motivated by any predetermined aim, outcome or end
product. Beauvoir writes:

It is certainly true that sexual pleasure does not have the same structure [*figure*] in woman as in man. [...] In woman [...] the goal is
uncertain from the start, and more psychic in nature than physiological; she wants sex excitement, pleasure in general, but her body
does not give [*projette*] any clear conclusion to the act of love; and
that is why coition is never quite terminated for her, it contains no
end (Beauvoir DSII 181–182/416).

Having no practical structure of means and ends, feminine desire also lacks
clear beginning and ending. Further, Beauvoir argues that the androcentric par-
adigm of desire has given a biased and incorrect notion of the localization of
erotic sensations and pleasures in the lived body. She refers us to the descriptions of women writers and points out that they do not depict sensual pleasure

as centered on any particular organ or body part but testify that pleasure may cover the whole body and extend to all organs.

> Feminine enjoyment [*joyssance*] radiates throughout the whole body; it is not always centered in the genital organs; even when it is, the vaginal contractions constitute, rather than a true [*véritable*] orgasm, a system of undulations that rhythmically arise, disappear and re-form, attain at times a paroxysmal condition, become vague, and sink down without ever quite dying out. Because no definite term is set pleasure strives for infinity (Beauvoir DSII 181–182/416).[14]

To summarize, Beauvoir argues that feminine desire differs from masculine sexuality in three respects: it lacks the practical intentionality of ends and means, it continues without any determinate beginning or ending, and pleasure disperses throughout the whole body without any clear focus on sexual organs. According to Beauvoir, most theories of desire reduce the specificity, multiplicity and continuity of feminine desire to some basic principle or origin, defined by reproductive ends. Beauvoir's claim is not that such explanations are futile or incorrect. Rather she argues that as they fail to take into account the whole diversity of experience, they cannot authorize any claims about the necessary structures of human existence.

In later feminist discussions, Beauvoir has been criticized for presenting women as apathetic or even frigid. There is a sound basis for such complaints: *The Second Sex* as well as Beauvoir's fictional works include many sections in which a woman is described as not responding to the caresses and tenderness of her lover. The aim of these descriptions, however, is not to establish any theory of women or feminine desire, biological, psychological, or metaphysical. On the contrary, Beauvoir rejects such attempts quite explicitly (Beauvoir DSII 9/33, Heinämaa 2003). If we study her writings carefully, and compare the scholarly works with the novels, we see that the negative descriptions only apply to specific circumstances. Besides them Beauvoir also offers different descriptions in which woman's desire is awakened by the caresses of her lover, and still others in which woman's passion is impatient and self-sufficient.

In the light of such comparisons, it seems that Beauvoir's contention is that a women in love [*amoureuse*]—a woman *as the lover*—experiences her own body and her lover's body in a particular way: as more sensual and more sensitive, as though transformed and intensified. In the novel *The Mandarins* (*Les mandarins* 1954), Beauvoir makes this difference explicit by describing the main character, Anne, first as living without any love and then, later in the story, as loving and saturated with desire. In the first situation, Anne gives her body to a casual lover in the interest of merely finding the forgotten possibilities of carnal pleasure. Even if she is able to enjoy her body, her pleasure is diffuse and distant. It does not arrest her attention, but remains in the margins of experience:

> I surrendered to his curiosity a skin which was neither cold nor warm. His lips circled round my breasts, glided over my belly, and descended to my labia. I hasty closed my eyes, and escaped to the pleasure which he extracted from me, a solitary remote pleasure, like a cut flower. Down there the mutilated flower burst suddenly into bloom, lost its petals, while he muttered words to himself, for himself, words I tried not to hear. But I... I was bored (Beauvoir M 96/119–120).[15]

Later in the story, Anne makes a trip to America, where she falls in love with a stranger. She is about to leave the man and return back home to Paris, but they meet again and she dares to ask if he wants her. His response is unexpectedly intense, it surprises her and fills her body with desire displacing all other aspects of life which sink into the past:

> 'I thought they were expecting you in Paris,' he said.
> 'I can always cable Paris. Would you like to keep me here a little longer?'
> 'Keep you? I'd keep you all my life!' he replied.
> He had hurled those words at me with such violence that I fell into his arms. I kissed his eyes, his lips; my mouth went down along his chest, touched the childish navel, the animal fur, the organ with small heartbeats. His smell, his warmth made me dizzy as with drink and I felt my life leaving me, my old life with its worries, its weariness, its worn-out memories (Beauvoir [1954] 1972 55/421).

Love, desire, and generosity [*générosité*] arrest the habitual actions and reactions of this woman. Familiar perceptions are abandoned, accustomed motions suspended, and pleasures and sensations connect in a new way forming a flow that carries through separation and longing.

Beauvoir's novels and essays present disinterested erotic love as an alternative to the operational activity of ends and means. Further, these works demonstrate that the alternative is not just open to women but equally to all humans. Thus the distinction between feminine and masculine eroticism presented in *The Second Sex* proves to be provisional. When we insert the descriptions of Beauvoir's treatise into the context of her other literary works, we obtain a more refined picture of human relations: What is crucial, is that we all are capable of relating to others in several different ways. We can live in the practical goal-directed attitude, but we can also relate to others, strangers as well as near ones, without any practical or theoretical interests (PC 83, cf. DSII

209/437). For Beauvoir, such a disinterested attitude is not just a necessary pre-
condition for ethics and aesthetics; it is also possible in carnal love and establishes a special form of eroticism. If we realize this attitude in our erotic
encounters, we can enjoy our own living and sensing bodies and the bodies of
others without manipulation, possession, or subjection.

Psychoanalyzing Things: The Slimy and the Feminine

Sartre's *Being and Nothingness* is well known for its highly negative accounts
which relate women to everything which is repugnant and base [*bas*]. Many
feminist scholars have criticized Sartre's analyses, similes, and metaphors as
misogynous, and several have also reproached Beauvoir for her uncritical repetition of his viewpoint.[16] In this last section, I argue that if we follow the dialogue between Sartre and Beauvoir in detail, we see that Beauvoir diverges
from Sartre's analysis in a crucial respect, and that *The Second Sex* includes a
strong critique of Sartre's presentation of feminine embodiment.[17] To see this
we need to study both works in detail.

At the end of *Being and Nothingness*, Sartre outlines a new philosophical appoarch which he calls "the psychoanalysis of things" [*psychanalyse des
choses*]: the aim is to disclose meanings inherent in things themselves (Sartre
EN 646, BN 765).[18] Sartre is not concerned with psychological images, mem-
ories, or phantasies of individual persons but aims at capturing the modes of
being that belong to things themselves as they are given in perceptual experience. His inquiry is not about our subjective impressions but about the objective meanings of material things (Sartre EN 645–647/764–766).

Language, literary similes, metaphors, and parables, offer clues for such
analyses, and thus they function in Sartre's analysis in a similar way to classical psychoanalysis. Sartre argues that if we study such hints, we will be able to
articulate the modes of being—"the ontological meanings"—that charaterize
material things and processes. We can identify, for example, the mode of being
that belongs to water and liquids. To this end, we would need to study the fluid
element in its different states, such as melting, oozing, and solidifying.
Similarly we can also investigate fire and its forms (smouldering, burning, and
sparkling) in the interest of capturing the ontological meaning of the fiery element. Sartre explains his approach by outlining an investigation into the element of snow:

> When for instance I wish to determine the objective meaning of
> snow, I see for example that it melts at certain temperatures and that
> this melting of snow is its death. [...] When I wish to determine the
> meaning of this melting [*fonte*], I must compare it to other objects
> located in other regions of existence but equally objective, equally

transcendent (ideas, friendship, persons) concerning which I can also say that they melt: money *melts* in my hands; I am swimming and I *melt* in the water; certain ideas—in the sense of socially objective meaning—"snowball" and others *melt* away; "how thin he has become! how he *has melted away.*" Doubtless I shall thus obtain a certain relation binding certain forms of being to certain others (Sartre BN 646–647/766).

To motivate his "psychoanalysis," Sartre develops an exemplary inquiry into the element of slime and the slimy [*visqueux*]. His idea is to analyze human experiences, and to expose the slimy as a common significative basis for a variety of our emotions and moral positions (Sartre EN 650/770, 653/776). The inquiry confronts us with a type of repulsion manifest in many different kinds of experiences. The objects of these experiences vary from concrete items to abstract entities, from material things to spiritual states: "a handshake is slimy, a smile is slimy, a thought and a feeling can be slimy" (Sartre EN 650/770). Sartre runs through a whole range of repugnance and disgust directed at evasive and sticky things: "oysters and raw eggs"; snails, leeches, fungus, and molluscs; bogholes and quick sand; liars, weaklings, and deceivers—everything "base" (Sartre EN, 650–652/770–773, cf. Merleau-Ponty 282–283/244–245).

At the end, Sartre summarizes that slime is an element or "a substance between two states," an intermediate mode between solidity and fluidity. Thus characterized, slime is a liquid which has started to solidify, has lost its flowing character, but has not yet reached the rigidity and firmness of solid objects. It is a thickening, dense and viscous liquid: pitch, gum, honey, tar—"the agony of water" (Sartre EN 654/774). As such it is attractive and yielding but deceptive. A solid object that falls into a slimy substance seems to keep its form for some time but actually starts to merge or fuse into the soft yielding material. The transformation is slow, all changes are inconspicuous, but in the end, no trace or impression of the object is left. The soft surface is even—"like the flattening of the full breasts of a woman who is lying on her back" (Sartre EN 654/755). Entities are not lost in slime as they are in water; instead they melt, dissove, and decompose in it (Sartre EN 656/774).

On the other hand, slime is adhesive, gluey, and sugary. It sticks to hands and sucks in everything that touches it or tries to move it. First it seems as if the slimy substance would yield and succumb, but this is deceptive, for its grip is tight and firm, even if passive:

> I open my hands, I want to let go of the slime and it sticks to me, it draws me, it sucks at me. Its mode of being is neither the reassuring inertia of the solid nor a dynamism like that in water which is exhausted in fleeing from me. It is a soft, yielding action, a moist and feminine sucking, it lives obscurely under my fingers, and I sense it like a dizziness: it draws me to it as the bottom of a precipice

might draw me (Sartre EN 655/776).[19]

Sartre's descriptions associate slime with decomposition and dying, or more generally, with all processes in which the temporality of life slows down and stagnates. Sartre argues, however, that the repugnancy of slime should not be confused with fear of death or with the anguish that we may feel for our own mortality. Rather, what is at issue is the horror [*horreur*] of an ideal, non-existential, possibility that consciousness could be arrested by being and could lose its temporality. According to Sartre, this cannot happen: consciousness is free activity by essence, and it retains its freedom even in embodiment and corporeality. However, the ideal possibility of a completely stagnated state of consciousness remains threatening even if it cannot be realized (Sartre EN 657/778).

In the very same analysis, Sartre also suggests that slime is associated with the feminine, and that the horror of slimy substances and feminine elements has the same signification basis. He writes: "Slime is the revenge of the in-itself. A sticky-sweet, feminine revenge" (Sartre EN 656/777). Finally, he extends his analysis to cover the proposed fear of female genitals: "The obscenity of the feminine sex [organ] is that of everything which *gapes open*. It is an *appeal to be(ing)*, as all holes are" (Sartre EN 660/782).

Sartre argues that the slimy and the feminine go hand in hand, and that together these qualities symbolize everything which is base and repugnant. His account suggests that the connection between slime and femininity is a structural feature of meaning, and that it functions as a basis for human experience of baseness (Sartre EN 652/772, 655/776-777). If this holds, then the association would not just be typical of some cultures or historical epochs but would be universally shared by all.[20]

Beauvoir's *The Second Sex* presents a modification of Sartre's description of "the feminine revenge." Beauvoir characterized the female sex organ as "mysterious," "concealed, mucous, and humid." She also compares feminine excitement to the preying activities of the mantis, the mollusc, and carnivorous plants. These sections are well known and often criticized for their misogynous undertones:

> Feminine heat [*rut*] is the soft throbbing of a shell. [...] woman lies
> in wait like the carnivorous plant; she is the bog in which insects and
> children are swallowed up. She is absorption, suction, humus, she is
> pitch and glue, an immobile appeal, insinuating and viscous
> (Beauvoir DSII 167, SS 407).

The Second Sex does not contain any explicit critique of Sartre. At most, one could argue that these sections are ironic and that they implicitly challenge Sartre's "psychoanalysis." We should not conclude, however, that Beauvoir settles for merely indirect critique. Her Sartrean descriptions should be inserted into, and read in, the context of her general argument about the ambiguity of human existence, and about the different ways of relating to this ambiguity.

Beauvoir accepts the Kierkegaardian notion of human existence as essentially paradoxical. The subject is in constant indecision between inwardness and externality, finitude and the infinite, temporality and eternity, solitude and bonding (MA 11-15/7-19). These paradoxes cannot be resolved (Beauvoir MA 186-187/ 133-134), they can only be endured, and executed in different ways. In *The Ethics of Ambiguity*, Beauvoir describes several alternatives: the infantile, the narcissistic, the serious, and the artistic. In *The Second Sex*, she distinguishes between two attitudes, one typical of men and the other characteristic of women. Following Kierkegaard, she argues that women tend to identify with the finite and the temporary, whereas men identify with the infinite and the eternal. These typical identifications have wide-ranging implications on our emotional, moral, and intellectual lives. In the case of men, the one-sided identification leads to a heavily charged notion of one's own embodiment. Beauvoir describes the typically masculine attitude as follows:

> [...] he [man] sees himself as a fallen god: his curse is to be fallen from the bright and ordered heaven into the chaotic shadows of his mother's womb. This fire, this pure and active inhalation in which he wishes to recognize himself, is imprisoned by woman in the mud of the earth. He would want to be necessary, like a pure Idea, like the One, the All, the absolute Spirit; and he finds himself shut up in a finite body, in a place and time he never chose, where he was not called for, useless, cumbersome, absurd. The contingency of flesh [...] also dooms him to death. This quivering jelly which is elaborated in the womb [...] evokes too clearly the soft viscosity [*viscosité*] of carrion for him not to turn shuddering away (Beauvoir DSI 245-256, SS 177-178, cf. DSI 274).[21]

The descriptions that Beauvoir presents of the feminine body are clearly similar to Sartre's. However, they do not contribute to a "psychoanalysis of things," but emerge from a Kierkegaardian understanding of human existence as paradoxical. Thus there is a crucial difference between Beauvoir's and Sartre's presentation: whereas Sartre proposes that the horror of feminine sex has an objective basis in the meanings of things and material processes, Beauvoir argues that such experiences have no objective basis but stem from an imaginary identification with eternity and spirituality, which is typical of men. Her claim is that the structure of meaning identified by Sartre is not universal or necessary but is merely dominant in the experiences and theories of men who struggle to identify with the one pole of human ambiguity: eternity, spirituality, consciousness, and freedom.

Such identifications are not unavoidable or necessary. Both sexes can cultivate both sides of their existence, flesh and spirit, and thus contribute to the emergence of new values and meanings. Beauvoir is not utopian here. Rather, she sees the revaluation as already happening, and she works to promote and express it. To obtain a full picture of her understanding of our experiences of femininity, we need to widen the perspective again and compare the descriptions of *The Second Sex* to those we find in her novels.

The early novel *Blood of Others* (*Le sang des autres* 1945) includes sections that are philosophically significant. Beauvoir presents us with very similar images to those in her treatise: the feminine body is identified with plants and molluscs, it becomes a tree, a blossom, a medusa, a spongy and moist surface with obscure magnetic powers.

The metamorphosis reminds us of those depicted by Sartre and represented by Beauvoir in *The Second Sex*. But here the transformation [22] is not negative: being described from a woman's point of view, it lacks the elements of disgust. The woman experiences her body as transforming, becoming animal, and even vegetative, but the transformation as depicted is not horrifying, it is liberating:

> There was only the flesh and blood hand stroking the nape of Hélène's neck; lips that were touching her cheeks, her temples, the corners of her mouth, until she felt enveloped in some pale, sickly vapour; she closed her eyes. She abandoned herself unresistingly to the charm which was slowly metamorphosing her into a plant. Now she was a tree, a great silver poplar whose downy leaves were shaken by the summer breeze. A warm mouth clung to her mouth; under her blouse, a hand caressed her shoulders, her breasts; warm vapours increased about her; she felt her bones and muscles melt, her flesh became a humid and sponge moss, teeming with unknown life; a thousand buzzing insects stabbed her with their honeyed stings. Paul picked her up in his arms, laid her on the bed and stretched himself beside her. His fingers wove a burning tunic along her belly; her breath came in quick gasps; she could hardly draw breath, she was sinking into the hearth of the night, she was our her depth; her eyes closed, paralysed by the net of burning silk, it seemed to her that she would never rise again to the surface of the world, that she would remain for ever enclosed in that viscid darkness, for ever an obscure and flabby jellyfish lying on the bed of magic sea-anemones (Beauvoir [1945] 1996 103–104/79–80).

Notes

1. I am grateful to Antti Kauppinen, Virpi Lehtinen, Pauliina Remes, Martina Reuter and Joona Taipale for their remarks and suggestions that have helped to strength-

en the argument and improve the presentation.

2. Historically both distinctions refer back to Aristotle's philosophy. Cf. Waldenfels 2004.

3. A detailed account of these connections is given in Heinämaa 2003.

4. Husserl develops his phenomenology of embodiment in the late work *The Crisis of European Sciences and Transcendental Phenomenology* (1936–1937, 1954), and in the second volume of *Ideas*. He worked on the latter during 1912–1928 with his two assistants, Edith Stein and Ludwig Landgrebe, but he never published the text. *Ideas II* was published posthumously in 1952, and it was known by Husserl's contemporaries in manuscript form.

5. Husserl's concept of *constitution* should not be mixed up with the Nietzschean concept of *construction* which is central in the philosophy of Foucault and his feminist followers, such as Judith Butler (1990, 1993). The Husserlian concept does not involve any sense of creation. See, Sokolowski 1964, Zahavi 2003 72–77. For a critique of the constructionist notion of sexual difference, see Heinämaa 1996.

6. For the problem of naturalization and naturalism in general, see Husserl [1911] 1965; for the naturalization of the living body, see Husserl IdII, Heinämaa 2003.

7. In "Cézanne's doubt"(Le doute de Cézanne 1945), Merleau-Ponty argues that art, and especially painting, discloses the primary level of perception on which the practical world of tools as well as the theoretical world of physical objects are based: "We live in an environment of man-made objects, among utensils, in houses, streets, cities, and most of the time we see them only through the human actions which put them to use. We become used to thinking that all of this exists necessarily and unshakeably. Cézanne's painting suspends these habits and reveals the base of inhuman nature upon which man has installed himself" (CD 21–22/16).

8. The quotation is from, *The Growth of the Mind: Introduction to Child Psychology* (p. 320), the English translation of Kurt Koffka's *Die Grundlagen der psychischen Entwicklung* (1924). Koffka, Kurt [1924] 1980: *The Growth of the Mind: Introduction to Child Psychology*, trans. Robert Morris Ogden, New York: Harcourt, Brace.

9. Sartre's account of perceptual experience is near to Heidegger's in emphasizing the practical relations that the subject has to the world.

10. Cf. Husserl IdII §36 145/153ff., but cf. §21 96/101, n.1.

11. We also tend to describe "primitive modes" of behavior—those of the animal and the child—in similar terms. See, for example, Freud's well known description of the fort-da game in "Jenseits des Lustprinzips" ([1920] 2003 52–53).

12. These descriptions are to be found in the sections discussing (i) the fundamental assumptions of psychoanalysis, (ii) male mythology of women's bodies, (iii) a young women's spiritual-bodily maturation, and (iv) lesbian love.

13. The most important alternative to this still common reading is presented by Bergoffen (1997), but see also Pilardi (1989) and Lundgren-Gothlin (1995).

14. Compare this passage to Luce Irigaray's well known characterization of feminine enjoyment: "But *woman has sex organs more or less everywhere.* She finds pleasure more or less everywhere. Even if we do not talk about the hysterization of her whole body, the geography of her pleasure is far more diversified, more multiple in its differences, more complex, more subtle, than is imagined—in an imaginary rather too narrowly focused on sameness" (Irigaray 1977 28/28).

15. The English translation of Les mandarins is unclomplete, an abridged edition. Especially sections describing erotic and sexual experiences have been omitted or abrideged. Cf. Klaw 1995 197ff.

16. See for example, Pierce 1975, Collins and Pierce 1976, Lloyd 1984 93–102, Pilardi 1989 21–27, Le Dœuff 1989, Grosz 1994 194–195. But for a different perspective, compare Zerilli 1992, Diprose 1998.

17. Here my approach is indebted to Michèle Le Dœuff's groundbreaking study *Hipparchia's Choice: An Essay Concerning Women, Philosophy, etc.* (*L'étude et le rouet* 1989).

18. In this project, Sartre is influenced by Gaston Bachelard who, in his *L'eau et les rêves*, studies meanings that belong to materials, and especially to water. Bachelard also spoke of the "psychoanalysis of plants" and named another work *Psychanalyse du feu* (1938). In addition to Sartre, Beauvoir's critique of psychoanalysis, drew from Merleau-Ponty's very different approach in *Phenomenology of Perception* (187/160, 184/157ff.). For a promising recent attempt to combine the conceptual frameworks of phenomenology and psychoanalysis see, Welton 1998,

19. Sartre elaborates: "Throw water on the ground; it *runs*. Throw a slimy substance; it draws itself out, it displays itself, it flattens itself out, it is *soft* [*molle*]; touch the slimy, it does not flee, it yields" (Sartre EN 655/775).

20. Compare Sartre's descriptions of slime and the slimy to Julia Kristeva's descriptions of *abjects* [*abjet*] in *Powers of Horror* (*Pouvoirs de l'horreur* 1980) and to Luce Irigaray's descriptions of mucous [*muqueux*] in *An Ethics of Sexual Difference* (*Éthique de la différence sexuelle* 1984). Kristeva does not refer directly to Sartre, but she is influenced by Mary Douglas' anthropological classic *Purity and Danger* (1966), which explains the horrifying character of slime by reference to Sartre's analysis (Douglas 1980 38). For a detailed account of this connection, see Grosz 1994 192–208.

21. Cf. Charles Baudelaire's poem "Carrion" (*Une Charogne*) in *The Flowers of Evil* (*Les fleurs de mal* 1855). See also Sartre's treatise on Baudelaire ([1947] 1967 77–78, 87–, 104–106, 119ff.).

22. The third part of Julia Kristeva's work *Le génie féminin* (2004) includes a highly interesting analysis of Colette's textual-bodily transformations which seem to be the main source of Beauvoir's account of femininity.

Bibliography

Arp, Kristana. 2001. *The Bonds of Freedom: Simone de Beauvoir's Existentialist Ethics*, Chicago, La Salle, Illinois: Open Court.

Baudelaire, Charles. [1855] 1988. *The Flowers of Evil*, trans. James N. McGowan, Oxford: Oxford University Press. Original *Les fleurs du mal*.

Beauvoir, Simone de. DSI: *Le deuxième sexe I: les faits et les mythes*, Paris: Gallimard, [1949] 1993. In English *The Second Sex*, trans. and ed. H.M. Parshley, Harmondsworth: Penguin, 1987.

———. DSII: *Le deuxième sexe II: l'expérience vécue*, Paris: Gallimard, [1949]

1991. In English *The Second Sex*, trans. and ed. H.M. Parshley, Harmondsworth: Penguin, 1987.

————. PC: *Pyrrhus et Cinéas*, Paris: Gallimard, 1944.

————. M: *Les mandarins I–II*, Paris: Gallimard, [1954] 1972. In English *The Mandarins*, trans. Leonard M. Friedman, London, New York, Toronto, Sydney: Harper Perennial, 2005.

————. MA: *Pour une morale de l'ambiguïté*, Paris: Gallimard, 1947. In English *The Ethics of Ambiguity*, trans. Bernard Frechtman, New York: Carol Publishing Group Editions, 1994.

————. [1945] 1996: *Le sang des autres*, Paris: Gallimard. In English *The Blood of Others*, trans. Yvonne Moyse and Roger Senhouse, Penguin, 1970.

Bergoffen, Debra B. 1995. "Out from under: Beauvoir's philosophy of the erotic," in Margaret A. Simons (ed.): *Feminist Interpretations of Simone de Beauvoir*, Pennsylvania: The Pennsylvania University Press, 179–192.

————. 1997: *The Philosophy of Simone de Beauvoir: Gendered Phenomenologies, Erotic Generosities*, Albany: State University of New York Press.

Butler, Judith. 1990. *Gender Trouble: Feminism and the Subversion of Identity*, New York: Routledge.

————. 1993. *Bodies that Matter: On the Discursive Limits of "Sex"*, New York: Routledge.

Collins, Margery L. and Christine Pierce. 1976. "Holes and slime: Sexism in Sartre's psychoanalysis," in Carol C. Gould and Marx W. Wartofsky (eds.): *Philosophy and Women: Toward a Theory of Liberation*, New York: G.P. Putnam's Sons.

Diprose, Rosalyn. 1998. "Generosity: Between love and desire," *Hypatia*, vol. 13, no. 1 (Winter 1998), 1–20.

————. 2001. *Corporeal Generosity: On Giving with Nietzsche, Merleau-Ponty and Levinas*, Albany: State University of New York Press.

Douglas, Mary. 1966. *Purity and Danger: An Analysis of the Concepts of Pollution and Taboo*, New York: Praeger.

Freud, Sigmund. [1920] 2003. "Beyond the pleasure principle," in *Beyond the Pleasure Principle and Other Writings*, trans. John Reddick, London: Penguin Books, 43–102. Original *Jenseits des Lustprinzips*.

————. [1931] 1991. "Female sexuality," in *On Sexuality: Three Essays on the Theory of Sexuality and Other Works*, trans. James Strachey, Harmondsworth: Penguin Books, 371–392. Original *Über die Weibliche Sexualität*.

————. [1932] 1979. "New introductory lectures on psychoanalysis: Femininity," in *New Introductory Lectures on Psychoanalysis*, trans. James Strachey, Harmondsworth, Middlesex: Penguin, 145–169.

Grosz, Elizabeth. 1994. *Volatile Bodies: Toward a Corporeal Feminism*,

Bloomington and Indianapolis: Indiana University Press.

Heidegger, Martin. [1927] 1993. *Sein und Zeit*, Tübingen: Max Niemeyer. In English *Being and Time*, trans. John Macquarrie & Edward Robinson, Oxford: Blackwell, 1992.

Heinämaa, Sara. 1996. "Women—nature, product, style? Rethinking the foundations of feminist philosophy of science," in Lynn Hankison Nelson and Jack Nelson (eds.): *Feminism, Science, and the Philosophy of Science*, Dordrecht: Kluwer, 1996, 289–308.

———. 2001. "From decisions to passions: Merleau-Ponty's interpretation of Husserl's reduction," in Ted Toadvine and Lester Embree (ed.): *Merleau-Ponty's Reading of Husserl*, Dordrecht, Boston, London: Kluwer, 127–146.

———. 2003. *Toward a Phenomenology of Sexual Difference: Husserl, Merleau-Ponty, Beauvoir*, Lanham, Boulder, New York, Oxford: Rowman & Littlefield.

———. 2004a. "Phenomenology of persons or ontological analytic of Dasein? A reply to Heiddegger's critique of classical phenomenology," paper presented at the international conference *Dimensions of Personhood*, August 13–15, 2004, University of Jyväskylä.

———. 2004b. "Sexuality and sexual difference: Questions in the phenomenological account of embodiment," paper presented at the conference *Embodied Mind*, June 14–16, University of Copenhagen, 2004.

Husserl, Edmund IdI. *Ideen zu einer reinen Phänomenologie und phänomenologischen Philosophie, Erstes Buch: Allgemeine Einführung in die reine Phänomenologie, Husserliana, Band III*, ed. Walter Biemel, Haag: Martinus Nijhoff, 1913. In English *Ideas: General Introduction to Pure Phenomenology*, trans. W.R. Boyce Gibson, New York, London: Collier, 1962.

———. IdII: *Ideen zu einer reinen Phänomenologie und phänomenologischen Philosophie, Zweites Buch: Phänomenologische Untersuchungen zur Konstitution, Husserliana, Band IV*, ed. Marly Bimel, Haag: Martinus Nijhoff, 1952. In English *Ideas Pertaining to a Pure Phenomenology and to a Phenomenological Philosophy, Second Book: Studies in the Phenomenological Constitution*, trans. Richard Rojcewicz and André Schuwer, Dordrecht, Boston, London: Kluwer Academic Publishers, 1993.

———. K: *Die Krisis der europäischen Wissenshaften und die transzendentale Phänomenologie: Eine Einleitung in die phänomenologische Philosophie, Husserliana, Band VI*, ed. Walter Biemel, Haag: Martinus Nijhoff, 1954. In English *Crisis of the European Sciences and Transcendental Phenomenology: An Introduction to Phenomenological Philosophy*, trans. David Carr, Evanston: Northwestern University, 1988.

———. [1911] 1965. *Philosophie als strenge Wissenschaft*, Frankfurt: Vittorio

Klostermann. In English "Philosophy as rigorous science," in *Phenomenology and the Crisis of Philosophy*, trans. Quentin Lauer, New York: Harper Torchbooks, 1965.

Irigaray, Luce. 1977. *Ce sexe qui n'en est pas un*, Paris: Minuit. In English *This Sex which Is Not One*, trans. Catherine Porter with Carolyn Burke, Ithaca: Cornell University Press, 1985.

————. 1983. *Amante marine, de Friedrich Nietzsche*, Paris: Minuit. In English *Marine Lover of Friedrich Nietzsche*, trans. Gillian G. Gill, New York: Columbia University Press, 1991.

————. 1984. *Éthique la différence sexuelle*, Paris: Minuit. In English *An Ethics of Sexual Difference*, trans. Carolyn Burke and Gillian C. Gill, Ithaca: Cornell University Press, 1993.

Käll, Lisa. 2002. "Beneath subject and object: The expressive body in light of the Sartrean gaze," paper presented at the 41st annual meeting of *The Society for Phenomenology and Existentialist Philosophy*, October 10–12, 2002, Loyola University Chicago.

Klaw, Barbara. 1995. "Sexuality in Beauvoir's *Les Mandarins*," in Margaret A. Simons (ed.): *Feminist Interpretations of Simone de Beauvoir*, Pennsylvania: The Pennsylvania University Press, 192–221.

Kristeva, Julia. 1980. *Pouvoirs de l'horreur*, Paris: Seuil. In English *Powers of Horror*, trans. Leon S. Roudiez, New York: Columbia University Press, 1982.

————. 2002. *Le génie féminin III: Colette*, Paris: Fayard. In English *Colette*, trans. Jane Marie Todd, New York: Columbia University Press, 2004.

Langer, Monika. 1998. "Sartre and Merleau-Ponty: A reappraisal," in Jon Stewart (ed.): *The Debate between Sartre and Merleau-Ponty*, Evaston: Northwestern University Press, 93–117.

Le Dœuff, Michèle. [1989] 1991. *Hipparchia's Choice: An Essay Concerning Women, Philosophy, etc.*, trans. Trista Selous, Oxford, Cambridge: Blackwell. Original *L'étude et le rouet*.

Lloyd, Genevieve. 1984. *The Man of Reason: "Male" and "Female" in Western Philosophy*, London: Methuen.

Lundgren-Gothlin, Eva. 1992. *Kön och existens: Studier i Simone de Beauvoirs "Le Deuxième Sexe,"* Göteborg: Daidalos. In English *Sex and Existence: Simone de Beauvoir's "The Second Sex,"* trans. Linda Schenck, London: Athlone, 1996.

————. 1995. "Gender and ethics in the philosophy of Simone de Beauvoir," *Nora: Nordic Journal of Women's Studies*, vol. 1, nr. 3, 3–13.

Marion, Jean-Luc [1983] 2002: "The intentionality of love, in homage to Emmanuel Lévinas," in *Prolegomena to Charity*, trans. Stephen E. Lewis, New York: Fordham University Press. Original *Phénomènes à la charité*.

————. [1994] 2002. "What love knows," in *Prolegomena to Charity*, trans. Stephen E. Lewis, New York: Fordham University Press. Original

Phénomènes à la charité.

Merleau-Ponty, Maurice. PP: *Phénoménologie de la perception*, Paris: Gallimard, [1945] 1993. In English *Phenomenology of Perception*, trans. Collin Smith, New York: Routledge & Kegan Paul, 1995.

———. [1945] 1995. "Le doute de Cézanne," in *Sens et non-sens*, Paris: Gallimard, [1966] 1996. In English "Cézanne's doubt," in *Sense and Non-Sense*, trans. Hubert L. Dreyfus and Patricia Allen Dreyfus, Evaston: Northwestern University Press, 1964.

Morris, Phyllis Sutton. 1999. "Sartre and objectification: A feminist perspective," in Julien S. Murphy (ed.): *Feminist Interpretations of Jean-Paul Sartre*, University Park: Pennsylvania State University Press.

Pierce, Christine. 1975. "Philosophy," *Signs: Journal of Women in Culture and Society*, vol. 1, nr. 2, 487–503.

Pilardi, Jo-Ann. 1989. "Female eroticism in the works of Simone de Beauvoir," in Jeffner Allen and Iris Marion Young (eds.): *The Thinking Muse: Feminism and Modern French Philosophy*, Bloomington and Indianapolis: Indiana University Press, 18–34.

Sartre, Jean-Paul. EN: *L'être et le néant: essai d'ontologie phénoménologique*, Paris: Gallimard, [1943] 1998. In English *Being and Nothingness: A Phenomenological Essay on Ontology*, trans. Hazel E. Barnes, New York: Washington Square Press.

———. [1947] 1967. *Baudelaire*, Paris: Gallimard. In English *Baudelaire*, trans. Martin Turnell, New York: New Directions, 1950.

Sokolowski, Robert. 1964. *The Formation of Husserl's Concept of Constitution*, The Hague: Martinus Nijhoff.

———. [1947] 1967. *Baudelaire*, trans. Martin Turnell, New York: A New Directions Paperbook. Original *Baudelaire*.

Waldenfels, Bernhard. 2004. "Leibliche Erfahrung zwischen Selbsheit und Andersheit," in Ulrich Bröckling, Stefan Kaufmann, und Axel Paul (eds.): *Vernunft - Entwicklung - Leben*, München: W. Fink.

Welton, Donn. 1998. "Affectivity, eros and the body," in Donn Welton (ed.): *Body and Flesh: A Philosophical Reader*, Oxford: Blackwell.

———. 1999. "Soft, smooth hands: Husserl's phenomenology of the lived-body," in Donn Welton (ed.): *The Body: Classical and Contemporary Readings*, Oxford: Blackwell, 38–56.

Zahavi, Dan. 2003. *Husserl's Phenomenology*, Stanford: Stanford University Press.

Zerilli, Linda M.G. 1992. "A process without a subject: Simone de Beauvoir and Julia Kristeva on maternity," *Signs: Journal of Women in Culture and Society*, vol. 18, nr. 1, 111–135.

Index

About the Contributors

Jodi Dean is a political theorist teaching and writing at Hobart and William Smith Colleges, Geneva, NY, USA. Her books include *Publicity's Secret* (Ithaca, NY: Cornell University Press, 2002), *Aliens in America* (Ithaca, NY: Cornell University Press, 1998), *Solidarity of Strangers* (Berkeley: University of California Press, 1996) and the edited collections *Cultural Studies and Political Theory* (Ithaca, NY: Cornell University Press, 2000) and *Feminism and the New Democracy* (New York: Sage, 1997). With Paul A. Passavant she edited *Empire's New Clothes: Reading Hardt and Negri* (London/New York: Routledge, 2004).

Cathrine Egeland holds a post-doc position at the Centre for Women's and Gender Studies, Univerity of Bergen, Norway. Egeland received her Ph.D at The University of Southern Denmark in 2001 on the disseration *But Gender Doesn't Have Anything to Do with It: Gender, Gender Barriers and Academia—Constructions of an Invalid Problem*. Her field of research is feminist philosophy of science. She has published articles on feminist philosophy, gender equality in Academia and feminist philosophy of science and knowledge production.

Elizabeth Grosz is Professor of Women and Gender Studies at Rutgers University, USA, and as of January 2006 she is adjunct Professor II at Centre for Women's and Gender Research (http://skok.uib.no) at the University of Bergen, Norway. She is the author, most recently, of *The Nick of Time. Politics, Evolution and the Untimely* (Durham, NC: Duke University Press, 2004) and *Time Travels. Feminism, Nature, Power* (Durham, NC: Duke University Press, 2005).

Sara Heinämaa is Senior Lecturer at the Department of Philosophy at the University of Helsinki, Finland. She has published several books and articles on existential phenomenology, focusing on the topics of perception, embodiment, end intersubjectivity. She is the author, most recently, of the book *Toward a Phenomenology of Sexual Difference: Husserl, Merleau-Ponty, Beauvoir* (Lanham, MD: Rowman & Littlefield, 2003).

Lisa Käll received her Ph.D. in Women's Studies in 2004. Her dissertation, entitled *Becoming Woman, Becoming Self, Becoming Other* makes use of phenomenological philosophy of lived embodiment and intersubjectivity and aims at reaching an understanding of the meaning of the notion of woman on the level of selfhood. More specifically, it explores the meaning of the notion of woman, from the two separate but interrelated perspectives of sexual difference and lived embodiment. Lisa is currently working on a second Ph.D. in philosophy at the Center for Subjectivity Research in Copenhagen, Denmark, where she also teaches.

Ellen Mortensen is Professor of Comparative Literature, and Director of Centre for Women's and Gender Research (http://skok.uib.no) at the University of Bergen, Norway. Her books are *The Feminine and Nihilism: Luce Irigaray with Nietzsche and Heidegger* (Oslo: Scandinavia University Press, 1994) and *Touching Thought: Ontology and Sexual Difference* (Lanham, MD: Lexington Books, 2002).

Johanna Oksala is a Research Fellow in the Department of Philosophy at the University of Helsinki, Finland. She has published articles on the philosophy of Michel Foucault, phenomenology and feminist theory. Her monograph entitled *Foucault on Freedom* (2005) is published by Cambridge University Press.

Tiina Rosenberg, Ph. D., is Associate Professor in Theatre Studies and Gender Studies at Stockholm University, Sweden. She has written extensively on performing arts, queer theory and feminism. Her latest books, *Byxbegär (Desiring Pants,* 2000) and *Queerfeministisk agenda (Queer Feminist Agenda,* 2002) deal with cross-gender performance, Queer Theory and feminism; *Besvärliga människor: Teatersamtal med Suzanne Osten, (Troublesome People: Theatre Talks with Suzanne Osten,* Stockholm: Atlas Böcker, 2004) is a book on Swedish feminist theatre; *Könet brinner! Judith Butlers texter i urval (Gender Is Burning! A Collection of Judith Butler's Texts,* Stockholm:

Natur och Kultur, 2004), and *Teater i Sverige (Theatre in Sweden*, cowritten with Lena Hammergren, Karin Helander och Willmar Sauter, Hedemora/-Uppsala: Gidlunds, 2004) is a new book on Swedish theatre history.

Kristin Sampson, Lecturer, Department of Philosophy, University of Bergen, Norway. She received her Ph. D. at the University of Bergen in 2006 with the dissertation "Ontogony—Conceptions of being and metaphors of birth in the *Timaeus* and the *Parmenides*." Research interests include ancient philosophy, feminist philosophy and ethics.

Vigdis Songe-Møller, Professor of Philosophy, University of Bergen. Major publications: *Zwiefältige Wahrheit und zeitliches Sein. Eine Interpretation des parmenideischen Gedichts*. Würzburg: Königshausen Neumann, 1980; *Tanker om opprinnelsen. Tidlig gresk filosofi fra Hesiod til Demokrit*. Oslo: Cappelen Akademisk Forlag, 1999; *Philosophy Without Women. The Birth of Sexism in Western Thought*. London/New York: Continuum, 2003.